INTERMEDIATE LOAN

READING IN THE EARLY YEARS

HANDBOOK

second edition

Robin Campbell

Open University Press
Buckingham · Philadephia

Open University Press
Celtic Court
22 Ballmoor
Buckingham
MK18 1XW

email: enquiries@openup.co.uk
world wide web: www.openup.co.uk

and
325 Chestnut Street
Philadelphia, PA 19106, USA

First edition published 1995
Reprinted 1995, 1996, 1998, 1999

First published in this second edition 2002

A catalogue record of this book is available from the British Library

ISBN   0 335 21128 3 (pb)

Library of Congress Cataloging-in-Publication Data
Campbell, Robin, 1937–
   Reading in the early years handbook/Robin Campbell.–2nd ed.
      p. cm.
   Includes bibliographical references and index.
   ISBN 0-335-21128-3 (pbk.)
   1. Reading (Primary)–Handbooks, manuals, etc.   I. Title.
LB1525 .C217 2002
372.4–dc21

                                                      2001045819

Typeset by Graphicraft Limited, Hong Kong
Printed in Great Britain by St Edmundsbury Press, Bury St Edmunds, Suffolk

CONTENTS

Acknowledgements   ix

Introduction   1

The entries   3

   alphabet   3
   apprenticeship approach   5
   assessment   7
   audience   10

   baseline assessments and standard assessment tasks (SATs)   12
   bilingual children   16
   book making   18
   books for babies   20
   Breakthrough to Literacy   22

   children's books   25
   classroom organization and management   27
   classroom print   30
   cue systems   34

   emerging literacy   37
   environmental print   40

   gender   43
   genres   45

guided reading   48
guided writing (mini-lessons)   50

hearing children read   52
home–school links   55

information and communication technology   59
illustrations   62
invented spelling   64

knowledge about language   68

language experience approach   70
library corner   73
literacy hour in the National Literacy Strategy   76
literature circles   78

miscue analysis   80

National Curriculum   84
non-fiction   87
nursery rhymes   90

onset and rime   92

paired reading (and buddy reading)   94
phonemic awareness   98
phonics   100
play activities   103
poetry   107
punctuation   110

reading drive   113
reading recovery   115
reading schemes   118
real books   120
real books approach   123
record-keeping   125
responding to miscues   128
running records   132

scanning and skimming   135
school policy   137

shared reading   140
shared writing (and interactive writing)   143
sharing a book   146
speaking and listening   149
story grammar   151
story readings   154
sustained silent reading   159

teacher's role   163
thematic work/topic work   165
time for literacy   167

whole language   171
words   174
writing   177
writing centre   180

your classroom   182

References   184

ACKNOWLEDGEMENTS

The writing of the first edition of this handbook originated from two main sources. First, there were the direct discussions that John Chapman and I had, at that time, about such a text. Those discussions considered how such comprehensive material might best be presented to the prospective audience of teachers, student teachers and interested others. Second, there were the frequent enquiries that I received from students, on initial teacher education and in-service courses, which suggested that a general text in a particular format might be helpful.

Since then, the popularity of the handbook has indicated that the format is helpful. However, developments in early years education, and reading and writing activities, suggest a second edition is required. For instance, in many countries, government initiatives have sought to control the teaching and testing of young children's literacy development (David *et al.* 2000), leading to such changes as the 'literacy hour' in England. Shared reading has acquired new meanings, as it is now associated with a class activity rather than an adult–child interaction. Also, the importance of onset and rime has become more widely recognized, the usefulness of shared writing is more apparent, literature circles are being used successfully with young children and other topics required a section. Most of the literacy activities from the first edition needed to be revisited and a few appeared no longer to be worthy of a complete section.

As with the first edition, the rewriting of the handbook was made easier by the support and comments that I received from colleagues around the world, who also have an interest in early years reading. I also had support from nearer to home and at home. The teachers and children who I had observed in classrooms engaged on literacy activities have guided the rewriting of this handbook. Even more directly, my wife Ruby, as a nursery/infant teacher, informed me, regularly and frequently, about classroom practice and challenged my interpretations of reality. When they were growing up, my children also taught me about literacy. Subsequently, and more recently, my grandchildren taught me daily and very directly about the process of becoming a reader and writer. I was able to share, enjoy, observe and then systematically record their literacy development. Indeed, part of that observation and recording of literacy development of Alice was brought together in a book (Campbell 1999a) and, occasionally, I make use of some of her reading and writing experiences in this handbook.

INTRODUCTION

There are many books on the teaching of reading and very often they are contentious because there are protagonists who would wish to argue for a particular method or the benefits of a new set of materials. Most recently, but in many ways reflecting the issues of the last 100 years or so, there have been debates about phonics teaching and alternative initial approaches to early reading. Such issues are not neglected in this handbook. Although the book attempts to be much wider in scope and deals with many aspects of the teaching and learning of reading and writing with young children, I do not avoid taking a stance on issues. The reader will find that research and references are provided as an aid to understanding contemporary issues in the teaching of reading.

How can the information be presented? Usually, books on the teaching of reading follow one of three formats. First, some books deal in considerable depth with a very specific aspect of reading. For instance, Alison Littlefair's (1991) book on *Reading All Types of Writing* deals very specificall with issues of genre and register and the implications for reading and writing across the curriculum. Second, some texts are somewhat broader in their scope and deal, perhaps, with an approach to the teaching of reading. My own book on *Reading Real Books* (Campbell 1992) provides us with an example, where an approach to early reading teaching is addressed. Third, there are also texts that try, more comprehensively, to provide an introduction to a wide range of ideas, topics and approaches to the teaching of reading. Marian Whitehead's (1999) *Supporting Language and Literacy Development in the Early Years* is an example of such texts, which typically have a broad title. Barratt-Pugh and Rohl's (2000) *Literacy Learning in the Early Years* covers nine specific topics, written by different authors, which explore important areas of literacy learning with young children.

This *Reading in the Early Years Handbook* belongs to the third category. However, there are some differences. First, the text deals specifically with the early years of reading development. That development is considered from birth to the pre-school nursery years and extends also to the initial years at school and, therefore, reception to Year 2 in the UK and kindergarten to grade two in the USA. Second, attention is given to aspects of writing. This is inevitable because writing and reading support each other. Writing, shared writing, invented spelling, and so on, support children's reading development and are therefore part of this text. Third, rather than following the usual chapter format, the book has been arranged rather differently, which readers have found to be helpful. It contains many short sections under a wide range of headings that are arranged in alphabetical order.

Each section is designed to provide an introduction to a particular topic, to provide some debate and to signal connections with other headings in the book by indicating in italics (e.g. *shared reading*) where further details relating to the subject can be found. Following each section, there are suggestions for further reading, where the particular subject can be considered in greater depth or from another perspective. Some sections also have a short passage – 'In the Classroom' – that highlights the debate with a practical example. The handbook can be used either as a conventional text and be read from cover to cover, or as a reference book where a particular topic can be found with ease without the need for an index and where some important insights are provided about subjects that are of particular interest to the reader.

THE ENTRIES

alphabet

a b c d e f g
h i j k l m n o p
q r s t u v
w x y and z
now I know my a b c
next time you can sing with me.

Many teachers of young children will have sung those six lines, to the tune of 'Twinkle, Twinkle Little Star', rather than reading them because it is a well-known alphabet song heard in many nursery settings and reception classrooms for 5-year-olds. The children enjoy singing that alphabet song in unison in the classroom and singly at home to their parents, just as they do other rhymes and songs. However, the alphabet song enables children to recite the letters. A progression, subsequently, is for the children to learn to recognize the letters and later to learn their sounds, Adams (1990) suggested. Learning the alphabet is important; however, the way it is learned is also important.

One of the simplest, yet most predictive, measures of future success at reading and writing is young children's knowledge of the alphabet as they enter school at 5 years of age (Riley 1996a, b). Without pursuing the various theories of reading, it is possible to see why that knowledge of the alphabet is so important. First, while reading, a knowledge of letters (and letter sounds) enables an emergent reader to use, for instance, the first letter of a word as a means of detecting what the word might be. Second, as the child writes, letters have to be written down to create an *invented spelling* or produce a conventional spelling. The letters of the alphabet are the child's building blocks for literacy.

However, directly teaching young children the letters of the alphabet does not appear to be the answer. As Riley demonstrated, knowledge of the alphabet has to be more broadly based. So it is a wider acquaintance with written language through *books for babies, story readings* and *sharing a book*, as well as engaging with *environmental print* supported by an adult and opportunities for mark making and *writing*, that is needed. These activities, and other broad-based literacy activities, enable young children to construct for themselves a firm understanding of the letters of the alphabet. That learning can then be added to as more specific alphabetic activities are introduced.

As well as singing alphabet songs, reading alphabet books such as *Animalia* (Base 1986) to the children at home and in school can be useful. *Animalia*, for instance, contains alliterations for each letter of the alphabet focusing on various animals, so the children enjoy hearing about the animals and learn about letters at the same time. The children will look at, and learn from, a collection of alphabet books in the *library corner*, especially if those books have also been read aloud by the teacher at some earlier time.

Using the children's forenames to create an interest in letters can also be useful. We know that the writing of their own name fascinates young children and, as Riley (1996a, b) noted, the ability to do so at 5 years old is another powerful predictor of future success at reading. Various studies have shown that the child's own name is one of the first words to be written by them (e.g. Schickedanz 1990; Campbell 1999a). Encouraging children to write their own name and developing an alphabet chart of the children's names in the classroom creates a lot of interest (Campbell 2001b). From such activities, the children's alphabet knowledge is consolidated and extended.

Further reading

Strickland, D.S. (1998) *Teaching Phonics Today: A Primer for Educators*. Newark, DE: International Reading Association.
Dorothy Strickland recognized that learning the alphabet was best done by giving some attention to letters in the context of enjoyable engagements with books and other print. However, she also listed a number of worthwhile activities that supported that learning, including teaching the alphabetic song. Focusing

on the letters of the child's name and using the child's name in a variety of contexts, reading alphabet books, making simple picture dictionaries available and developing an alphabet chart in the classroom at the child's eye level are all useful.

apprenticeship approach

An 'apprenticeship approach' to reading was given considerable impetus in the UK by the publication of a short text by Liz Waterland (1988) entitled *Read with Me: An Apprenticeship Approach to Reading*. That booklet was developed from Waterland's dissatisfaction with the teaching of reading in primary classrooms. In particular, she was concerned that there appeared to be many children who could read but in practice seldom did so. Or, the children could read but did so hesitatingly and with little apparent sense of making meaning. Such concerns led her, in her own infant classroom, to move away from reading schemes and a skills model of early reading teaching.

Instead, she proposed a move towards recognition of language as a whole, where the text to be read is vitally important and the adult acts as a guiding friend. In making these suggestions, the apprentice-ship approach demonstrated its links with *whole language* in the USA (Goodman 1986) and *real books* in the UK (Campbell 1992). The approach also emphasized the links with parents, who have contributed so much to their children's *emerging literacy*, and who are encouraged to maintain that support in tandem with the school. And much of that support for the child as a developing reader is based on *sharing a book* with a teacher/parent/adult. Thus opportunities are provided for the children to see many 'experts' at work with literacy (Coles 1990).

Sharing a book is based on the notion of children contributing what they are capable of at that moment. Initially, therefore, the role of the child may be to listen to the story being read by the adult and making few contributions to the reading. But, with a growing knowledge and increased confidence, the child gradually takes on a more prominent role (Guppy and Hughes 1999). Importantly, as Waterland (1988) has indicated, the child is encouraged to read with, rather than to, the adult. And that is a reading that allows the child to take on the role of an apprentice who gradually does more as learning takes place.

However, just because the child is reading with, rather than to, does not mean that in the classroom the teacher is no longer assessing the child's growth as a reader. Observations of the child as a reader (and writer) are made and recorded so that the teacher is aware of the child's development as a reader. And, in that analysis, a note is made of the child's growing knowledge of letters and sounds because, Waterland (1988) argued, being able to check on the initial letter (or initial letter combinations) in a word is helpful. But that skill of knowing the letters and sounds develops from the child's meaningful readings and is built upon by the teacher. It is that way round rather than the letters and sounds being the starting point out of which eventually reading develops.

Of course, the approach also includes other literacy practices. So listening to *story readings*, periods of quiet reading, *paired reading*, the use of sentence makers, as in *Breakthrough to Literacy*, and *writing* are all provided. The expectation is that the children will be learning as apprentices supported by the person who at the time knows more about reading. Therefore, the teacher, parent and other adults have an important supportive role to play in this approach.

Further reading

Waterland, L. (1988) *Read with Me: An Apprenticeship Approach to Reading*. Stroud: Thimble Press.
This short booklet describes the events that led Liz Waterland to change to a different form of teaching and instigate what she refers to as an apprenticeship approach to reading. She indicates in the booklet the influence that other writers such as Goodman, Smith and Meek (as well as Huey 1908) had upon the changes she made. The booklet, of course, gives a more detailed account of the approach than is provided above.

Waterland, L. (ed.) (1989) *Apprenticeship in Action: Teachers Write about Read with Me*. Stroud: Thimble Press.
This text demonstrates that Liz Waterland was not alone in her attempts to develop apprenticeship-type approaches in primary schools. The work of several teachers, headteachers and advisers are brought together who, at these various levels, have provided more holistic learning experiences for the children in their classes, schools and districts. These various contributors indicate not only what they perceive to be the benefits of the approach, but also the problems encountered as they changed their practices.

Beard, R. and Oakhill, J. (1994) *Reading By Apprenticeship? A Critique of the Apprenticeship Approach to the Teaching of Reading*. Slough: NFER.
The authors of this book welcome some of the features of the apprentice

approach. In particular, they highlight reading aloud to young children, using appealing books and the value of children using books which they create themselves. Nevertheless, they do criticize the notion of an apprenticeship in learning to read and they also express concerns about the lack of systematic teaching of phonics.

Geekie, P., Cambourne, B. and Fitzsimmons, P. (1999) *Understanding Literacy Development*. Stoke-on-Trent: Trentham Books.
The Australian authors indicate that they wrote this book as a direct response to Beard and Oakhill's (1994) critique. They indicate that they view learning as being social, collaborative and cultural. Therefore, a community of learners rather than an adult-run model of instruction is suggested. Rather than dealing in the abstract with those ideas, classroom examples are provided to demonstrate, for instance, children learning through guided participation.

assessment

It is inevitable, and appropriate, that teachers of young children will make assessments of the children's reading and writing in the classroom. The very nature of teaching involves the observation of children, an assessment of what is being achieved, an evaluation of that achievement and a subsequent teaching based on that cycle. 'Evidence of children's achievement arises naturally from good teaching' (QCA 1999b: 12). So, as teachers, we make assessments daily and they inform our on-the-spot teaching. However, the assessments also have a more long-term effect because, on the basis of the evaluations that we make, there may be more major alterations to the classroom organization for literacy teaching and learning. Furthermore, we also have to think about collecting together those assessments to inform other teachers and parents about the progress of children. That implies some form of *record-keeping*, so that the information can be given in a detailed and systematic manner. For some teachers, the assessments and records are also required in a particular format to meet the demands of the *National Curriculum*.

How might the teacher of young children set out to assess the diverse literacy achievements of the children in the classroom? Yetta Goodman (1989) provides a useful framework in suggesting that the teacher might informally and formally observe, interact and analyse the literacy activities of the children. We can place that in the context of some of the sections of this book.

First, the teacher will observe informally throughout the school day; as the children engage, for instance, in *play activities*, the teacher will note which children are involved in such activities and the range of *writing* being produced by the children in that context. Of course, such observations may tell us about the organizational needs of the play area as well as informing about the children's use of literacy. More formally, the teacher might decide to collect the writing from the play area for a period of time to make a more complete evaluation of the extent to which the area is encouraging writing and the nature of that writing.

On occasion, the observations will lead the teacher towards informal interactions with the children. For instance, the teacher might observe a child writing in the play area, or elsewhere, and during that observation a particular aspect of writing might be noted. The teacher might then stop to have a short interaction with the child, centring the discussion on an aspect of writing (e.g. content, development of the writing, etc.) or features of transcription (e.g. letter formation, spelling, etc.). But the teacher will not just wait for opportunities for informal interactions to occur, but plan formally for interactions to take place. So *sharing a book* requires a careful *classroom organization* so that it can proceed satisfactorily. During such interactions, the teacher has an opportunity for the regular assessment of the progress of each child's reading. With a 5-year-old, the teacher might assess the way the child handles the book and uses the illustrations and print to construct the story. With older or more advanced readers, the teacher might make a note of miscues to determine the language *cue systems* being utilized or concentrate on a discussion of the book to consider the child as a reflective reader of the book.

The interactions and the observations include, to some extent, analyses of the children's literacy. When *sharing a book*, there is the opportunity for the teacher informally to collect and analyse the miscues of a child. The procedures suggested for a *miscue analysis* (Goodman *et al.* 1987) would not include teacher support. Nevertheless, as a child produces miscues in the classroom, a teacher with a knowledge of miscue analysis will analyse those miscues and the child's use of the language *cue systems* and respond accordingly. More formally, the teacher might have a system for analysing the literacy progress of each child. With writing, the most common feature in the busy early years classroom is for a collection to be made of the child's writing. That collection, as part of a portfolio, enables the teacher to analyse the child's writing development and to pick out particular aspects for a detailed assessment of development. So the child's growth from *invented spellings* to becoming a conventional speller can be noted and, perhaps, features of spelling that might be creating a problem can be detected. Many other aspects of writing can be analysed from that collection, as well as during the writing conferences that are arranged by the teacher.

Although assessment is a natural part of teaching, it has been highlighted in recent years when teachers have had to consider the attainment targets of the *National Curriculum*. Teachers have been critical of the time demands placed upon them by the assessment procedures of that curriculum. Yet, in another sense, those assessments, using *baseline assessments and standard assessment tasks (SATs)*, have been insufficient. They occur at one set time in the year, whereas assessment and evaluation have to be part of everyday teaching and learning where reading and writing are observed in many literacy activities. So *shared reading* and *shared writing*, *guided reading* and *guided writing* and other times that the children engage with literacy are all used for assessment.

Parents can provide some help in the assessment of early literacy. For instance, when reading cards are passed from school to home and back again, both teachers and parents are likely to comment upon the children's reading. Comments from the parents can provide insights into the reading strategies and interests of the children as well as giving the parents' perspective on reading growth. And children can be involved in the assessment procedures. They can be asked what they need to do to improve a piece of writing and, although their answers may initially be limited, nevertheless it is an important step along the path towards self-evaluation. Self-evaluation will be a key feature of the children's future literacy learning.

Further reading

Goodman, Y. (1989) Evaluation of students, in K. Goodman, Y. Goodman and W. Hood (eds) *The Whole Language Evaluation Handbook*. Portsmouth, NH: Heinemann.

The first chapter in this collection of papers is by Yetta Goodman. It is an important chapter because it provides the framework of literacy assessment and evaluation for the subsequent sections in the book. In it, Goodman outlines the notion of informal and formal observation, interaction and analyses and provides suggestions for each of these. The subsequent chapters in the book extend that introduction and frequently provide classroom examples.

Barrs, M. and Johnson, G. (1993) *Record-keeping in the Primary School.* London: Hodder & Stoughton.
Myra Barrs and Gillian Johnson provide examples and debates about the assessment of children's language development. They do this by linking to the ideas contained in the Primary Language Record that was developed at the Centre for Language in Primary Education in London. The examples indicate how progress can be monitored regularly in a way that supports learning.

audience

In Denny Taylor's (1983) book on young children learning to read and write within the context of the family, she noted how the children would often write notes to other children in the family or to their parents. Of course, with the youngest children, those notes might be difficult to decipher, even though children receiving such notes might claim to be able to read them. An important feature of that writing was that the notes were being written for a real purpose and with a genuine audience in mind. Such opportunities for writing may arise naturally within the home. The teacher in the nursery or infant classroom will try to replicate those natural writing occasions. Therefore, the teacher will try to provide opportunities for writing where there is an obvious audience and a purpose for communicating in print.

The writing that can occur during *play activities* is one example where children find it natural to write notes for an audience of other children. The nature of the play will determine the purposes for the writing, but messages, instructions and letters are all likely to be produced for other children as well as notes for oneself. Such natural writing will be assisted where the teacher has arranged the play area for a particular activity and with numerous materials for writing and reading. Then, prescriptions, telephone messages, shopping lists and form filling might appear for a real purpose as part of the play.

The teacher can encourage writing in different contexts. For example, letters to children who are absent from school or are in another class enable the children to write with a real audience in mind. The children can also write for other children as part of *book making*, with varying support from the teacher. Frequently, such books are to be found in the library corners of infant classrooms. This writing of books also encourages children to consider the conventions of print, such as *punctuation*, because they will want the books to look like the printed commercial texts available in the library. So the influence of the audience is not only to provide a real purpose for writing, but also to encourage the writer to consider the needs of the reader during the production of that writing.

The teacher can suggest further audiences for writing in addition to other children. Parents are an obvious example. Letters informing about activities in the classroom, or used as invitations to events, can be commonplace. But there are many other occasions to write to, or for, parents. Margaret Lally (1991) described how, in one nursery class-room, the teacher and children worked together to produce a notice to remind the parents to close the high latch on the nursery gate. The children contributed to that notice during a shared writing session as the teacher demonstrated aspects of the construction of print. A fur-ther outcome, as we might expect from 3- and 4-year-old children, was that many other notices were produced by them over the next few days as they imitated the behaviour of their teacher.

The writing by the children can be extended outwards from the parents to the wider community. So a letter to a policeman or police-woman, or other guest, after a visit to the school can be viewed as writ-ing for a real audience. However, the audience can also be imagined (although perhaps real to the children). Jeanne Price (1989) described how the children in her nursery classroom became involved in writ-ing letters to a ladybird after the reading of Eric Carle's (1982) *The Bad Tempered Ladybird*. The return letters from the 'ladybird' ensured that the children remained interested in writing to that audience. However, these letters also helped the children to begin to perceive some of the conventions of letter writing and to begin to produce the salutation, closure and signature that are typically evident in a letter. In addition to extending the audience out beyond the classroom, there are also opportunities for children to write for themselves. For older infants, this might include a diary or journal, but the younger children also write for themselves. During play activities, for instance, children write lists for their own use – a shopping list is an obvious example. In one reception class, the children created shopping lists of food to be purchased for the classroom snails (CLPE 1999).

All of these examples are indicative of the ways in which the teacher can try to provide a variety of audiences for the children's writing. Of course, the teacher can also be the audience for some of the writing. Connie and Harold Rosen (1973) suggested that young children assume that their teacher will be interested in their writing. Therefore, the teacher can act as an audience for some of the children's writing. However, the aim will be to create a diversity of audiences because that will encourage the writer to consider the reader as he or she writes and, therefore, to match the writing to the purpose and audience.

Further reading

Hall, N. (ed.) (1989) *Writing with Reason: The Emergence of Authorship in Young Children.* Sevenoaks: Hodder & Stoughton.
The subtitle of this book indicates that it has as a central purpose the consideration of the child as an author. For a child to act as an author, it requires that the child has the responsibility for selecting what is written on the paper. And that means that he or she needs to be aware of the audience for whom he or she is writing. The twelve chapters in this book are written in the main by classroom teachers. They provide examples from nursery and infant classrooms where the children were writing to a variety of audiences; for example, writing dialogue journals with their teacher, contributing to the classroom notice board, writing book reviews for the other children, as well as writing to the ladybird that we noted above.

baseline assessments and standard assessment tasks (SATs)

Standard assessment tasks (SATs) are national tests that were devised in conjunction with the *National Curriculum* in England and Wales. For Key Stage 1 children aged 6 and 7 years, most are expected to reach Level 2 attainment targets by the end of Year 2. Most children of this age group are expected to work at Levels 1–3. Subsequently, baseline assessments were added for all children entering school at 4 or 5 years of age. In addition, there are SATs for the older children, with Key Stage 2 being tested with 10- and 11-year-olds towards the end of Year 6.

The baseline assessments cover the five areas of reading, writing, speaking and listening, mathematics, and personal and social development (SCAA 1997). As some of those areas have more than one collection of test items, there are eight assessment scales altogether. For instance, three areas are covered in the reading assessments: reading for meaning and enjoyment, letter knowledge and phonological awareness. In each of those, four items are assessed; therefore, there are 32 items in all eight scales. In reading for letter knowledge, the increasingly more difficult items are 'recognizes own name', 'recognizes five letters by shape and sound', 'recognizes 15 letters by shape and sound' and 'recognizes all letters by shape and sound'. The expectation is that most children will achieve the first item, 40–80 per cent the second item, 20–60 per cent the third item and less than 20 per cent the final item, which is set at about Level 1 of the National Curriculum.

As noted in the section on the *National Curriculum*, the target for Level 2 in reading at Key Stage 1 is that:

> Pupils' reading of simple texts shows an understanding and is generally accurate. They express opinions about major events or ideas in stories, poems and non-fiction. They use more than one strategy, such as phonic, graphic, syntactic and contextual, in reading unfamiliar words and establish meanings.
>
> (QCA 1999a: appendices, p. 5)

To assess those aspects of reading, each child reads a book from a short graded booklist. The teacher and child read together at first so that the child becomes familiar with the book. Then, when a specific section is reached, the child carries on reading alone. A *running record* is maintained for that section. At the end of the reading, a discussion takes place to determine the child's understanding of the story and ability to express opinions about it. The reading and discussion provide the evidence to be compared with performance descriptors (QCA 1999d) to complete the assessment.

As the reading assessment is from a book of interest to the child and the writing assessment is of a piece of independent writing, those assessments would appear to be appropriate for young children. However, there have been concerns about SATs and now about baseline assessments. In particular, there are concerns about high stakes testing, pressure on the child and influence on the curriculum.

The first national testing using SATs at Key Stage 1, for 7-year-olds, took place in the summer of 1991. The first year of testing demonstrated that there were problems with the tests and the equal application of them in all schools (even with monitoring processes in place). Furthermore, the publication of the results and their interpretation created something of a public furore; this was especially the case with reading and writing in the core subject of English. Although changes were made, teachers had become disenchanted with this mode of testing, in part because it did not appear to add greatly to their knowledge of the children. Therefore, in many schools, the tests were boycotted; even when the tests had been conducted, the results were not forwarded to the authorities for publication. Such disquiet led to a major review of the assessment procedures for the National Curriculum (Dearing 1993), which led to a substantial slimming down of the testing in the 1994 national tests.

Although the testing is now less demanding of time, major concerns remain. The use of the results makes the assessment a form of high stakes testing. The results are used to rank schools and, therefore, teachers, although often the results appear to reflect the social backgrounds of the school. The baseline assessments create a different complication. The scores from these will be used to create a 'value added' aspect when the SATs results are known. Whitehead (1999) raises the question about encouraging a modest baseline score to help value added! Such questions and issues are inevitable with high stakes testing and have also been noted outside the UK (Hoffman *et al.* 2001).

With such high stakes, the SATs assessments inevitably become the key part of schooling and daily teaching becomes dominated by the nature of the test: 'teaching to the test' is also noted in the USA (Kohn 2000: 29). In England, a simple example of this is the way in which *punctuation* has been elevated in importance by the nature of writing assessments. The ability to demarcate a sentence with a capital letter and full stop is an important criterion for achieving Levels 2 and 3. As a result, some teachers and children restrict the writing in terms of content to concentrate on that aspect (Anderson 1993). It is not that punctuation is unimportant for young children. The emphasis on accuracy in sentence demarcation has changed the nature of teacher support in classrooms for young children, which may not have been in their best interests.

Many children quickly become aware of teacher and parental pressure to do well in the assessments. Inevitably, for some children, that creates pressure and worry, which may be inappropriate for 6- and 7-year-olds. Because of the considerable amount of time that is devoted to SATs, a major concern for teachers working with young children is that it seems to reduce dramatically the time that is available for teaching each summer term. Furthermore, the time available for other important areas of the curriculum – including the arts, music and physical education – appears to be diminished. The tests have become the curriculum – Level 2 books are stocked by local shops and have become the most sought-after books by parents and many schools.

The reporting of assessment results to parents is a problem because no account is taken of the age of their children. Although, in theory, Key Stage 1 should test attainment at 7 years of age, many 6-year-olds are tested. There is inevitably a range of eleven months in the ages of the children tested. As might be expected, the results of the test in any one class reflect the ages of the children as much as they reflect the attainment of the children. In the early stages of SATs, 86 per cent of the children on Level 1 were born in the summer – that is, the youngest in the class (NUT 1991).

Although the SATs have associated problems and interpreting the results has been fraught with difficulties, this does not mean that an assessment of children's development as literacy users is not required. We need to know about children's progress so that their strengths and weaknesses can be determined and literacy activities can be provided to help them further. And, as part of the *home–school link*, parents should be kept informed of their children's progress. Assessment is an integral part of the teacher's monitoring of the classroom. Whether SATs in their current format are a useful part of that assessment is yet to be determined.

Further reading

QCA (1999d) *English Tasks Pack Key Stage 1*. London: Qualifications and Curriculum Authority with Department for Education and Employment.

This pack includes a range of materials giving instructions for carrying out the standard assessment tasks at Key Stage 1. There are also forms for recording the results. In particular, the Teacher's Handbook, as a part of the pack, indicates all the details for the SATs. It includes samples of children's writing that provide examples of the levels. Packs of this kind are produced each year thus any changes in the demands placed upon the children can be detected.

SCAA (1997) *Baseline Assessment Scales*. London: School Curriculum and Assessment Authority.

This booklet provided the first details of the baseline assessment to be carried out with children starting school, that is 4- and 5-year-olds. The Qualifications and Curriculum Authority provides updated information on this assessment procedure on its website: www.qca.org.uk. Included in that information are the various accredited schemes for baseline assessment and an indication of which scheme the various local education authorities use.

bilingual children

Some children have the advantage of being bilingual. Most typically in the UK, they are children who have a home language and then learn English as an additional language at school. Drury (2000) suggests that 8.5 per cent of children in primary schools in the UK are in that category. Of course, for the teachers and other adults who teach them, there are challenges in meeting the language and literacy needs of the children. Inevitably, those children have a wide range of linguistic, cultural and learning experiences as they enter pre-school or school. To meet that diversity, the teachers will need to bear in mind certain principles leading to particular strategies.

Eve Gregory (1996) suggested a first principle of building on the children's existing knowledge – working 'from the inside-out'. To achieve that, adults working in early years settings need to know as much as possible about the family's approaches to literacy to build upon what already exists. Drury (2000) noted that home visits and parental involvement enabled staff to draw on the child's previous experiences and interests as a starting point for literacy learning, and bilingual adults can help in particular to assist the child with routine classroom interactions. Initially, a *language experience approach* will be used for some of the child's early experiences with English. In addition, Gregory (1996) suggests the use of puppets and songs as a means of modelling chunks of language orally and notes the importance of *play activities*. And a home–school reading programme that families feel comfortable with adds to the recognition of what the child brings to the setting. Kenner (2000) also emphasizes the value of parents working alongside the children. She shows how parents writing alongside their children in a nursery classroom provided a model of literacy and encouraged the children to write in their home language as well as in English.

From another perspective, Gregory (1996) also suggested working 'from the outside-in'. A key feature of that approach is the important role of stories, with the first task for the teacher being the careful selection of *children's books* that are interesting to the children, worthwhile and contain attributes of rhyme, rhythm and repetition. Minns (1997) also argued that reading aloud from storybooks, and a variety of other texts, over and over again needs to form a key part of the teaching and learning of reading with emergent bilingual children. So *story reading* and *shared reading* are important features of the early years classroom for all children. During shared readings, bilingual children are able to repeat chunks of language that have been modelled for them by the teacher and that can be read as the words are repeated. These chunks of language can gradually be increased as the children's confidence with the additional language is developed. Linking the story theme to other aspects of the curriculum then helps to support the children's understanding of language and literacy.

Although the importance of *sharing a book*, or listening to children reading, is not part of the *literacy hour* strategy, Gregory (1996) suggested it as a means of supporting individual bilingual children. Occasionally, using a *miscue analysis* provides a greater insight into the children's development as readers and their strengths. It can become a valuable part of the record of the child's progress. Also, just as with other children, the use of *paired reading* – an older child reading with a younger child – can have benefits for both children. In this instance, it may have the additional benefit of the older child being able to communicate in more than one language with the younger learner.

Further reading

Gregory, E. (1996) *Making Sense of a New World: Learning to Read in a Second Language*. London: Paul Chapman.
This book is a very useful guide to supporting young children from a variety of backgrounds who are learning English as an additional language. Gregory's proposal to meet the child's needs by starting from the known inside-out and introducing the unknown outside-in is detailed in this text. Many practical suggestions, firmly derived from theory, are provided. These suggestions are contextualized in classroom examples with many bilingual children from different backgrounds.

Kenner, C. (2000) *Home Pages Literacy Links for Bilingual Children*. Stoke-on-Trent: Trentham Books.
This book also has many insightful examples of bilingual children from a variety of backgrounds developing as literacy users. However, the emphasis here is on these children writing. Many of the examples are drawn from Kenner's research carried out in a south London nursery class. Some of the examples demonstrate the young children writing in two languages as they explore matters of interest to them.

book making

Children enjoy making books, whether as a member of the class or group making a collaborative book, or working independently on an individual book. The children's enthusiasm for this activity is enhanced because the task appears to them to be manageable and the end product is typically worthwhile. Indeed, the value of this activity is such that Burman (1990) suggested that class and individual book making should be regular features of classroom practice.

The class or group book can be constructed in a variety of ways. For instance, a class book might be developed as part of a *shared writing* with the teacher. It could be a rewriting of a story that the teacher and children construct. Often that would be a story that had been enjoyed previously in a *story reading*. Anderson (1995) reported working with 6- and 7-year-olds who created a rewriting of *The Very Hungry Caterpillar* (Carle 1969). In the rewriting, the caterpillar became 'she', some of the foods eaten were changed and several adjectives were added. All of that encouraged the children to think about story structure, sentences and words. After completing the rewrite, the text was printed from a computer and put into a book format. Once placed in the class library, it became one of the most frequently read books, probably because it was the children's authored book.

The class book can also be constructed from children's individual pieces of writing. The children are encouraged to draw and write about some aspect of a story that has been enjoyed. Subsequently, the teacher creates a sequence with the children's writing and sticks them into a large book. In doing so, only one page from a two-page-spread might be used. On the opposite page, the teacher prints carefully some of the words from the child's writing. In doing this, the teacher's print recreates the story, but always using the words from the writing of the children. Once placed in the classroom library, these books become very popular. Again the children have authored the book and the teacher's clear print supports them in their reading of it.

When it comes to creating individual books, there are again different approaches that can be adopted. One simple way is for the children to write and draw on sheets of paper, which are then stapled together or stuck into small books that have already been prepared by an adult. An alternative approach is to create an eight-page booklet that the child then writes in directly. Johnson (1995: 9) described the construction of such a booklet, which he called an 'origami book'. Quite simply, the book is constructed by folding a single sheet of paper twice vertically, once horizontally and cutting the centre fold. Once folded out into an eight-page booklet, the children take great delight in authoring the books.

Johnson (1995) argued that the booklet was ideal for young children to use. A front cover and end piece that can be used for a blurb and details of the author still leaves the middle six pages for writing. These six pages, or three double-spread pages, provide a structure for young children to write a story with a beginning, middle and end. The booklets can also be used to write in other *genres*. Young children can use the booklets to write recipe books, create books on animals, dinosaurs and a wide range of other topics of interest to them. That the book is soon completed and that ownership is with the child author encourages young children to engage in this activity. Furthermore, a great deal of literacy learning occurs as the children decide on the cover, construct the details for the end page and develop the writing of the story or topic.

In the classroom

The story *It's My Birthday* (Oxenbury 1993) has as its theme the making of a cake. That various animals collect all of the ingredients adds to the attraction of this book for young children. After the story had been read to a reception class of 5-year-olds, some of the children decided to make their own recipe books. The children used the eight-page origami booklets for their recipes. One child described how to make a fruitcake:

1 mix the egg.
2 mix the butter and sugger.
3 mix the Flour and Frot.
4 mix it alltogetheer
5 pot it in a tin
6 Bac in the ovn.

(Campbell 2001a: 85)

In the writing by the 5-year-old, a mixture of upper- and lower-case letters was used. Some of the words were written with the child's *invented spellings*, whereas other key words were written accurately. Nevertheless, the sequence within the recipe indicated a substantial amount of thinking by the child. Furthermore, she was motivated to create her own recipe book using a booklet made in the classroom.

Further reading

Johnson, P. (1995) *Children Making Books*. Reading: Reading and Language
  Information Centre, University of Reading.
Paul Johnson has been very influential in the development of book making
for young children. In this sixteen-page booklet, he provides clear information
on the construction of a variety of books by young children. Drafting, book
formats, words and pictures and illustrations are among the topics covered. At
the same time, he indicates the benefits that accrue from engaging in this
activity, not only in English but in other important curriculum areas as well.

books for babies

Babies love to have books shared with them. The book sharing, enjoyment of the *illustrations* and conversation around the text can start
during the first year of life for the baby and extend to other pre-
school years for the young child. And it is not only babies and young
children who enjoy *sharing a book*. The parents or other adults involved in the sharing are likely to take pleasure in the activity as well.
Once it is established as a time when the adult and child share a book
together, then the child is likely to request a book sharing at various
times in the day. Dorothy Butler (1998) emphasized the importance
of this topic in the title of her book, *Babies Need Books*.

The starting point for *sharing a book* with babies is the pleasure that
it gives. Many parents conclude the day by sharing a book with their
child because it helps to settle the child. A book sharing can also calm
a baby or child at other times of the day. Fortunately, there are many
delightful *children's books* that are now available to read with young
children. Libraries and bookshops have a wide range of books for the
very youngest of children.

The sharing of books is valuable beyond the important emotional
benefits that it brings. First, the baby and young child grow up knowing
about literacy. For instance, children who have had books shared with
them at home know about books. At the simplest level, they know how
to handle books and use them and may learn to do so by their first
birthday (Campbell 1999a: 17). Features such as left-to-right directionality
are learned incidentally and the importance of print in the process of
reading becomes known. Of course, many young children at home who
share books daily with parents or other adults move far beyond those

beginnings and learn to read to some extent before going to school. Such learning has been reported in books on the literacy development of young children before starting school (e.g. Schickedanz 1990; Martens 1996; Campbell 1999a). Positive results have also been reported from such projects as Books for Babies (Millard *et al.* 2000) and Bookstart (Wade and Moore 2000), where parents were given books and encouraged to share them with their babies from 9 months of age.

A constant feature of children sharing books in their first five years is the request for a re-reading. Children love to have stories repeated that they already know. This is partly a desire to remain with the familiar; however, with each reading, children also gain a greater ownership of the text. During those repeat readings, children learn more about their own environment and about the wider world. It is also from those repeat readings that many children begin to remember the words of whole books and to relate them to the print on the page – they learn to read. Of course, that requires parents who are patient, who ask children about the text, who respond to the questions posed by the children and who encourage them to join in with the repetitive features that are found in books for young children.

Once the children move on to school at 5 years of age, they are immediately familiar with activities such as *story reading, shared reading* and *sharing a book*. They are well prepared to understand the literacy activities of the classroom. Indeed, because the sharing of books has enabled them to know about reading and writing, their progress in those areas is likely to be accelerated. There is also a message for the teachers of young children: sharing books with young children is enjoyable and promotes literacy. Therefore, *story reading* to the class is a very important part of the school day. And for those children who have not shared books with adults at home frequently, then that activity is much needed.

Further reading

Campbell, R. (1999a) *Literacy from Home to School: Reading with Alice.* Stoke-on-Trent: Trentham Books.
This book recounts the details of a five-year longitudinal study of a child from birth to 5 years of age. Throughout those five years, Alice (the granddaughter of the author) had books read with her regularly and frequently by her parents and grandparents. A key message of the book was that the frequent *sharing of a book* with Alice supported her literacy development. Other literacy activities took place incidentally, including opportunities to write and sing nursery rhymes. Nevertheless, the transcript evidence from the shared *story readings* indicated the way in which Alice became a reader and writer before age 5.

Wade, B. and Moore, M. (2000) *Baby Power*. Handforth: Egmont World Ltd.
In this forty-eight page colourful text, there are, arguably, three main strands.
First, parents are encouraged to share books with their babies from 9 months
of age. The importance of the activity is stressed and several strategies during
the sharing of the book are suggested. Thus encouraging the child to fill in the
gap by saying the familiar phrase or rhyme is suggested, as is encouraging the
child to predict what they think will happen next in the story. Second, there
are some simplified results from the Bookstart Project that demonstrate the
educational benefits from reading regularly to a young child from 9 months.
Finally, there is a small section that helps in the selection of books for young
children.

Breakthrough to Literacy

In primary classrooms in the 1970s, many teachers were using a *language experience approach* with very young children (and, for good reasons,
some aspects of that approach are maintained in infant classrooms
today). The emphasis of that approach – to get children to talk, write
and read about their experiences and interests, with support from the
teacher – was also the basis for Breakthrough to Literacy. In paragraph
7.14 of the Bullock Report (DES 1975), where a language experience
approach is advocated for the youngest children in school, a link is
made to 'Breakthrough' (the shorthand term used by many teachers for
the materials and approach). But, first, what is Breakthrough and what
are the principles on which it is based?

The teacher's manual (Mackay *et al.* 1970: 3) indicated that Breakthrough integrated 'the production (writing) and the reception (reading)
of written language' and, furthermore, that written material 'should
from the very beginning be linked to [the children's] own spoken language'. Therefore, as with a language experience approach, the children
were to use their own experiences and interests to form the basis for
their reading materials. However, with Breakthrough, the children were
aided in this task by the provision of some materials. In particular, the
sentence maker (a card with slots to allow for the insertion of smaller
printed inserts) and the smaller word inserts and blank inserts (for the
children's own special and personal words) were a major feature of
Breakthrough. These materials enabled children to compose sentences
and longer pieces of prose by inserting the words into the sentence

maker in the appropriate sequence. The use of the children's special and personal *words* is an important feature of the approach.

There was also a word maker, which looked like a smaller sentence maker, with letter inserts that encouraged the children to build up unknown words. Additionally, there were some Breakthrough books, nursery rhyme materials and a magnet board for language demonstrations. When Jessie Reid (1974: 92) conducted her evaluation of Breakthrough to Literacy, she noted a number of positive features that were linked to that usage. In particular, she indicated that it made the children 'progressively aware of the way language works': the existence of words, the structure of sentences, the nature of bound morphemes (-s, -es, -ed, -ing) and the terminology of language (e.g. letter, word, sentence, etc.). Waterland (1988) added that it provides an opportunity for children to play with writing independently of the teacher; she advocated its use as part of an apprenticeship approach.

However, concerns have been expressed about aspects of the materials and their use. First, at a practical level, the maintenance and storage of the materials can be a problem and, unless the teacher is very organized and careful, pieces can be lost on a daily basis. Second, as the Bullock Report (DES 1975: 103) noted, 'whether or not the knowledgeable teacher needs this particular material once the [language experience] approach is well established is open to question'. Bullock was suggesting that it might only be those teachers who are not yet confident enough to engage in a language experience approach who need to use Breakthrough to Literacy.

Furthermore, it was the sentence maker and the word cards that were argued to be central to the process, because they helped young children overcome two difficulties when writing: 'their lack of manual dexterity in handling a writing tool and the difficulty they have in spelling words' (Mackay *et al.* 1970: 3). Therefore, handwriting and spelling were key reasons why some teachers wishing to use a language experience approach adopted Breakthrough. However, these supposed difficulties might be viewed differently now.

Children need to write to develop their motor skills related to handwriting; however, in the future, skill at the keyboard may be more relevant than handwriting. And before arriving at school children will, of course, already have been scribbling and making marks, which leads to drawing and writing. As teachers, we need to support that and help to develop handwriting by guiding, instructing and encouraging individuals, groups and the class as needed. The Breakthrough manual recognized that need and devoted a chapter to the teaching of handwriting but away from the process of composing.

The difficulty that children have in spelling words would now be seen in the context of children's own *invented spellings*. During the process of writing, children have to consider each word on the basis of their knowledge of that word, their developing awareness of English phonology (Read 1971) and their increasing familiarity with the letters of the *alphabet*. In the process of attempting to construct the word, children are engaged actively with literacy and, with support from the teacher, gradually become more proficient users of written language. Furthermore, such an engagement with writing, letters and sounds helps children in their reading development. Therefore, children's unconventional spellings are viewed as a developmental process leading towards literacy rather than as a difficulty hindering writing. Such a view now requires a change of attitude on the part of the teacher, especially in relation to the spellings produced by young children.

So the perceived difficulties that in part led to the development of Breakthrough might not be seen in the same light today. Rather than avoiding handwriting and spelling through the use of materials, many teachers would want children to engage in those activities to further their learning.

Further reading

Mackay, D., Thompson, B. and Schaub, P. (1970) *Breakthrough to Literacy: Teacher's Manual*. London: Schools Council/Longman.
The teacher's manual for Breakthrough to Literacy was first published in 1970 and provides a most useful guide to both the theory and practice of the materials. There are very detailed suggestions for the use of each of the materials in the classroom, as well as chapters on working with parents and record-keeping. In several ways, the manual not only describes the materials, it also provides an introduction to aspects of linguistics, because the purposes for the materials are outlined.

Reid, J.F. (1974) *Breakthrough in Action: An Independent Evaluation of 'Breakthrough to Literacy'*. London: Schools Council/Longman.
In her evaluation of Breakthrough to Literacy, Reid indicated several positive features linked specifically with the use of the materials (these were noted above). However, her evaluation also noted some of the practical problems that teachers face when using the materials. Examples of children's writing, some interviews with children and an awareness of the classroom at work enable the reader of this book to gain a good insight into the use of this material with young children.

children's books

The books available for children today are numerous, varied and many are of a high quality. That is important because such books play an important role in young children's literacy development. Starting with *books for babies* and developing into *story readings* and *sharing a book* at home and in school, children's books are a source of great pleasure for children and for the adults who share those books with them. However, in addition to the pleasure that is gained from books, Bruner (1968) argued that story provides one way of thinking about reality. Children learn from the books that are read with them and which eventually they read for themselves.

What are the features of high-quality books? Rhodes (1981) suggested that books for young children are often predictable books, featuring repetition, rhythm and rhyme – the three R's of language and story as Wade (1990) referred to them. These features, which were also noted by Gibbons (1999), capture young children's attention. However, the repetition is typically one of phrases and sentences rather than of words – that was used by some of the earliest reading schemes. They add to the story rather than being designed to teach a word. So in *Good-Night Owl* (Hutchins 1972), the repetition of 'and owl tried to sleep' adds to the story line as well as creating a rhythm in the text. And when children hear that repetition during a *story reading*, they are quickly able to join in with the reading. In *Slinki Malinki, Open the Door* (Dodd 1993), the repetition is even more extensive. After each 'mischievous adventure', Slinki Malinki and Stickybeat Sid move on and 'Slinki Malinki jumped high off the floor, he swung on a handle and opened a door'. Because of that repetition on every other page, children are quickly able to predict part of the story when they hear it read aloud. Other books by Lynley Dodd have a very strong rhyming element. For instance, in *Hairy Maclary from Donaldson's Dairy* (Dodd 1983), each of the dogs in the pack has a rhyme to its name just as Maclary/dairy did. Often, it is the repetition and rhyme that create the rhythm in the book. However, in the classic *Rosie's Walk* (Hutchins 1968), it is the journey across the farmyard in which the rhythm is developed. In the Dr Seuss books, such as *Green Eggs and Ham* (Seuss 1960), the repetition and rhyme elements create a rhythm throughout the text.

It is enough that children enjoy story books. From that enjoyment is created a desire to want to continue to engage with books. However, far more is taken from books than enjoyment. As Whitehead

(1987) noted, skills, cultural heritage and personal development are all linked to children's books. As a starting point, children learn how to use books as they hear them being read and manipulate them themselves. Other skills are also learned, including phonological development from the rhymes in stories and nursery rhymes (Meek 1990). More specifically, the *onset and rime* elements are apparent in many of the picture books mentioned above; this aspect of letters and sounds is learned as the books are read. And it goes beyond letters and sounds. As Taylor (1990) noted, children learn about syntactical structures and other aspects of language during their contact with worthwhile books. But they also learn of a wider world as they transact with books. Within many of the books enjoyed by children, there is history, geography and science – or making a cake in *It's My Birthday* (Oxenbury 1993) – none of which is taught explicitly; rather, it is learned from the story. Many stories contain aspects of social relationships that enable the children to learn about themselves and others. *Alfie Gets in First* (Hughes 1981) is a delightful story, but it also tells about children's adventures, fears, relationships and problem solving and it tells about community, adult relationships, support and friendship. But it is read because it is a delightful story enjoyed by children.

Because they are so important, children's books need to be readily available for the children in early years settings. The *library corner* should contain many books, *story readings* should occur daily or more frequently and time for reading such as *sustained silent reading* should be organized for reception classes and beyond. McQuillan (1998) argued that it is important to provide more access to reading materials and more opportunities for reading to support children's reading development.

In this section, I have only mentioned seven titles of children's books from the many thousands that are available. How does the busy teacher ensure that past classics and new favourites are known and available? Some texts contain annotated lists of children's books (e.g. Wade 1990; Bennett 1991; Trelease 1995), which provide a good starting point. Other listings appear from time to time in various journals and magazines; annual awards also inform us of highly regarded new texts. Visits to children's libraries can suggest books to bring into the classroom. Then there are the discussions with colleagues that help a teacher to build up a repertoire of authors and books. All of that helps us to bring children's books and children together.

Further reading

Meek, M. (1988) *How Texts Teach What Readers Learn*. Stroud: Thimble Press. This forty-eight page booklet argues for worthwhile children's books that enable young children to learn about reading and writing and to read and write. Meek's account, in particular, of an adult sharing *Rosie's Walk* (Hutchins 1968) with young Ben demonstrates the learning with that polysemic text. Because books like that function at different levels, children learn countless lessons. Meek debates other books briefly to demonstrate the wealth of learning about literacy and the wider world that are to be found in many of the children's books now available.

classroom organization and management

In the classroom setting, the teacher is responsible for twenty, thirty or more children. In such circumstances, the literacy activities that are provided can flourish only when the teacher has devoted a good deal of attention and effort to the prior organization of the classroom and, subsequently, to classroom management as well as to the *time for literacy* and the *teacher's role*. These are key, albeit basic, issues for the teacher. For the moment, let us consider the organization of the classroom.

A starting point for that organization is the physical arrangement of the classroom furniture. Because literacy activities require individual interactions, groupwork and whole-class sessions, the tables, benches, chairs and mats, as well as the partitions, cupboards and walls, need to reflect that requirement. The teacher needs to ensure that there is a sufficiently large space for whole-class sessions, including the very important *story readings*, where the children can sit in comfort without being too close to one another. Often, the overall organizational requirements will be reflected in the grouping of the children's tables and chairs into blocks catering for four to six children, of a number of bays or areas to cater for specific purposes (e.g. *library corner*) and some small bays to allow for individual work.

The organization of the furniture needs to ensure that there is space to help the children to work undisturbed next to other activities being undertaken in the classroom, as well as allow the teacher space to move between the activities. It also allows the children to move from one activity area to another as they complete their work. In this way, they can collect materials from clearly labelled drawers, boxes and cupboards, consult charts among the *classroom print*, and consult dictionaries or information books as necessary. It is part of the management of the classroom by the teacher to monitor the movement of the children and to ensure that such movement is purposeful. Ease of movement is important because it enables the teacher to support, guide and encourage the children in their various activities. It also enables the teacher to find a place to interact with an individual child before moving on to another area. How the furniture is laid out can also encourage child–child as well as teacher–child interactions.

The furniture in nursery and infant classrooms is arranged in a general manner but is also arranged very specifically for a number of areas more clearly designated for literacy activities. The teacher will need to determine how best to organize the classroom for the *library corner, listening area, writing centre* and a play area or home corner for *play activities*. This makes a very considerable demand upon the space in the classroom, as well as on the ingenuity of the teacher. But such efforts are worthwhile, because each of the areas provides many opportunities for literacy involvement that contributes to the children's literacy development. The careful organization of the classroom is a prerequisite for effective literacy teaching and learning.

In many ways, the classroom organization might be regarded as the easy part! How will all the activities be managed once the children are in the classroom? Many teachers find that creating a structure or framework to the day is the first part of classroom management. For early years teachers in England, with Key Stage 1 classes beyond the reception or kindergarten year, that framework is determined currently by the inclusion of a *literacy hour* (DfEE 1998) with its clearly defined structure (they also have to organize for a numeracy hour). Beyond that literacy hour, the school day is naturally defined by start and finish times, and the inclusion of the lunch break and other breaks during the day. Linking literacy activities to these boundaries is a relatively common practice. *Story readings*, for instance, are often placed at the end of the school day (Trelease 1995). Placed there it brings the school day to an enjoyable, quiet and reflective finish. Yet many teachers of very young children want to use stories as a stimulus for drawing, painting, play activities, drama, movement and writing. Therefore, having the start of the day devoted to story reading begins to be attractive. Some nursery and infant teachers find it easy to reach a compromise – they place story readings at both the beginning and the end of the school day (Campbell 2001a). They do so because of the benefits that are derived from engagement with stories.

Sustained silent reading, when used in early years classrooms, would also appear to be best placed alongside one of the natural breaks in the school day (Campbell 1990a). In part, this is because it involves the whole class and making arrangements for it is logically linked to the lunch break, for instance, when the children have to be brought together anyway.

That merely allocates two major literacy activities to the structure of the day. What about the rest of the day and the provision of other important literacy activities? Many teachers of the youngest children, at the foundation stage in England (QCA 2000), create a structure in which several activities are available for the children throughout the school day. The children then move between these activities, which include other curriculum areas as well as literacy, so that there is always something worthwhile available for them. Ideally, the children do not have to wait for the teacher to become involved with an activity, as the teacher's prior preparation ensures that there are interesting, worthwhile and appropriate activities readily available. And because the children do not have to wait for the teacher to tell them what to do next, there will be fewer problems maintaining order (Goodman 1986).

Of course, even when a structure is in place, the teacher still has to manage the moment-by-moment happenings in the classroom. Cambourne (1988: 95) noted in relation to a literacy activity time, that the teacher needs to move around the classroom to 'observe, evaluate, interact, teach, redirect, refocus, demand, pursue, question, clarify, analyse, support, celebrate, coerce, coax, cajole, sympathise, and empathise'. Although we can debate whether some of these suggestions are totally appropriate, nevertheless the quotation neatly indicates the complex task of managing in the classroom. The list provides an insight into some of the strategies that teachers use to manage the classroom, maintain a good working atmosphere and keep events and the children quietly under control.

As part of classroom management, Holdaway (1979) indicated that it is useful to think in terms of positive teaching as a principle for governing teacher–child interactions. So, in relation to making predictions during *shared reading* with a big book, it is possible to say 'Yes' or 'It could be' rather than being negative and corrective. Such a strategy would appear to be helpful in aiding the management of a busy classroom.

Finally, all teachers know how difficult it is at times to manage transitions – for example, into the story reading at the end of the day. Yet here, too, the positive principle might be applied. Wherever possible, teachers need to use interesting and beneficial activities to bridge the gap from one set of activities to another: 'They didn't settle easily so we sang a favourite song and a nursery rhyme or two' (Holdaway 1979: 66). So, the two or three minutes that it takes to tidy and get ready for story reading can be filled in part with *nursery rhymes* or other worthwhile literacy activities. This is not to understate the difficulties or to fail to recognize the demands placed upon the teacher. However, the transitions that can create disorder can instead be transformed into short activities. These activities support the management of the class and contribute at the same time to the children's literacy development.

Further reading

Burman, C. (1990) Organizing for reading 3–7, in B. Wade (ed.) *Reading for Real*. Buckingham: Open University Press.
The chapter by Chris Burman is one of ten contributions in this very helpful book edited by Barrie Wade. There are two strands to the chapter. First, there is a case study of the organization, teaching and support given to 6-year-old Kevin as he developed as a reader in an infant classroom. There is then a debate on the classroom environment that provides the context for that learning to take place.

Cambourne, B. (1988) *The Whole Story: Natural Learning and the Acquisition of Literacy in the Classroom*. Auckland: Ashton Scholastic.
Brian Cambourne's book is 'about children learning to read and write' (p. 1). In the text, he explores a model of learning as applied to literacy learning. However, his exploration of the theoretical is related very closely to the events of the classroom. The analysis of the classroom includes sections on the organization of space and of resources. He makes the point that even an average-sized room can be organized so that it is not overcrowded. Although we would all probably prefer to have a classroom with plenty of room, with planning the classroom can be organized for the spaces that are required for literacy learning – and that is demonstrated in this book.

classroom print

Teachers of young children will be aware that most of them – whether 3, 4 or 5 years of age – will arrive at school with some awareness of, and knowledge about, *environmental print*. That being the case, teachers will want to capitalize on that knowledge by bringing some of that environmental print into the classroom for displays, play activities and discussion. However, teachers can also extend the use of contextualized environmental print by developing various examples of classroom print.

Teachers will not want to develop classroom print simply for its own sake. Instead, classroom print will be such that it can be seen to serve real purposes. Furthermore, teachers should not be content just to provide meaningful classroom print displays, but should also ensure that time is spent discussing the print with the children and responding to their enquiries about it.

So what forms of classroom print might be made available? In part, of course, that will be determined by the age of the children and their experience with literacy. Nevertheless, lists of various types of classroom print are given in several texts (e.g. Cambourne 1988; Campbell 1992). However, a starting point could be environmental print. Goodman (1986) suggested that children might be taken for walks to look for environmental print and such questions as 'Why is the print there?' and 'What does it say?' can be raised. This can then lead to the development and display of environmental print in the classroom. For instance, the children could collect pictures or examples of road signs – or make their own – and display them. Their discussion of these signs with their teacher can lead to aspects of road safety as well as encouraging literacy development.

With the very youngest of children, attendance charts can be used, which they are asked to sign each day. This is an important task for young children, because of the considerable interest they have in beginning to recognize, and have control over, the production of their own names. Harste *et al.* (1984) describe with examples the development of children's writing of their own names in a context in which a teacher of pre-school children has asked them to sign in each day. Although the teacher was concerned with whether the activity was successful, the examples of the children's 'scribbles' indicated differences between scribbled writing and scribbled drawing. The examples also demonstrated how the children were gradually developing more sophisticated and conventional representations of their names. All classroom print activities have to be as meaningful as this, because contextualized environmental print is being replaced by less contextualized classroom print.

A daily message board can be used to inform the children about important happenings during the day, as well as indicating the activities that are immediately available. This can work as well for children emerging as literacy users as for children who are beginning to gain some independence with reading and writing. For those children who are not yet able to read in a conventional manner, the teacher will have to spend some time talking about the messages on the board and perhaps reminding the children of those messages throughout the school day.

A bulletin board can be used to extend the usefulness of the message board by telling the children about other events later in the week or in the very near future. This separation of function can be useful, as the children's attention will not then be distracted from the daily immediacy of the message board. Regular, albeit short, discussion of the contents of the board will be needed, especially with the younger children.

Functional labels can supply important information to the children. Drawers, cupboards and boxes of equipment can be labelled to inform the children of their contents. The children have a real purpose for reading the labels and this enables them to work with some degree of independence from the teacher. Furthermore, the teacher is able to engage in important literacy interactions, rather than spending time supplying pencils, paper and other materials. But we need to remind ourselves that the functional labels must serve a real communicative purpose. Simply attaching a 'chair' label to a chair serves no real purpose; however, a 'pencil' label on a drawer containing pencils can be useful and is functional (Donaldson 1989).

Nursery school and reception/kindergarten children love to sing short songs, recite nursery rhymes and poems, and take part in language games, some of which can be displayed on large charts. These charts can be constructed by the teacher and the children during a *shared writing* activity. They then form part of the classroom print and the teacher and the children can engage with them on a frequent basis. During such activities, the *shared reading*/singing begins to resemble the interactions that occur with big books and the children will gain similar benefits from the experience. In particular, the children will note some of the conventions of print (e.g. *left-to-right directionality*, top-to-bottom reading, space either side of a word, etc.) as their teacher links the oral words to the written print.

Birthday charts are also significant to young children, as they indicate the timing of a very major event in every child's life. And such a chart can be used to relate an individual child's birthday to the birthdays of the other children in the classroom. They can also be used to teach sequences of time, including the months of the year, the days of the week and the numbers from 1 to 31.

A weather chart can be linked to the daily message board on which a child might be nominated to record the weather. Children will enjoy having the responsibility for recording the weather. And with the very changeable weather in the UK, a morning and afternoon recording could be appropriate! This activity also brings together a number of curriculum areas (e.g. reading, writing and science) in a natural way.

Although the message board can be used to nominate children for particular responsibilities, this can lead to the board becoming overcrowded and, therefore, less easy to read. Some teachers prefer to have a separate chart of job responsibilities, with the children's names changing on a weekly or even daily basis. And because of these regular and frequent changes, it will form the focus for brief but regular teacher–child interactions.

Around the room may be hung charts that tell the children about the activities available in a particular corner or centre. For example, in the listening area, there might be instructions about the number of children who can use the area at any one time, as well as informing the children about the use of the equipment and the tidying up procedures at the end of the day. Another more general chart might list the classroom rules and expectations. The children can contribute to these rules and expectations as the teacher debates the list with them and reminds them of expected behaviour and responsibilities.

Among these different wall charts and displays will be some derived from the children's own work. In the library corner, for instance, might be displayed the children's book reviews. This might be more appropriate for those children who have developed their writing; however, a picture of a main character with just the name underneath can also enliven the corner. Alphabetic wall charts and sources of reference can also be part of the classroom print as well as a *word* wall, as described by Cunningham and Allington (1998). Furthermore, labels to describe and explain the displays and exhibitions as well as graphs, derived perhaps from the birthday or weather charts, all add to the classroom being rich in print.

To use Brian Cambourne's (1988: 101) phrase, teachers need 'to flood the classroom with useful wall charts' and, having done so, they need to use the charts, update them on a regular basis and, importantly, discuss them with the children. These discussions give the children the opportunity to reflect on the messages and to learn about literacy.

Further reading

Cambourne, B. (1988) *The Whole Story: Natural Learning and the Acquisition of Literacy in the Classroom*. Auckland: Ashton Scholastic.

In this book, Cambourne stresses how important it is for the teacher to organize time, space and resources in the classroom. And one of these resources is classroom print. He argues that the classroom should be flooded with useful print and that the teacher and the children should talk about that print on a frequent basis. He provides a list of wall charts that might be usefully displayed and discussed.

Cunningham, P. and Allington, R. (1998) *Classrooms that Work: They can All Read and Write*. New York: Longman.

One of the many literacy activities suggested in this book is having a word wall. Quite simply, the word wall is a wall area in the classroom where key words can be listed alphabetically. However, it is not sufficient just to have a word wall; the authors argue that teachers must 'do' word walls. Teachers and children have to talk about the words on the wall. To make that manageable, Cunningham and Allington suggest that teachers should be very selective about the words that are listed on the wall [such as the high frequency words listed in the *National Literacy Strategy* (DfEE 1998: 60–1)] and that no more than five should be added each week. The word wall should be positioned so that it is clearly accessible to all the children in the class. It should have big bold print, possibly using different colours to help pick out the words. Cunningham and Allington also suggest that the words should be clapped (using the syllables), chanted and written regularly. For teachers, the issue is one of considering how best to help the young children to develop a visual memory of some key words.

cue systems

When *sharing a book* or as part of a *hearing children read* interaction, several miscues will be noted. These deviations from the text can be examined in detail using a *miscue analysis*. Such an analysis will provide information about the language cue systems that the children might have used. This information, built up within an extended read or with a young reader over a number of occasions when he or she reads aloud, tells the teacher about what the child is attempting to do during the reading. It can provide insights into which cue systems the child might be using effectively or not so effectively. To gain most benefit from a miscue analysis, therefore, it is helpful if the teacher has some knowledge of language cue systems.

Language cue systems can be considered at two levels. First, we can explore the graphophonic, syntactic and semantic cue systems in a relatively simple way, as might be the case in a miscue analysis in the busy classroom. Second, these systems can be explored in far greater depth, where a detailed analysis of the language cues might indicate the complexities of the systems that the young child uses.

It is often easy to recognize when a child is using the graphophonic cue system. In particular, we might expect young readers to pick up on the cue provided by the first letter of a word. They see that first letter, recognize it and then produce the sound that is often associated with it. Eventually, attention might also be paid to the final letter(s), the length of the word or a cluster of letters in the middle of a longer word. Comparing miscues with text words enables us to detect the graphophonic strategies of children. Second, children also use the syntactic cue system as they read. They may not be able to articulate their knowledge of sentence structure, but their miscues often demonstrate this implicit knowledge. We can analyse these miscues to see the way in which children try to keep their reading in organized sentences. Usually, for instance, the miscues will be of a noun for a noun, a verb for a verb, and so on. Third, children try to maintain a meaningful read when involved with a book. The miscues that are produced will demonstrate the use of the semantic cue system, as words of similar meaning are offered as substitutions. Such an emphasis upon meaning may sometimes lead the child to ignore the graphophonic cues. Of course, it is not the case that children simply use one or other of the cues. In many instances, it is apparent that children make use of all of the cues to read a text and that the miscues produced have some degree of graphophonic, syntactic and semantic similarity or appropriateness.

However, using language cue systems is more complex than the above might suggest. The graphophonic cue system provides readers with the orthographic written symbols of the alphabetically written English language and these symbols indicate the conventions of our spelling. The sound or phonological system enables us to turn these written symbols into oral language. But it is not just the letters and words that are represented graphically. Punctuation is also represented on the page; apostrophes in particular are represented as part of a word and have to be dealt with by children. Next, the syntactic cues deal with the ways in which words, sentences and paragraphs are brought together within a text. Although we tend to study syntactic cues by considering the complete sentence, it is possible to consider the child's awareness of word features, in what Kenneth Goodman (1994) refers to as the lexico-grammatical language cue system. So although the syntactical feature of sentence order might be of prime importance, we can also look at the way in which children use the inflection system of bound morphemes (-ed, -s, -ing) and the function words (e.g. 'the') that carry less meaning but are instrumental in creating sentence patterns. Finally, the semantic cue system is used to create meaning and children demonstrate their attempts to maintain that meaning in the miscues that they produce. However, Goodman (1994) refers to the semantic–pragmatic cue system, which serves to remind us that a reader has to consider the context to extract the fullest meaning. A text might be written straightforwardly to convey a particular meaning, or it might be written to convey a subtle message. The use of words in the text and the context in which they are written are important pragmatic features.

A knowledge of the language cue systems used by children enables the teacher to be more reflective in terms of the support that might be given during a reading interaction. And on the basis of the diagnosis made during a miscue analysis, it also helps the teacher to determine which literacy activities might be developed further.

In the classroom

6-year-old Alan, while reading with his teacher from a book, demonstrated his understanding of the syntactic cue system. The text sentence to be read was:

The giants live in the castle.

However, Alan read it as:

The giant lives in the castle.

So having miscued 'giants' and read 'giant', Alan was confronted with a difficulty with the word 'live'. He either had to self-correct and read 'giants' or he needed to produce another miscue of the verb so as to maintain his reading as a sentence. Alan changed the verb ending, therefore creating a miscue chain, and, in so doing, he demonstrated his implicit understanding of sentences.

Further reading

Gollasch, F.V. (ed.) (1982a) *Language and Literacy: The Selected Writings of Kenneth S. Goodman. Vol. I: Process, Theory, Research.* London: Routledge.

Gollasch, F.V. (ed.) (1982b) *Language and Literacy: The Selected Writings of Kenneth S. Goodman. Vol. II: Reading, Language and the Classroom Teacher.* London: Routledge.

Fred Gollasch has collected together a number of Kenneth Goodman's articles in Volume 1 of this text. The main sections are concerned with the reading process and miscue analysis. Therefore, not only are there some key articles that address the cue systems directly (including 'Reading: a psycholinguistic guessing game', pp. 33–43), but also most of the articles contain some reference to the language cue systems. Although Volume 2 does not look at the language cue systems in any detail, one of the articles, 'Behind the eye: what happens in reading' (pp. 99–124), is useful.

Goodman, Y., Watson, D. and Burke, C. (1987) *Reading Miscue Inventory: Alternative Procedures.* New York: Richard C. Owen.

This book is referenced in the section on miscue analysis and the main emphasis of the book is to provide the details of the means of exploring a child's reading. However, the second chapter of the book explores the theoretical understandings of a holistic view of reading and includes a good introduction to the language cue systems. It serves as a useful starting point for an exploration of this subject.

emerging literacy

Teachers of young children, whether in the nursery, pre-school classroom or the reception or kindergarten classroom when the children start school, have to consider how to help the children develop as readers and writers. In part, that consideration will be based upon views that the teacher has about children as learners and the extent to which each child is perceived to bring to school knowledge and skills about literacy. In recent years, the notion of emerging literacy has developed as a way of viewing children as literacy learners, as intensive – and often longitudinal – case studies have produced evidence about children's learning to read and write at home and at school. The evidence from these studies (e.g. Schickedanz 1990; Martens 1996; Campbell 1999a) has suggested that children were engaged with literacy in many different ways during their early years. This engagement provides the basis for literacy to emerge from each child.

But why use the term 'emergent'? Nigel Hall (1987) suggested that there are four reasons for doing so. First, the term indicates that the development of a child as a literacy user comes from within. It is children who make sense of all the print data that surround them during their early years, supported by interactions with adults about that print. Second, emergence implies a gradual process that takes place over time – literacy development does not wait until the school years to begin. Literacy emerges while the child is at home engaged with print in a variety of ways. Third, emerging literacy recognizes the abilities that children have to make sense of the world. It perceives children as active learners constructing a sense of their environment, an environment that includes a substantial amount of print. Fourth, literacy only emerges if the conditions are right, so there has to be meaningful print and engagement with adults who support the child's enquiries. There also has to be respect for the child's literacy performances. So when children produce their emergent readings (which might be meaningful but not yet constrained by the conventions of the print) of a story book or they begin to write with *invented spellings*, adults need to accept and support such efforts.

These reasons for using the term 'emergent' help to demonstrate key aspects of the role of the child in the learning process. Teale and Sulzby (1989) developed this further in their consideration of emergent literacy. They suggested that a portrait of young children as literacy learners should include several features, some of which can be linked directly to Hall's (1987) list. First, they indicated that learning to read and write begins very early in life. Of course, it is not easy to determine the extent of such early learning or when it begins, but we do recognize the encounters that very young children have with literacy, and we can speculate on the learning that might be taking place. Children in the first year of life are often read to by their parents and grandparents and are often informed of print in the environment. Each of these interactions help children to learn about literacy. And opportunities to write, even though they may at first only appear as 'scribbles', also help children to emerge as literacy users.

Second, children learn about literacy from real-life settings. In part, this is because of contact with *environmental print*, but it is also derived from their observations of adults using books, newspapers and magazines. Many children, therefore, see adults using print for real purposes and they begin to see the ways in which literacy can support particular goals. Third, it is literacy that emerges rather than reading or writing; as Teale and Sulzby (1989: 3) indicated, 'reading and writing develop concurrently and interrelatedly in young children'. They extended this to argue that oral language proficiency is also related to growth in reading and writing. Finally, they emphasized that children emerge as literacy learners through their active engagement with written language. Young children need the support of adults who can facilitate such learning by demonstrating, suggesting and guiding the children's efforts. (Teale and Sulzby refer to literacy as a complex sociopsycholinguistic activity, which emphasizes the role of parents and others and, subsequently, the teacher, in helping the child to emerge as a literacy user.)

Emerging literacy may well appear to place the emphasis on learning rather than on teaching, but it does not deny the important role of the adult. So what does emergent literacy suggest for practices in the classroom? Teachers will want to build upon the literacy that has already been learnt at home and in many instances replicate some of the practices that the children have already experienced. Therefore, a classroom should be rich in print, most of which serves a real function and some of which is drawn from the environment, thereby creating a link with the reading with which the children are familiar. Teachers should read stories to the children on a daily if not more frequent basis and use such *story readings* to develop activities of drama, painting and writing that are stimulated by the stories. Additionally, the *play activities* that are provided should be developed to encourage the children to engage with literacy; again, this will reflect some of the experiences the children will have had at home. In part, the play activities will encourage the children to write, as will some of the story readings, and the teacher should encourage meaningful *writing* knowing that the children's involvement with letters, words and sentences will help them to develop further their emerging literacy.

Further reading

Hall, N. (1987) *The Emergence of Literacy*. Sevenoaks: Hodder & Stoughton.
Nigel Hall's book, as the title indicates, is about the concept of emerging literacy. It provides a good deal of theory to substantiate what he refers to as the rediscovery of emergent literacy. It is a rediscovery because, as presented in this book, there is a historical background to these ideas. Emergent literacy is contrasted with other literacy assumptions, which, for instance, might have emphasized reading readiness – where the role of the teacher might have been to get children ready for reading, therefore denying many of the experiences that the children brought to school. The final chapter in the book is devoted to emergent literacy and schooling, where practices to be developed by the teacher to support emergent literacy are suggested.

Strickland, D.S. and Morrow, L.M. (eds) (1989a) *Emerging Literacy: Young Children Learn to Read and Write*. Newark, DE: International Reading Association.

Reference was made above to the work of Teale and Sulzby, the authors of one of the twelve chapters in this book. The authors of the other eleven chapters are also considered authorities on the topic of young children learning to read and write. Reference to another one of the chapters, by Lesley Mandel Morrow, is made in the section on the *library corner*. The book is very useful for teachers of young children, as it provides many practical ideas, as well as a theoretical background, related to the encouragement of an emerging literacy in children. In their useful follow-on text, many of the original contributors reappear, although there are also some new contributions with fifteen chapters in all:

Strickland, D.S. and Morrow, L.M. (eds) (2000) *Beginning Reading and Writing.* Newark, DE: International Reading Association.

environmental print

Most children in the developed world are surrounded by print in their homes and immediate environments. Importantly, this print is contextualized. For example, when a child sees the word 'cornflakes', it is likely to be on the cornflakes box. The pictures, colours and writing on the box as well as the contents of the box immediately assist the child in determining the connection between the word, or initially the logo, and the product. So the contextualized nature of environmental print supports the child's learning.

In the home, children's toys are often labelled with their 'names' and the boxes the toys were purchased in are covered in print. Print also appears on the labels of their clothes and, more directly, as writing on the T-shirts they and those around them wear. Many children also see a wide variety of printed materials brought into the home – newspapers, magazines, cookery books, telephone directories, and so on. Furthermore, television programmes, especially during the introduction and conclusion, include a lot of print, as do many commercials – to which children often appear to pay a good deal of attention.

Outside the home, there are street names and road signs, and the names and notices on and in buildings. A wealth of print also confronts children in supermarkets: the print on labels and boxes again, the signs on shelves, the special-offer posters and the directional signs.

Children are aided in their search for a meaning to such print by seeing adults responding to and using the print and talking about it.

Even more directly they are supported when adults talk with them about the logos and the print. Where that happens, the children will be helped to understand the nature and message of the environmental print.

Case studies of young children learning to read and write help us to see the way in which environmental print, and parental comment about that print, supports the child's learning. Baghban (1984) provides an example in her book, which details the growth of her daughter's reading and writing. Giti was able, we are informed, to identify the broad yellow 'M' for McDonalds by the age of 20 months. Furthermore, she was able to do so whether the 'M' was outside of a McDonalds, on an advert or on a cup. As we might expect, children do appear to be able to recognize environmental print. They do so with a confidence that enables them to read that print with the contextualized support gradually reduced. So, initially, children might be able to recognize the logo together with all the background features, before recognizing the logo in isolation. Finally, they are able to recognize the logo as a word or letter(s), written with normal script letters and without colour (Goodman and Altwerger 1981).

Laminack (1991), in his study of his son Zachary, also provides many examples of contact with and recognition of environmental print. These began at the age of 13 months with Zachary's recognition of a 'Stop' road sign, when he responded to his father's question 'What does it say?' by replying 'Stop the truck'. At the age of 3 years and 11 months, he was able to indicate how he worked out some of the subtle differences in signs. At that time, he was able to discriminate between the drinks available from a vending machine: 'The diet Sprite has two yellow words and the regular Sprite just has a red dot'.

Another way of considering children's growth in their understanding of environmental print is to note how they are able to recognize a label or logo with a gradually developing accuracy and appropriateness. Harste *et al.* (1984) found that when asked about logos, children might first provide a functional response (e.g. 'a toothbrush' for Crest toothpaste) that might later become a categorical response (e.g. 'toothpaste') and, finally, a specific response (e.g. 'Crest'). And that development they argued was related to the opportunities and experience the children have to transact with the print and to be supported by an adult. Linda Miller (1999) extended this view by suggesting that activities involving environmental print also help to create links between the educational setting and home.

Because many children start school familiar with, and able to read, a good deal of environmental print, we can support their literacy by using that print in the classroom. Although classroom print includes other varieties of print, environmental print can also be displayed usefully. And print from the environment can be included in the materials for play activities, so that the literacy aspect of the play is encouraged. Where environmental print is used in this way, the school creates a bridge between the literacy experiences that the children bring from their homes and neighbourhood with those of the classroom. Such a link has benefits for the literacy awareness and literacy development of the children.

In the classroom

A visit to a supermarket on almost any day of the week will provide evidence of the power of environmental print. Young children, under 5 years of age, will be 'helping' one of their parents with the shopping. And that help will include selecting, from a wide range of similar products, the particular brand that the child, or the family, wishes to purchase. That young children so often appear to succeed in their selection is an indication of their use of the logo, colour, shape and print of the product.

5-year-old John was able to replicate these experiences in his classroom, because the classroom teacher had developed a collection of grocery boxes. This enabled John and his classmates to place the boxes in categories, to write shopping lists, to shop for a product and to inform each other about the products:

John: I'm getting some cornflakes.
Steven: So am I.
John: They're not cornflakes. They're Frosties. You can see it on the box.

Although we cannot tell what John could see on the box, he was paying attention to key features that provided the message for him.

Further reading

Hall, N. (1987) *The Emergence of Literacy*. Sevenoaks: Hodder & Stoughton.
Nigel Hall's book is about young children who, before entering school, have already begun to demonstrate that they are becoming literate. He makes the point that the text is not about those few children who reach school able to read and write, in the conventional sense of those words. Rather, it is a book about all children who are growing up in a Western, print-oriented society. These children emerge as literacy users because they construct their own know-

ledge about print. An important section of the book is devoted to children's contact with environmental print. Here reference is made to several research articles, which demonstrate the role of environmental print as one of the foundations of children's emerging literacy.

Harste, J.C., Woodward, V.A. and Burke, C.L. (1984) *Language Stories and Literacy Lessons.* Portsmouth, NH: Heinemann.

This book provides a detailed account of 3- to 6-year-old children learning to read and write. It provides many observations of children's encounters with language; such evidence provides language stories from which we can begin to deduce literacy lessons. Some of these observations were of children's encounters with environmental print. The examples demonstrate the ways in which environmental print can support children's literacy development. Indeed, they show that children often read boxes more conventionally than they read books because the boxes are more familiar to them.

Miller, L. (1999) *Moving Towards Literacy with Environmental Print.* Royston, Herts: UK Reading Association.

This minibook is one in a series published by the UK Reading Association. Here Linda Miller explores environmental print as it is used in early years classrooms. After considering some of the research evidence, she emphasizes the need for adults to support children's encounters with this print – just as they have to be supported as they talk about *classroom print*. There is an extensive listing of the opportunities for using environmental print in early years classrooms.

gender

In a chapter on language and gender, in her book *Developing Language and Literacy 3–8*, Ann Browne (1996) explored this complex issue. She articulated differences between the sexes that are apparent in speaking, listening, reading and writing in young children. Here it is mainly reading and writing that are considered. In reading among young children, it is boys who have most difficulty. As Browne noted, 'girls learn to read more quickly, with more ease and with greater success than boys' (p. 172). That success is accentuated as children move through school. By the time they are sitting external examinations at 16 years of age, girls as a group are far more successful in England. Of course, considerations about gender require us to think through how all children are being supported (Baxter 2001). A major issue currently is how boys are helped towards literacy in the early years. This is reflected, for instance, in the title and contents of *Boys and Reading* (Barrs and Pidgeon 1998), an edited book that explored this issue. Pahl (1999) argued that boys are involved with different narratives than girls. They are especially involved in model making, construction, drawing and other physical activities, including mapping their actions on the page. They learn kinaesthetically. The teacher can use these physical activities, and the narratives derived from them, as the basis to support literacy. However, that is often not the case and the interests of the boys in pre-school and infant classes may be seen as less relevant to the curriculum. The outlet for physical activity was expressed differently by a headteacher who suggested taking classes out for a five-minute run in the playground in the morning (Hinds 2000). It was suggested that following such activity, all children are able to concentrate better on their work.

Boys' interests also suggest a greater range of non-fiction books needs be to available in the classroom. Inevitably, the content of these books is set out differently, so that for young children reading non-fiction can be more difficult than reading stories. The teacher needs to read-aloud from *non-fiction* books on occasions to help the children to understand the format and language of such books. *Guided reading* also provides an opportunity to explore non-fiction books; both Browne (1996) and Barrs and Pidgeon (1998) suggest the use of single-sex groups at times for such activities. Browne (1996) also suggests the use of such groups to consider the 'least preferred choices of reading material'; that is, girls come together to read information texts and the boys to read stories together. Whatever arrangements are set up, the objective is to support children's involvement with and understanding of various *genres* of books and to encourage their reading.

In the early years setting, there is often a lack of role models for boys. The teachers and other adults in the early years setting typically are female. However, several strategies can be adopted to overcome this. The involvement of older boys, male teachers or visitors, fathers and grandfathers in the classroom can help to create an image of the male as a reader. For instance, many settings attempt to bring a male into the classroom during *sustained silent reading* and the idea of *paired reading* with an older boy reading with a younger boy is widely used. Additionally, the teacher can provide books for the children whereby boys and males are seen as readers, as well as books containing animals as readers, such as in *Can't You Sleep Little Bear* (Waddell 1988).

Ensuring reading and writing in a variety of contexts, including the use of word processing and computer programmes, is also useful in supporting boys' literacy development. As part of *home–school links*, debating gender issues with parents can be useful. For instance, talking about fathers finding time to read with a son can be used to discuss the importance of that activity for young boys. We should recall that boys do not necessarily have difficulties with reading. Paul, Raja, Adam and Zachary all made good progress with literacy in their early years (Bissex 1980; Doake 1988; Schickedanz 1990; Laminack 1991). They did so because the adult support they had at home ensured that literacy learning occurred.

Further reading

Pahl, K. (1999) *Transformations: Children's Meaning Making in a Nursery*. Stoke-on-Trent: Trentham Books.
Part of this book on meaning making in nursery settings considers boys and meaning making in particular. Boys are noted to be busy in nursery settings, but they are often busy doing particular things that differ from what the girls are doing. They are especially engaged in physical activities such as making models, models that are often linked to play around active characters (such as Power Rangers, Batman, Spiderman and Captain Hook at the time of the study). Pahl argues that the boys' modelling can be used to develop their narratives and 'provide a foundation for early literacy activities' (p. 89).

Barrs, M. and Pidgeon, S. (eds) (1998) *Boys and Reading*. London: Centre for Language in Primary Education.
The ten chapters in this book consider various aspects of boys and reading. The books in the classroom, teaching arrangements, involvement of males in the classroom and the use of *information and communication technology* are among the many topics covered. The text extends far beyond the early years and there is, for instance, a case study of a secondary school and the strategies adopted to support the literacy development of boys. Nevertheless, there are many aspects debated that are relevant to the early years. The various school initiatives that are noted provide many useful suggestions.

genres

Although genre might be thought to be more of an issue for the junior and secondary school teacher, children in the infant classroom also require experiences that enable them to cope with the various genres that they meet in the infant classroom and the wider environment. An exploration of different genres demonstrates this to be the case. Alison Littlefair (1991, 1992) suggested that texts might be considered as falling into one of four major categories of genre.

The first, the literary genre, forms a central part of young children's reading. After all, storybooks are for many children the texts that introduce them to books. As teachers, we might occasionally group books into subgroups of that genre when we put together collections of *nursery rhymes*, folk tales, *poetry*, animal stories, adventure stories, and so on. It is probable that children will have considerable experience of being read to, and reading for themselves, within that genre. However, young children are likely to meet other genres and require adult support, at least initially, to help them with the demands of that writing.

The expository genre contains more objective writing and infant children begin to explore that genre as they write, for example, about their own experiences or science experiments, or as they get information by reading non-fiction books. The procedural genre may be evident in classroom print, as notices and lists of instructions inform children about classroom activities. Many teachers of young children use written recipes with groups of children engaged in cooking, which brings home very forcibly the importance of following with some accuracy the procedures in such writing. Fourth, the reference genre will be brought to the children's attention in the infant classroom as they are introduced to dictionaries. But the children will need to access sequential information in other texts; simple encyclopaedias are an example.

At this point, perhaps, we need to remind ourselves that, in the early years classroom, it will be the literary genre that provides most of the children's reading experiences. But it will also be evident that the other genres are not something waiting to be introduced in later years, but rather they will be part of the literacy experiences of the children almost as soon as they start school. This being the case, the teacher will want to demonstrate those genres from time to time. For instance, extracts from information books will be read to the class occasionally, which will help the children to begin to perceive the different register of language that is often used in such texts. So although it might be left to the older children to examine more analytically some of these differences, younger children will at least begin to appreciate the different use and flow of language that will then help them with their own readings. Occasionally, a child might wish to read an information book with a teacher as part of *sharing a book*, where support from the teacher is provided for those more unusual texts.

Littlefair (1991, 1992) suggests that, although some writers use genre and register interchangeably, it might be better to consider them separately. The subject being written about will influence the register, as will the relationship with the audience for that writing. And that will determine the vocabulary to be used and the grammatical structures. We all understand that, because we write in different registers according to the task in hand. Very young children – some before they enter school – soon realize that a shopping list is constructed differently from a message or story.

A key task for the teacher of young children, then, is to ensure that there is a range of written materials that the children can experience. In addition to the many storybooks in the classroom, there should also be books written in other genres. Furthermore, the teacher needs to demonstrate, share and work alongside the children to support them in their understanding of the various forms of writing.

In the classroom

In the early years classroom, the teacher will occasionally read from a book in a genre other than the narrative. In the brief extract below, the teacher was reading to a class of thirty 6-year-olds from a text, *Famous Cities: London* (Quest 1979), which provided some historical evidence for a project that the children were exploring:

Candina: It burnt a lot of the houses.
Teacher: Yes, it burnt a lot of the houses, didn't it. Shall we find out?
    Fire was a frequent threat to the city of London.
    Why was it a threat?
Claire: Because the fire could burn the people's houses down.
Teacher: Why could it burn the houses down?
Candina: Because they were so close together.
Teacher: So close together and they were made of?
Children: Wood.
Teacher: That's right.
    Since many London houses were wooden, fires could spread rapidly.
    They could spread quickly couldn't they?

Even in this short extract, we can see how the language in the text could be more problematic for the children, especially if their main contact with books was through stories. The teacher was giving more explanations during the reading for that reason. Nevertheless, the children, by hearing such texts read occasionally, would begin to appreciate the nature of the discourse patterns in such books.

Further reading

Littlefair, A.B. (1991) *Reading All Types of Writing: The Importance of Genre and Register for Reading Development.* Buckingham: Open University Press.
Littlefair, A.B. (1992) *Genres in the Classroom.* Widnes: UK Reading Association.
The first of these books is the more substantial both in size and in content; the second is directed more firmly towards the classroom teacher. Nevertheless, both books extend the brief introduction to the subject given here. The 1991 title also makes links to the National Curriculum in England and Wales and demonstrates how, at each key stage in English, there are expectations of the children's knowledge of, and ability to work with, different genres.

guided reading

Guided reading is a group activity. Typically, it is organized for a group of six to eight children with the text carefully matched, as far as possible, to the children in the group. Therefore, the group is relatively homogeneous and each child has a copy of the book. The teacher then devotes fifteen to twenty minutes with the group. Guided reading is useful, Mooney (1990) suggested, because in the classroom it provides the opportunity for young children to read with support from the teacher. However, this should be developed after the younger children have experienced many *story readings* and *shared readings.* Only then will the children be ready for the first reading of a new text. As Hill (1999) notes, the selection of the books is important; she suggests that what is required are texts that 'are supportive and there is some challenge for the children' (p. 131).

The questions asked during *shared readings* help young children with strategies to explore new texts during a guided reading. For Mooney (1990), an important part of the group activity is that the children are guided towards particular ways of working. For her it is not about concentrating upon letters or words. Rather, it is an activity that helps children develop towards independent readers 'who question, consider alternatives, and make informed choices as they seek meaning' (p. 47). In her short book, Mooney demonstrates how children can be encouraged to predict, sample, confirm and self-correct by the careful questioning by the teacher.

Fountas and Pinnell (1996) suggested that guided reading can be divided into three phases: before, during and after reading. Before reading the book, the teacher should discuss it with the children. Smith and Elley (1994) argued that this is an important time within guided reading, as the children are guided to organize some background information in advance of reading the book. The discussion is about meaning rather than the mechanics of the print. During the reading, the teacher should listen to the children as they read. With the youngest children, that is all the teacher does, quite literally listen to them as they read. However, as the children increasingly read silently, the teacher might ask a child to read softly to them for a moment so that the child's strategies and reading can be noted. At the end of the reading, there may be no follow-up on occasions. At other times, the story might be discussed and key ideas from the reading debated. Smith and Elley suggested that the follow-up could result in rewriting the story, reading aloud in pairs, responding to written questions and other activities.

In England, guided reading has become a key part of the *literacy hour* – 'guided reading should be a fundamental part of each school's literacy programme' (DfEE 1998: 12). In that hour, guided reading was put forward because it was considered to have advantages over *hearing children read* on an individual basis (Beard 1999); first, because it increased the time that children were able to spend on reading and, second, because it creates a helpful social context for reading. However, some teachers remain reluctant to lose the benefits of working alongside a child *sharing a book* or *hearing children read*. Indeed, Smith and Elley (1994) suggested that, depending on the organization of the classroom or the needs of the child, there might be occasions when guided silent reading takes place between the teacher and one child. Furthermore, as Fountas and Pinnell (1996) noted, there are other literacy activities that need to occur, including *literature circles*, which is a different form of group reading activity.

Further reading

Fountas, I. and Pinnell, G. (1996) *Guided Reading: Good First Teaching for All Children*. Portsmouth, NH: Heinemann.
This book provides a very comprehensive discussion of guided reading. Half of the 406 pages are appendices, including an extensive list of appropriate books for use with groups. As well as considerable detail on working with small groups, there is a chapter on managing the class. *Classroom organization and management* is, of course, very important for literacy activities.

Mooney, M. (1990) *Reading To, With and By Children*. Katonah, NY: Richard C. Owen.

Margaret Mooney demonstrates how guided reading might be used in the classroom with different age groups. She provides details of the teacher working with emergent readers, early level readers and fluent readers. With emergent readers, she suggests working towards the author's meanings rather than focusing on individual words. Of course, the teacher needs to use different strategies with different age groups. However, the principle of working with a group of six to eight children and perhaps working with two groups in any one day should be maintained.

Hill, S. (1999) *Guiding Literacy Learners*. York, ME: Stenhouse.

As guided reading has become a frequent feature of primary classroom life, so texts have been published with a focus on this literacy activity. This text provides a detailed consideration of the organization and structure of guided reading. The many classroom examples help to illuminate aspects of the activity and there are practical guidelines for teachers.

guided writing (mini-lessons)

Guided writing, like guided reading, is a group activity. And like guided reading, guided writing is typically, although not always, organized for a group of six to eight children. The children are brought together for an activity that meets their needs at that time. So the teacher attempts to create a group that is relatively homogeneous. In England, guided writing is a part of the *literacy hour* (DfEE 1998) for year one and two children. However, the suggestions for the use of guided writing are relatively limited, demonstrating its recent development in early years classrooms. Within the literacy hour, the teacher devotes fifteen to twenty minutes to the activity.

In the USA, guided writing is more frequently referred to as a 'mini-lesson' (e.g. Graves 1994). Although as much as twenty minutes might be spent on this activity, it is often considerably shorter. For instance, Lucy Calkins (1983) noted how effective mini-lessons of five to ten minutes were, albeit it with third and fourth graders. Of paramount importance is the subject of the mini-lesson and how much time should be given to the activity to support the children's learning now and to help them to move forward to independent writing in the future.

When the subject of the mini-lesson is determined, a class session might be considered appropriate. For instance, Wyse (1998) debated a guided writing time given over to topic choice. From that session, involving a whole class discussion, a wealth of different ideas was created for the children to think about. Those topics can then form a list that can be returned to from time to time to support children who may find it difficult to get started with their writing. There are other broad areas of writing that might be considered with the whole class; for example, finished writing, including redrafting and proof reading, and classroom processes such as bookmaking.

In addition to these broad areas, Wyse (1998) also suggested *shared writing* as a mini-lesson because it helps the very youngest children to see 'the process of writing and focus on composition' (p. 4). He noted that eventually shared writing can be used to cover more specific areas, such as initial letter strategies and phonic knowledge. However, in the first instance with the younger children, *shared writing* may be the most appropriate mini-lesson for them. During that time, they would be given insights into the process of writing, the reasons for writing and aspects of conventions. As the children engage with *play activities* or use opportunities for *writing*, so the learning from the mini-lesson can be explored.

Consideration of broad areas of writing may have to be revisited occasionally. But once they have been part of a mini-lesson, many of the children will use the ideas to develop their writing. However, some of the more detailed features of writing may require more frequent revisits to support the children's learning. Helping children to learn more about transcription features, such as punctuation, spelling and handwriting (although keyboarding is becoming more important), can be dealt with during a mini-lesson, but might require several sessions to establish the children's learning. Grouping the children can be useful when helping with those fine details of writing.

Although teachers will have in mind what needs to be learned, that does not necessarily imply direct teaching by them. As Graves (1994) suggested, listening to children to determine how much is known is a good starting point. Then, using their writing, the books they are reading and their collaborative discussions to further their learning reduces the abstract nature of the process of writing for young children. Guided writing or mini-lessons are included from time to time to help the children with their writing. However, it is *writing* that is the real goal. Guided writing is a support activity to help children to write more effectively.

Further reading

Graves, D. (1994) *A Fresh Look at Writing*. Portsmouth, NH: Heinemann.
The work of Donald Graves is cited frequently when aspects of writing in the primary school are considered. In this text, chapters twelve and thirteen deal with features of mini-lessons. The first of these chapters looks at mini-lessons concerned with the conventions of writing. It demonstrates, in particular, the way in which the details of punctuation in writing can be explored with young children.

hearing children read

The Bullock Report (DES 1975) was not alone when it noted the widespread use of 'hearing children read' as a practice in infant classrooms in the UK. Of the teachers of 6-year-old children who were surveyed for that report, many indicated that they heard their children read daily. This was especially true for those children who were regarded as poor readers. But in most of the 1417 classes that were surveyed, even the ablest of readers in the class were heard reading three or four times a week. Such a commitment to hearing children read continued in the 1990s (HMI 1992).

So what is the nature of the one-to-one interaction – hearing a child read? In most respects, it is similar to the fourth part of the sharing a book sequence. So:

- the teacher and the child discuss parts of the book;
- the child reads to the teacher (and the child does so because she has reached that point in her development as a reader where reading in a conventional way has become possible);
- the teacher listens to the reading and supports the child where that appears to be required;
- finally, the teacher and the child discuss some aspect of the book at the end of the reading.

This indicates that the role of the teacher is not a passive one. Instead, it requires an active listening to the child reading, with the teacher ready to support, guide, instruct or encourage as necessary.

However, if the teacher is listening to many children, and on a regular and frequent basis, there is a need to remain alert to the nature of the activity and ensure that it has not become ritualized (Goodacre, undated). In a ritualized interaction, the teacher might be distracted from the reader to other children or events in the classroom. Or, all interactions might begin to look alike because the teacher has become concerned with getting through the list of readers rather than ensuring, as is needed, that there is a quality to the activity. The teacher responds according to the needs of the child and develops the interaction from an analysis of the child's reading. It was because of concerns about this interaction that Southgate *et al.* (1981) suggested that, for older children (the Extending Beginning Reading Project explored the reading development of 7- to 9-year-olds in classrooms), there might be less frequent but more extended sessions of the teacher and the child with a book. Such sessions, they suggested, might include a range of activities, including the child reading aloud and a discussion of the book, but also from time to time a detailed *miscue analysis*, a checking on comprehension or exploring the vocabulary of the book.

It is inevitable that when a teacher hears a child read the child will produce miscues. I consider *responding to miscues* elsewhere; however, teachers should bear in mind several principles to guide their actions. Because we want children to remain active learners, teachers should use the notion of minimal distraction as a guiding principle. And, where support is given, other principles include helping the reader with the current miscue, to do so in a way that might help with that word on another occasion and to suggest future reading strategies.

For some children who have become fluent readers, who are branching out in their reading (Guppy and Hughes 1999), the nature of the interaction needs to be altered. Although there may be reasons for listening to the child read, such as to note intonation, expression, awareness of punctuation and fluency, just hearing the child may not be the best practice. At this point, it may be better to discuss the book being read and others that have been read. A child who is aware that the discussion is going to take place can be encouraged also to have selected a particular passage to read to the teacher. That passage might be chosen to share something of interest with the teacher or to debate something that is considered complex. At other times, the teacher might select a short passage for the child to read. But a reading by the child is not the main event in the activity when the child is an independent fluent reader.

Hearing children read can play a useful part in the primary classroom, but it requires careful *classroom organization and management* for it to occur. The teacher needs to ensure that the interaction is not interrupted and that the activity develops to meet the needs of the child as well as helping the teacher to determine the progress being made.

In the classroom

To keep each child engaged actively with the text when the teacher is hearing a reader, the principle of minimal distraction should be applied. So when 6-year-old Brian was reading to his teacher, his various repetitions, self-corrections and comments received no response from the teacher during part of his reading.

> *Brian:*   Next . . . next they find a house made of . . . a house made of jelly.
> Ha, ha!
>   'This will not do . . . This will not do, says one of the little kittens. The children will eat it all up . . .'
> And it will wobble!
>   '. . . all up and then there will be no house left'.
> And it would wobble.
> *Teacher:* It would wobble. Go on then.

On this occasion, Brian's enjoyment of the story – in particular, the thought of a jelly (or jello) house – meant that eventually the teacher was brought into the interaction by Brian's insistent comments. On another occasion, when the reader might be producing many miscues that detract from the meaning of the passage, then mediation from the teacher would be required. But, during Brian's reading, the teacher appropriately remained in the background.

Further reading

Arnold, H. (1982) *Listening to Children Reading.* Sevenoaks: Hodder & Stoughton. In this book, listening to children reading is considered within a historical perspective and there is a consideration of what is involved in the reading process. The word listening is used to denote the active role of the teacher. Helen Arnold uses transcripts of the practice in the classroom to demonstrate the teacher's active role. Miscue analysis as a means of diagnosis in a busy classroom is also debated.

Campbell, R. (1988) *Hearing Children Read.* London: Routledge.
This book is devoted entirely to the activity of hearing children read. It sets the scene by describing an infant classroom in which a child was heard reading by the teacher. It details the purposes that teachers have in mind when they

hear children read. However, the main part of the text describes and analyses teachers hearing children read, with many transcripts providing the basis for that description and analysis. The book concludes with some guidelines for hearing a child read based on the earlier transcript evidence.

Southgate, V., Arnold, H. and Johnson, S. (1981) *Extending Beginning Reading.* London: Heinemann Educational.

The findings from the Extending Beginning Reading Project are reported in this book, a project that explored the reading development of 7- to 9-year-olds in classrooms and considered the classroom practices to support that reading development. The report was critical of hearing children read, as the authors witnessed the event with its many disruptions and overly simple teacher responses to miscues. They proposed less frequent, but longer, individual reading consultations with a variety of activities during each consultation.

home–school links

Children arrive at school with some literacy learning already having taken place. Although the literacy experiences of the children will have varied, as Shirley Brice Heath's (1983) study of two communities separated by only a few miles in Carolina, USA, demonstrated so vividly, nevertheless all children will reach school with some knowledge of literacy. One problem for the school is to match that previous learning with appropriate teaching strategies that can build on those initial foundations. But this can be made less problematic if home–school links are established in some form. For example, links might be established with parents before the children enter school and particular literacy experiences might be encouraged. Or, it might involve close collaboration between the school and home once the children have started school, in which case the school and home might together develop certain literacy activities; *sharing a book* is one of the literacy activities that is used frequently to create such a link.

The benefits that can accrue if home–school links are developed were emphasized by the Plowden Report (DES 1967). In particular, it noted that, when parents became involved and encouraged their children during literacy activities, those children were likely to make good progress with reading and writing. Subsequently, studies like the Haringey Project (Hewison and Tizard 1980) demonstrated how simple home–school procedures can help in children's reading development. Parents were encouraged to become involved with their children's reading in the form of hearing them read. The children took books home to read to their parents two to three times a week. A reading card, with the book, was used to structure the reading and to allow comments to be passed between the teacher and parents. Children who had this type of support made better progress with their reading than children with other forms of school support. However, the gains made by these children were not always apparent one year after the completion of the project. This ties in with many other projects that have aimed to support children in some aspect of their learning. It serves to remind us that the development of home–school links is a long-term endeavour. Once established, the links need to be maintained and developed further to serve the needs of the children.

Since those initial attempts to establish the value of home–school links, many more projects have been initiated and reported upon; Wendy Bloom (1987) provides details of some of these projects. One feature common to all successful projects is preparation for the partnership; success is not guaranteed but has to be worked for. Two examples, one from pre-school support and the other related to the early years at school, demonstrate such careful attention to organization.

The Sheffield Early Literacy Development Project (Weinberger *et al.* 1990) developed as a collaborative project, which included the city's education department. Because it was recognized that knowledge of literacy on entry to school was a strong predictor of later literacy attainment, the project was based on the pre-school period. The project concentrated on three aspects of literacy: *environmental print*, looking for print in the home and local environment; *sharing a book*, in a one-to-one interaction; and *writing*, introducing materials for the child. It suggested three key roles that parents could adopt as a model for their children: first, reading a paper and writing notes or shopping lists, etc.; second, providing opportunities, by providing the materials or drawing attention to environmental print, etc.; and third, providing encouragement, by praising achievement, including success in a non-conventional form (e.g. *invented spellings*). Subsequently, some of the comments made by the parents were indicative of the changed views that they developed and of the support that they gave their children for literacy as a result of this project.

In contrast, Davis and Stubbs (1988) encouraged the establishment of home–school links in several primary schools. They did so as part of their encouragement for *sharing a book* to support children's development as readers. They recognized that although most early years teachers make valiant attempts to share a book with many of the children in their classes, such an aspiration is fraught with difficulties. The size of classes and the need to support children in a range of literacy activities often mean that a teacher will share a book with fewer children than might be appropriate and the quality of the interaction can be undetermined by those other needs. A home–school *sharing a book* programme can therefore be useful. But that does require an initial meeting to help the home and school to develop a working partnership, and it probably requires some form of booklet to indicate key features of the *sharing a book* practice. Furthermore, the use of a reading/comment card or reading diary helps teachers and parents to develop similar views of the reading process and give the children similar forms of support. When a teacher writes in the reading diary 'We looked at this book together and I've read the story to Brian', that helps the parents. It gives an indication that it is appropriate to spend time discussing a book and for the child to hear the story before being asked to contribute to the reading. However, it is not that single comment, but rather many comments over a period of weeks and months, which will contribute to a shared view of reading and support for reading.

A variety of home–school link programmes will be developed by schools. However, *sharing a book* is often at the heart of those collaborative attempts to support young children's literacy learning. Nevertheless, for any home–school programme to succeed, there is a need for initial careful planning, an organization that maintains the link on a daily basis and the will to sustain the link on a long-term basis. The extent of home–school links today is emphasized by the various initiatives from government in the UK. For instance, there is a free magazine, *Parents and Schools*, with useful information and ideas for parents. A website (www.parents.dfee.gov.uk) provides additional information for parents with internet access and there is a formal expectation that Year 1 and 2 children will complete one hour of homework per week focused mainly on reading and writing.

In the classroom

3- and 4-year-olds in a nursery classroom of a primary school were encouraged to take a book home each evening to share with their parents. And their parents were encouraged to read the book to their children. Whenever possible, the nursery teacher discussed the book with each child as the book was changed:

Teacher: What was your book about?
Jamie: About Spot going to the seaside.

Teacher: Did you like the book?
Jamie: Yeah, 'cos it was lovely.
Teacher: Which part did you like best?
Jamie: The bit where Spot got splashed – I get splashed in the bath.
Teacher: Do you? Okay, so do you want to get another book for tonight?
Jamie: Yeah.
Teacher: So what have you got there?
Jamie: It's another Spot story – I like Spot.
Teacher: What do you think Spot is going to do now?
Jamie: Go to the doctor's.
Teacher: Who do you think he will see?
Jamie: His friends.

Here, Jamie, who was nearly 4 years old, had the opportunity to talk about his books, to relate the story to his own experiences and to reflect on his choice of book. The home–school link facilitated teacher–child discussions at school and story readings at home.

Further reading

Weinberger, J., Hannon, P. and Nutbrown, C. (1990) *Ways of Working with Parents to Promote Literacy Development.* Sheffield: University of Sheffield Division of Education.
This twenty-eight page, A4-size booklet is very practical in its orientation. However, it does back the practical suggestions with theoretical views and there are references to several key texts. The booklet includes a jigsaw framework as a means of maintaining some form of record-keeping of the children's achievements. The parents were encouraged to participate in that process by shading in the pieces, as the children demonstrated their literacy behaviours. A more extensive debate on home–school links and strategies is contained in another book by one of the above authors:

Weinberger, J. (1996) *Literacy goes to School.* London: Paul Chapman.

Beverton, S., Hunter-Carsch, M., Obrist, C. and Stuart, A. (1993) *Running Family Reading Groups.* Widnes: UK Reading Association.
Although family reading groups link teachers and librarians with parents, they do not have as their main aim the teaching of reading, albeit that might be an indirect outcome of the meetings. Instead, the aims are 'to promote a love of books and voluntary reading' and 'to widen children's and adults' experience of children's books' (p. 9). These aims are achieved during a series of meetings in which discussions are held and children and adults review books that they have enjoyed. The authors stress the need to consult and plan to achieve

success with these meetings and they suggest strategies for setting up and running a family reading group.

information and communication technology

Information and communication technology (ICT) is an exciting addition in the lives of young children. Many children are introduced to ICT in some form at home. There is also the experience of working with ICT in the pre-school and infant classroom, as it is part of the National Curriculum in England for children in Years 1 and 2 (DfEE 1999). There are opportunities for writing, presenting work effectively and using tables to express ideas using a computer. Using CD-ROMs or the internet to access information is readily learned by young children. There is also the possibility of setting up a link with another classroom or school to exchange writing, ideas and information using email.

One example of ICT is the use of a computer to write. Using a word processor, the children can draft, redraft, edit and produce a final good copy without constantly rewriting the story, or other piece of work, by hand. In some instances, the children might just engage with one aspect of that process and be supported by the teacher more directly at other stages in the process. For instance, when Moore and Tweddle (1992) described a Year 2 class writing 'badger stories', the children began by working in small groups and told their stories directly into a cassette-recorder. Subsequently, the teacher produced a transcribed story for each of the groups. The children in each group then read their story, debated it and amended or redrafted it as necessary. Finally, an edited copy was produced, which the children illustrated and developed as a book. Each of the books was then read out to the other children in the class. The production of such books, some of which may become part of the classroom library, is a major benefit of using computers as word processors (Graves 1994). The children enjoy seeing themselves as authors, like to read their own books and the books add to the print resources in the classroom. In another example of the computer being used to write with 5-year-olds, Dawn Nulty (2001) indicated that it provided support in three ways. First, it allowed the child freedom to compose at the keyboard; second, it provided the opportunity for sensitive teacher intervention; and third, it alleviated the problem associated with the secretarial aspects of writing. The writing examples that she provided by the 5-year-olds and then 7-year-olds demonstrated how well the computer was put to use.

Many teachers encourage children to work together at the word processor. The stories that are then drafted, for instance, are debated as part of a collaborative exercise within a small group. Such discussions involve children talking about language; for example, spelling and punctuation are discussed directly and features such as story structure are discussed implicitly as the story is produced. Although the practical reason for grouping the children at the word processor may be to make best use of limited resources, a positive outcome is that the children often benefit from the discussions about language. Indeed, it is such collaboration when working at a word processor that many teachers in the National Writing Project (SCDC 1990) saw as the main advantage of such work.

Accessing information from the internet, or CD-ROM, is readily learned by young children, although it does require a facility with reading to make best use of that information. As to software that promises to teach reading, or aspects of it such as phonics or spelling, then teachers have to ensure that the materials are worthwhile. Some of the early materials required a series of conditioned responses rather than thought from the children (Wray and Medwell 1991). In such circumstances Whitehead (1999: 55) argued, 'there is no necessity to buy . . . expensive software which promises to teach pre-school children all about the alphabet, phonics and spellings. These materials will not allow the children to ask their own questions about print and invent their own experimental systems for writing'. Wepner and Ray (2000) consider some of the features that might be evident in the more useful software that develops, reinforces and extends children's knowledge. They suggest that 'visual, auditory and kinaesthetic modalities' (p. 170) should all be used to support the development of concepts.

Writing messages to other children in the classroom, or extending that to writing emails to children in other classes or schools, may be more appropriate for the older children in the early years. Nevertheless, that activity provides an opportunity for children to write for a real *audience*, to consider carefully what is to be written, and to develop further their use of the keyboard and computer skills. The computer aids children's literacy development and, even when not being used, Phinn (2000) suggested it should be left turned on with a poem screen saver. That poem then becomes a part of the *classroom print* to be talked about and to extend the children's interest in *poetry*. Additionally, the children can write their own poems and rhymes into the computer as screen savers.

In the classroom

Two events with pre-school children demonstrate clearly the way in which the youngest children were learning about modern technologies for information and communication. First, an adult was talking with a small group of children about an aspect of the environment. As the debate continued, she asked a 3-year-old 'How do you think we could find about it?' The reply was an unexpected, 'We could try www dot bbc dot co dot uk.' Presumably that knowledge of where information on the internet might be accessed had been gleaned from watching television. Nevertheless, it demonstrates how the youngest of children develop an understanding of the possibility of using computers to surf the web for information.

Second, in a corner of a pre-school classroom, an area had been set aside as a post office for *play activities*. The materials included many that encouraged literacy learning – message pads, forms, paper, pens, pencils, notices, booklets, telephone directories, and so on. One girl was sitting at a table that included a 'qwerty' keyboard. After a few moments, she began to sing to herself the *alphabet* song and, as she did so, she typed each letter of the alphabet on the keyboard. Although not typing a message or story, she was consolidating her knowledge of the alphabet, learning about the keyboard and establishing a foundation for using the computer to write in the future. She and other 3- and 4-year-old children in the classroom were developing a familiarity with the world of ICT.

Further reading

Moore, P. and Tweddle, S. (1992) *The Integrated Classroom: Language, Learning and I.T.* London: Hodder & Stoughton.
This book is one in a series, produced in the UK, which deals with 'Teaching English in the National Curriculum'. Moore and Tweddle focus on the use of computers to support language development in both primary and secondary classrooms. Several case studies are presented in the text, one of which explores a Year 2 class writing stories, with the aid of a word processor for the production of final copies. It was recognized that many classes have just one computer and that strategies have to be developed to use that computer and integrate it into the daily events of the classroom.

Barratt-Pugh, C. and Rohl, M. (2000) *Literacy Learning in the Early Years*. Buckingham: Open University Press.
One of the chapters in this book is devoted specifically to information communication technologies and literacy learning. Martyn Wild provides a snapshot of four early years settings in which ICT was being used to support literacy learning. Developing a website and using other websites, sending and receiving emails, reading interactive storybooks and curriculum investigations were all part of those descriptions. The snapshots demonstrate how young children are involved in literacy learning as they participate in a variety of ICT activities. Of course, this is a rapidly developing area and new texts are appearing all the time.

illustrations

Teachers of young children will be aware of the way in which the covers on books attract the attention of children who are beginning to emerge as readers. Many books should be displayed in library corners with their front covers showing, so that the illustrations can help the children in selecting a book. Margaret Meek (1988) noted that a well-illustrated cover could be used to initiate a discussion about the characters and setting of the story, so that the child is well prepared for the story and will already have anticipated some possibilities for the plot.

As a simple, although important, starting point, the illustrations in early reading books can be seen as to lure children into the book. The illustrations can attract the children's attention and encourage them to engage with books. And the bold pictures and bright colours frequently do exactly that. Jill Bennett (1991) noted that 16-month-old Joe would rush off to get a Spot book (*Where's Spot?* by Eric Hill 1983) when asked 'Shall we read a book?' Although Joe was unable to read the print, he was able to engage with the pictures and, with that particular book, help to find Spot's hiding places by opening the doors, lids and flaps. Spot, as Bennett noted, is probably one of the best loved picture book characters of recent times. To emphasize that view, in another study (Campbell 1999a: 13), 7-month-old Alice can be seen enjoying *Spot's First Words* (Hill 1966) with her mother. Yet the illustrations in these books are very simple with little or no background, the emphasis of the pictures being on the characters, especially Spot. Nevertheless, children from 1 to 5 years of age appear to be captivated by the representations of Spot. They are attracted to the Spot books, and others, in part because of their illustrations, but also because of the enjoyable interactions that they have with significant adults.

The illustrations in many of the excellent picture books that are now available do far more than just attract children to the book. In many early reading books, the illustrations are an important part of the story. For instance, in Eric Carle's (1988) *Do You Want To Be My Friend?*, the illustration of an animal's tail leads to the side of the page and takes the reader on to the next page. And, in the much loved *Rosie's Walk* by Pat Hutchins (1968), the illustrations play an even more prominent part in the story. Hearing the words of that story without any knowledge of the book, or the pictures, will only provide the listener with part of the story. The fox, a central character of the story, is never mentioned in the text, but it is there on every double-page spread and plays an important part in the development of the plot.

The illustrations in many picture books are brightly coloured and that appears to be part of the attraction. But the illustrations do not have to be in full colour; more importantly, they need to be there for a purpose, supporting the text, or part of the text, or creating a character, or suggesting a setting, or developing the plot.

When these purposes are met, then illustrations can provide an important contribution to the child's development as a reader, because they capture the child's involvement and engagement with the book. But the illustrations often do more than that because, having become interwoven with the narrative, they are important in helping the child to understand and become engaged with the story. In her book *Pictures on the Page*, Judith Graham (1991) demonstrates this with great skill; she concludes that the illustrations have the potential to create readers, a conclusion which reminds us as teachers of our important role in selecting worthwhile books for the classroom *library corner*.

Further reading

Bennett, J. (1991) *Learning to Read with Picture Books*, 4th edn. Stroud: Thimble Press.
As the title of the book suggests, it argues that children can best learn to read when presented with picture books (real books) rather than reading scheme books. A substantial part of the text is devoted to a list of books that might be used to help young children to read and to continue reading. This list includes brief descriptions of the books. Jill Bennett demonstrates the way in which many of the books have words and pictures that are closely connected. Indeed, she uses these examples to show that the illustrations add to the story that is being told.

Graham, J. (1991) *Pictures on the Page*. Sheffield: NATE.
In this text, Graham provides a very detailed account of the importance of illustrations in picture and early reading books. She argues that much of a character, setting, story and theme can be conveyed through carefully executed and detailed pictures. In that sense, she is suggesting that children can learn story grammar as much from pictures as from words. The debate that she presents is informed by both theoretical insights as well as numerous examples of illustrations from many different books. These carefully selected pictures support the argument of the importance, in picture and early reading books, of illustrations, for they demonstrate how they support the child in his or her reading.

Evans, J. (ed.) (1998) *What's in the Picture? Responding to Illustrations in Picture Books*. London: Paul Chapman.
Janet Evans brings together several writers from the UK, USA and Australia who contribute to the debate, from various perspectives, on the importance of illustrations. One of the chapters, for instance, is an interview with the author and artist Anthony Browne, who stated that 'I deliberately make my books so that they are open to different interpretations' (p. 195) – a comment that emphasizes the critical response that is required of young emergent readers as they engage with books. In another chapter, Brenda Parkes demonstrates how nursery children develop an understanding of text as they respond critically to those illustrations.

invented spelling

Children in a nursery setting, although only 3 years old, can be encouraged to write. The use of a *writing centre*, or table, which the children can visit, whenever they wish, can be instrumental in that encouragement. However, more important perhaps will be the attitude of the teacher towards the children's efforts at writing. If the teacher conveys an acceptance of, and an interest in, a child's efforts, then that may contribute substantially to the child being encouraged to continue exploring written language. And that acceptance, by the teacher, may need to start with the 'scribbles' that children produce. However, what soon becomes evident is that writing scribbles can be differentiated from drawing scribbles. They can be differentiated because, as the children become more aware of the conventions of writing, so their own writing becomes more linear. Either they produce a joined-up squiggle across the page or they write separate shapes and other marks, which Judith Kalman

(1991) refers to as 'pseudoletters' – which could be letters but are not. At 2 years 5 months, Alice was able to distinguish between drawing and writing as she drew a picture of 'Grandad smiling', alongside which were marks that she suggested were 'd, d, b, i, d' (Campbell 1999a: 52).

Those pseudoletters can eventually take on other attributes of writing, so that there may be no more than two of the same shapes written side-by-side, there may be gaps between groups of letters and, for some children, 'bear' may require more letters than 'butterfly' because it is a bigger creature. In one sense, the writing is real writing rather than scribbles (at least as that word might be interpreted), because the children are writing according to the rules that they perceive govern writing production. Eventually, real letters will replace the various marks as the children learn from the print in the environment, the *classroom print* and literacy activities such as *shared reading* with big books. However, the letters, although recognizable, may be difficult to decipher as words, because initially they may not be governed by the sounds of oral language.

When the children begin to use the sounds of oral language to construct words or invent spellings, then we have a better chance of reading their writing (invented spellings are also sometimes called 'developmental spellings' or 'phonic spellings'). Charles Read (1971) indicated that children bring some knowledge of English phonology, learnt in the pre-school years, to their first encounters with both reading and writing. Therefore, we can begin to follow the children's writing because it is rule-governed. Initially, we might expect that consonants would be more predominant than vowels in early invented spellings. Donald Graves (1983) suggested that five general stages of invention might be noted in the spellings of children. First, the initial consonant might be used to represent the word (e.g. 'G' for 'grass'). Second, the initial and final consonant might be used (i.e. 'GS'). Third, the initial, final and also any interior consonant might be written (e.g. 'GRS'). Fourth, to those consonants might be added a vowel place holder. That vowel may not be the correct vowel, but it might appear in the correct position (e.g. 'GRES'). Finally, the child moves to a conventional spelling of the word, 'GRASS'.

Richard Gentry (2000) also provides a view of children's spelling stages that moves beyond the invented spellings to conventional spellings. He suggests five stages of how the child thinks about spelling:

- *Precommunicative*: letters are put together but without matching to sounds.
- *Semiphonetic*: spellings contain some letters that match sounds.
- *Phonetic*: sound-based strategies dominate.

- *Transitional*: letter patterns and letter sequences are used as well as sounds.
- *Conventional*: adds to store of words that can be spelled correctly.

Children's progress with invented spellings may not be as tidy as the above sequences suggest, however. In part, this is because visual memory also influences each child's invented spellings. This should not surprise us, as print that surrounds children gives them support as they write. One of the first words which children might write conventionally is their own first name. Although this might be guided initially by the child's phonemic awareness, most children see their name in many different contexts, which will offer the opportunity of developing a visual memory for that word, as will many other experiences of print for other words.

Although children will move gradually towards conventional spellings, teachers should not just stand by and wait for it to happen. The many literacy activities in the classroom will give general support to the children, but additionally the teacher will also help more directly when talking with each child about the writing that has been produced. The content of the writing may be the main emphasis of that discussion or writing conference, but the teacher might also talk about one of the invented spellings, particularly high-frequency words, to guide the children towards conventional spellings. And the *classroom print* might be used to draw the children's attention to the conventional spellings of some words.

Although the teacher guides the children towards conventional spellings, the advantage of encouraging them to write freely, even though that means that the writing may contain many invented spellings, is that the children have to engage actively with sounds and letters to produce the writing. They have to think about the sounds, letters and the representation of those letters on the page. That engagement is an important part of learning to write conventionally; indeed, both Goodman (1990) and Adams (1990), working from different perspectives, suggest invented spellings are a helpful part of young children's writing development. Furthermore, it will be obvious that such activity might be helpful when the child is reading, because the thought applied to sounds and letters in writing can be used to help the child give sounds to the letters and words when they are reading.

In the classroom

6-year-old Sam produced a piece of writing unaided, in his infant classroom. The writing, a short story, contained numerous invented spellings as well as some conventional spellings:

one day a pig wos
rolin in sum mud and h
met one of His frens
and they Playd two
geva and they the
frma cam and tod them
to get Bac in they stiy
He wos vere cros

The writing, which can be read quite easily, demonstrates Sam's strengths as a literacy user. He is able to spell conventionally many of the words. He is also able to construct, or invent, the other words using his knowledge of letter shapes and letter sounds. These invented spellings suggest that Sam's phonemic awareness and knowledge of phonics will help him to develop further as a reader and a writer.

Further reading

Graves, D. (1983) *Writing: Teachers and Children at Work*. Portsmouth, NH: Heinemann Educational.
This book includes a chapter devoted entirely to spelling, in which the author indicates the five general stages of invention that he believes operate as children develop their spelling. The chapter also stresses the active role of the teacher in guiding children towards more conventional spellings.

Temple, C., Nathan, R., Temple, F. and Burris, N.A. (1988) *The Beginnings of Writing*. London: Allyn & Bacon.
This book is divided into three main parts, one of which deals with 'The beginnings of spelling'. There are many examples of children's spellings within the context of their writing. The authors debate the progress that children make from pre-phonemic spelling (using letters without reference to sounds) to early phonemic, letter name and transitional spelling (which can be related to the first four stages suggested by Gentry) and, finally, conventional spelling. They provide suggestions for the teacher to support the children's move to conventional spelling. These suggestions indicate both general support from the literacy activities of the classroom as well as more specifically bringing the children's attention to some examples of conventional spellings.

knowledge about language

As young children talk, listen, write and read within the context of a variety of experiences, they learn to use each of these aspects of language with increased sophistication. This is important, because children learn about a wide range of subjects through language. So children learn to use language and to learn through language and, in doing so, they also demonstrate their knowledge about language. This knowledge is in the main implicit, but nevertheless it will be demonstrated during the children's talk, writing and reading. For instance, when children talk, they demonstrate their developing knowledge about the structure of sentences with each of their utterances. When they write, their invented spellings are indicative of knowledge about orthography, phonology and sequences of letters. And in their reading, a miscue analysis will provide information relating to the children's knowledge about parts of speech as they typically substitute nouns for nouns, verbs for verbs, and so on. Yet, despite their knowledge about language, the children may not be able to articulate that knowledge or indeed have the terminology of language to describe their knowledge. Recent debates and developments have considered what children might be expected to know and the extent to which that knowing might be articulated.

In the UK, the Bullock Report (DES 1975) influenced many aspects of language across the curriculum and it raised the issue of children learning about language but not in the sense of being taught formal grammar. It was the Kingman Committee (DES 1988a) that developed this idea more specifically. While recognizing the opposing views of the direct teaching of grammar versus no explicit teaching of language structure, the Committee suggested:

> We do not recommend a return to that kind of grammar teaching. It was based on a model of language derived from Latin rather than English. However, we believe that for children not to be taught anything about language is seriously to their disadvantage.
>
> (p. 12)

The report went on to describe a model of language that included: the forms of the English language; communication and comprehension; acquisition and development; and historical and geographical variation. Such a model, it was suggested, might be used to inform the training of teachers as to how the English language works and to inform professional discussion of all aspects of English teaching. Subsequently, the LINC (Language In the National Curriculum) Project was set up to develop materials for professional use (Carter 1990). The conflicts that arose between LINC and government ministers in the UK as those materials were developed, demonstrated the political debates relating to language education in the 1980s. But how did all of these debates and developments affect teachers and children in early years classrooms?

First, the debates suggested that teachers gain by knowing about language. As is argued in the *whole language* section, teachers need to have a knowledge about language that can inform their planning, teaching, monitoring and evaluation of children's progress in literacy. Second, the debates suggested that when talking with children about language, it is appropriate to use the terms that most adequately describe language being used. But as the Kingman Report emphasized (DES 1988a: 13), 'these terms must be acquired mainly through an exploration of the language pupils use, rather than through exercises out of context'. And the very specific example that was given in the report was that of teacher–child conferences to discuss written work. Quite simply, it was suggested that terms such as word, sentence and paragraph would be used to talk about the child's writing. So the teacher should not feel restricted by avoiding technical terms. Indeed, it is now part of the curriculum in England, where the use of a technical vocabulary to discuss reading and writing is part of the National Literacy Strategy (DfEE 1998). However, with young children we are reminded that such technical language should be offered as part of discussions and in an unobtrusive manner (Whitehead 1999). That is what many teachers of young children do when, for instance, they read a story to the class. Words such as author, illustration, character, paragraph, sentence, full stop, noun and adjective might all be used at various times. Although some of these words help to describe features of a book or story grammar, others are more specifically related to the forms of the language. All of this helps children to acquire a language about language that subsequently will enable them to become more reflective about their own language. But it is acquired in the early years informally during the interactions within meaningful literacy events, supported by an informed teacher.

Further reading

DES (1988a) *Report of the Committee of Inquiry into the Teaching of English Language* (*The Kingman Report*). London: HMSO.

This report provided a model of the English language for use in the teaching of English. It was influential because it set the foundations for parts of the National Curriculum in England and Wales and it provided a basis for a further discussion of what might be learnt about language and how that learning might take place. Of course, the document did not concern itself in the main with the early years. But there were features, some noted above, that were of importance to the infant classroom.

Carter, R. (ed.) (1990) *Knowledge about Language and the Curriculum: The LINC Reader*. London: Hodder & Stoughton.
This book contains a collection of articles under two main headings: 'Knowledge about language – some key issues' and 'Language and the curriculum'. In the first, the Kingman model of language is developed 'to make it pedagogically sensitive' (p. 6). A key part of that development was, then, to ensure that teachers would recognize the relevance of the model for classroom practice. In the second part, the articles are more practical in their orientation and, at least two of them, those by Yetta Goodman and Margaret Meek, are of direct interest to the early years teacher.

Bain, R., Fitzgerald, B. and Taylor, M. (eds) (1992) *Looking into Language: Classroom Approaches to Knowledge about Language*. London: Hodder & Stoughton.
This collection of articles is very much based in the classroom. The articles report on the work of teachers helping children (including young children) to learn about language. There are many transcripts that highlight the ways in which teachers introduce the terminology of language, and examples of the written work of children that demonstrate their knowledge about language.

language experience approach

When the Plowden Report (DES 1967) on primary schools in England was published, it included brief accounts of practices observed in schools. It noted that:

> it is quite common for writing to begin side by side with the learning of reading, for children to dictate to their teachers and gradually to copy and then to expand and write for themselves accounts of their experiences at home and at school. Often these accounts also serve as their first reading books . . . Much of the writing derives from the experiences of individual children, much from the excitement of a shared visit.
>
> (pp. 218–19)

Although the report did not refer directly to a language experience approach at that point, the description above does include many of the elements that would be a recognized part of such an approach used both then and today.

In particular, the sequence starts with the experiences of the individual children or from shared visits or experiences. Then there might be a dictation to the teacher, the copying of the dictation by the child and the use of that dictation as a first reading book as part of a language experience approach in the classroom with young children. Nora Goddard (1974), in her distinguished book on the language experience approach, included all of these elements in her discussion of the approach. In particular, she argued that the teacher of young children needs to make use of children's experiences, interests and feelings as a basis for developing literacy. Furthermore, she suggested the approach has the advantage of bringing together the four modalities of language (speaking, listening, writing and reading) within one activity.

The practical consequences in the classroom would be that the teacher would wish to encourage each child to talk about those experiences and interests which had been thought about. That which had been talked about could then be expressed in drawings, paintings and in writing. For the very young child, that writing might have to be dictated to the teacher and the child could subsequently copy the writing. The writing might also provide the basis for a reading book for the child. The collection of writing by a child, or the writing by a number of children, can be used as part of the reading resources of the classroom. When that reading material is organized and presented in an appropriate way, it can form part of the reading collection in the *library corner*.

Many teachers in the UK have made widespread use of language experience approaches as well as derivatives of it (e.g. *Breakthrough to Literacy*). Indeed, aspects of the approach are still being used in many schools, especially the attempts to link children's literacy activities to that which has been experienced and is known, as we noted with *bilingual children*. However, there are some issues that need to be considered. Holdaway (1979), although recognizing the many positive features of the approach, was concerned that the writing and reading might become dull and repetitive. That is, for some children, the experiences that they dictate to their teacher might relate to common and frequent events without variation (e.g. watching television, shopping with a parent, etc.). However, such obstacles can be overcome. Goddard (1974) suggested that, although the starting point for writing and reading might be the experiences that the children bring to school, it is an important part of the teacher's role to provide other experiences and interests. So the children can talk about and, therefore, write about visits outside of school, about visitors to the school, collections within the school and experiences encountered second-hand through the stories that are read to the class. Such class experiences can lead to individual writing but also to group or *shared writing*, where the teacher composes a description or account based on the various inputs from the children (Hornsby 2000). During this process, the teacher is able to demonstrate the ways in which spoken language is used and developed as it is presented in a written format.

The dictation of writing to the teacher by individual children is another contentious area. From a practical point of view, this has always been a problem for teachers with even moderately large classes. Being a scribe for each of the children in the class can create unproductive queues for the children and a difficult task for the teacher. Some teachers, in an attempt to overcome such problems, developed their skills as touch typists using jumbo print typewriters, so speeding up the writing of the dictations and producing 'book-like' print at the same time. However, we also need to consider whether it is in the best interests of the children for the teacher to act as scribe (Goodman 1991).

Our insights of children as active constructors of knowledge, and the many examples we now have of children developing as writers (e.g. Schickedanz 1990), lead us to question the notion of the teacher as scribe as a constant feature of a language experience approach. Many teachers now wish to see children writing on their own using *invented spellings*, rather than eventually copying the dictated writing produced by the teacher. In such circumstances, children have to consider actively the letters, sounds, words, sentences and eventually some of the other conventions of print as they write. All of this helps them to develop their literacy.

Nevertheless, the key principle of the language experience approach is likely to underpin a good deal of the work in the early years classroom. That is, the children's experiences and interests, from both outside and within school, will be used to encourage *writing, shared writing*, reading, *play activities*, drama, painting and model making, so that the children's involvement with literacy in those contexts has meaning and purpose.

Further reading

Goddard, N. (1974) *Literacy: Language Experience Approach*. London: Macmillan Educational.

Joyce Morris, in her introduction to Nora Goddard's book, states that the text is 'the best possible exposition of language-experience approaches to literacy'. Perhaps this view is based on the fact that not only does the book provide interesting classroom examples of the approach in practice, but it also includes a clear reference to the theoretical and historical underpinnings of the approach. And it does not neglect to deal with many of the important and demanding roles that confront the teacher when using the language experience approach.

Stauffer, R.G. (1970) *The Language-Experience Approach to the Teaching of Reading.* New York: Harper & Row.
This text was written by one of the key exponents of the language-experience approach in the USA (I use the hyphen here because Stauffer includes a section on the importance of the hyphen to denote the linking of language-experience rather than, as he notes, the less dynamic language and experience). There are many connections between the approach as it was developed in the UK and in the USA. However, the text does demonstrate a stronger emphasis on the dictations to the teacher and there is a complete chapter on 'dictated experience stories'. Furthermore, there is a more formal emphasis given to word recognition. Yetta Goodman (1991: 386) argued that 'taking dictation from children and then having them read it became a way to teach children words and other sub-skills', thus ultimately taking the approach away from initial principles. Nevertheless, this book provides many interesting insights into the approach as it was being developed in many English-speaking countries.

library corner

The books that are made available for children to read are central to the organization for literacy in the early years classroom. And the quality of those books is of considerable importance, as noted in the sections on *children's books* and *real books*. However, how the books are displayed, the general ambience of the area and the availability of spaces where the children can read the books in comfort also require attention. Careful thought needs to be given to the setting up and maintenance of the library corner in the classroom.

A survey of 120 primary schools and 470 classrooms by HMI in the UK, during the autumn term of 1990, indicated the widespread acceptance of the need for a library corner (HMI 1991). Almost all the classrooms had a library corner, or reading area as it was called in the report. In the classrooms through to Year (or grade) 2, the corner was most usually carpeted, had bookshelves and some comfortable seating.

But the value of the area for reading varied considerably, depending on how well it was organized and maintained. Therefore, the organization and day-to-day management of the library corner is very important.

The first thing the teacher must consider is the physical setting of the library corner. Most teachers want the daily use of the corner to be integrated into the literacy activities provided. Quite literally, a corner of the classroom is most often used, as it provides two physical boundaries as well as two walls for displays of books, book covers, posters and the children's pictures or reviews of books that they have enjoyed. It is insufficient to think only of the walls as boundaries. One further side, and perhaps part of the fourth side, needs to have bookshelves, noticeboards or small cabinets, so that the corner is more clearly distinguished from the rest of the room. And these boundaries will also include some surfaces at child level for table-top displays. Carpeting the floor brings two benefits: first, there is the comfort of the soft flooring and, second, there is a reduction in noise that helps the children to concentrate on their reading. Soft chairs, large beanbags and a sofa all add to the comfort of the library corner. A few large soft toys and puppets of some well-known story characters acquired over time reinforce the messages from storybooks. One objective will be to make the corner a very inviting place to visit, which will be enhanced if attention is given to its physical appearance.

However, the books are the reason we want the children to visit the library corner; therefore, the selection and variety of books available is very important. Storybooks will make up a substantial part of the collection, but there will also be anthologies of *nursery rhymes* and fairy tales, picture and *poetry* books, *alphabet*, information and reference books, and each category will need to cater for children at different stages of development. Morrow (1989) suggested that five to eight books per child is the minimum number of books required to stock a library. Not all the collection can be displayed with their covers showing, so shelving that allows for the spines of books to be displayed is important too.

As part of the management of the library corner, the books that are shown front-on will need to be changed or rotated on a regular basis. Furthermore, the teacher should add to the collection as often as possible, ensuring the children are aware of recent additions. Occasionally, it is useful to have a book of the week, which has been read to the class, talked about and made readily available by providing more than one copy. At other times, there can be an author of the week or month, when as many of that author's books as possible are displayed. A thematic display, with a variety of authors, can also stimulate interest in a range of books and might include both storybooks and information books.

The management of the library corner need not be restricted to the teacher. Morrow (1989) suggested that children should be involved in the planning and development of the area. In particular, she suggested that they might help to develop the rules and arrange a rota for keeping it tidy. If there are notices in or around the library corner (e.g. 'Only six children in the library corner at one time please'), it will help to establish the rules, as well as adding to the *classroom print* that is used for real purposes. A lending system, whereby each child has a library card that indicates the book they have taken home, provides another functional use of literacy. Involving children in the management of the library corner was noted by HMI as an important feature of successful reading areas.

Nevertheless, class teachers should monitor the corner constantly and ask themselves: Is the area attractive? Has it been changed for good purpose often enough? Do the children use the facility with respect? Are all the children making use of it? Are the discussions about books, and the library corner generally, demonstrating the children's interests in books? Such monitoring will enable teachers to evaluate and develop further this important part of classroom provision. In some classrooms, such evaluation leads to other literacy activities being added to the corner so that it becomes a literacy corner, or centre, rather than more simply a library corner. A simple addition is that of a listening area where two or more children can listen to a taped story while following the words in the book in front of them. The use of headphones ensures that the other children are not disturbed by the activity and it enables the children to listen again and again to a well-loved story and to link the story to the print in the book. The inclusion of a *writing centre* and some computing facilities also extends the library corner into a literacy centre. In each classroom setting, decisions have to be made as to whether to develop the room with a library corner, with other literacy activities elsewhere in the room, or to have a large literacy centre including a library section. In each case, the arrangement is designed to support the children's literacy development.

Further reading

Morrow, L.M. (1989) Designing the classroom to promote literacy development, in D.S. Strickland and L.M. Morrow (eds) *Emerging Literacy: Young Children Learn to Read and Write*. Newark, DE: International Reading Association.

The chapter by Morrow is about more than just the library corner. It includes a debate about the organization of the classroom as a rich literacy environment and the benefits that can accrue for the children; she provides examples from classrooms of children engaged with literacy, which add to the picture presented. However, part of the chapter is about the literacy centre, which includes a library corner, writing area, oral language area and additional language arts materials. Such an area is argued to be the focal point of the room and the library corner is a major part of the centre. Morrow considers some of the important features of the library corner and several of her suggestions are included above.

literacy hour in the National Literacy Strategy

The development of The National Literacy Strategy (DfEE 1998), which included the use of a literacy hour, led to profound changes in the way that literacy was taught in primary schools in England. In particular, the literacy hour was 'intended to promote literacy instruction' (p. 8) and, as we shall see, there is substantial time given to the teacher instructing the whole class. Initially, reception classes with children of 5 years of age and younger were included in the prescription. However, subsequently, with the development and description of a foundation stage for children from 2 to 5 years (QCA 2000), reception classrooms were no longer required to utilize a literacy hour. Nevertheless, in many schools a literacy hour was maintained for the 5-year-olds or at least introduced to them in the later stages of the school year.

The structure of the literacy hour was detailed in The National Literacy Strategy (DfEE 1998); Beard (1999) subsequently provided the rationale. Four distinct parts were mooted for the hour. First, there is a *shared reading* or *shared writing* time with the whole class for 15 minutes. Second, there is another whole class time of 15 minutes that is devoted to word, sentence or text level work. It is during this time that a 'systematic, regular and frequent teaching of phonological awareness, phonics and spelling' (DfEE 1998: 11) is expected to occur. Third, approximately 20 minutes is devoted to group and independent work. During this time, activities such as *guided reading* and *guided writing* take place with the teacher working with one or two groups of six children each while other children work independently. Finally, in the fourth element, a plenary session takes place with the whole class in which the activities of the day are reviewed or consolidated.

One of the benefits of the literacy hour is the clear unequivocal focus that is placed upon literacy for one hour each day. It is important that adequate time is devoted to literacy by the children. Others have suggested that longer periods of time are required for literacy. For example, Cambourne (1988) notes that two hours a day are devoted to literacy in some Australian schools, while Cunningham and Allington (1998) suggest two and a half hours of *time for literacy* during the course of the day in the USA (Campbell 1999b). A second benefit is that the literacy hour has ensured that useful literacy activities, such as *shared reading* and *shared writing*, have become a very substantial part of the primary school day. Previously, although debated and explained earlier by Holdaway (1979), only a few teachers in the UK had used these activities. The opportunities to see reading and writing being modelled would appear to be beneficial to young children.

However, although The National Literacy Strategy suggested that there would need to be a continuation of the time devoted to *story reading*, there was a danger that those read-alouds might not be maintained (Campbell 1998). Of course, the *shared reading* of big books has similarities to a *story reading*. However, in the literacy hour, the emphasis is on *shared reading* being used to consider words, sentences and text rather than emphasizing enjoyment of the story. The use of *story reading* to introduce a variety of books and authors and create an interest in and enjoyment of reading remains important.

In part, perhaps because of the emphasis on literacy instruction, there appears to be less time devoted to children doing – in this case, reading and particularly writing. Margaret Cook (see Fisher 1998) suggested that time needs to be provided for the children to engage in extended *writing*. Furthermore, teachers reported that, based on their experience of working with the literacy hour, 'there was insufficient emphasis on writing' (Smith and Whiteley 2000: 36). This is perhaps inevitable if the teacher continues to instruct the whole class for more than half of the time – there will be little time available for the children to write regularly.

A more critical view of the literacy hour, especially for young children, was offered by Whitehead (1999). In particular, she expressed concerns about the prescriptive nature of the hour. The professionalism of the teacher is reduced if the guidelines for each term are followed strictly. Frater (2000) notes that teaching and learning are least appropriate in classrooms where there is a literal following of the hour prescription. There is also concern about the amount of time that children spend sitting and listening to the teacher instruct. (The literacy hour does not appear to be based on young children as learners constructing meaning from experiences.) The emphasis upon instruction in word, sentence and text is also a cause for concern. Because linguists are able to describe language in great detail does not necessarily mean that it should be taught to children. The dissection of texts is also a worry. For Whitehead, quality books and poems need to be loved by children and meanings developed from them by the children. The development of the literacy hour appeared to be linked more to the teaching of older primary school children.

Further reading

Browne, A. (1998) *A Practical Guide to Teaching Reading in the Early Years.* London: Paul Chapman.
This book was published as the National Literacy Strategy was being put into place and the literacy hour was being piloted in some schools. Nevertheless, the text usefully explores some of the teaching strategies that were being included and considers the teaching and learning that is developmentally appropriate for young children. The book has a theoretical base but also provides many helpful practical suggestions for teachers.

Fisher, R. (ed.) (1998) *Hours of Literacy.* Teaching in Practice Series (TIPS) No. 4. Royston: UK Reading Association.
In her introduction to this book, Ros Fisher describes the literacy hour, debates some of the key elements in it and notes some of its theoretical justification. Then, Margaret Cook looks beyond the hour at other activities that might still need to be organized in the classroom including, importantly, *story readings* by the teacher and time for *extended writing* as well as considering the long-term planning required by the school. The subsequent chapters provide more detailed information on the literacy hour being used in a variety of classrooms, including with young children.

literature circles

Like *guided reading*, literature circles are usually developed as a group activity. However, each of these activities has different purposes. In *guided reading*, the emphasis is on reading the book and developing the children's strategies to succeed in that task. Rather than being organized to develop reading strategies, literature circles 'enable children to think more deeply about text as they talk with one another and co-construct new understanding' (Fountas and Pinnell 1996: 1).

So the child reads and develops an understanding of a book. Within a literature circle, the child has the opportunity to expand upon and critique those initial understandings in talk with other children and the teacher.

Typically, a literature circle has six children reading the same book and, wherever possible, chosen by the children from a wide collection of books. A short picture book might be read completely in one session, with the children immediately beginning to talk about their under-standing of the book. With older children, it might be agreed to read a larger book a chapter at a time and to discuss that before proceeding with the reading. The teacher acts as a guide during these discussions. For the very youngest children, the teacher might read the story aloud (Roser and Martinez 1995) and then concentrate upon the children's understanding during a follow-up discussion as a literature circle. Teachers of nursery and reception children will know how insightful young children's comments can be during an interactive story reading, as when they comment on some aspect of the story and relate it to their own experiences and lives. It is these comments, understandings and reflections that the teacher will try to extend during literature circles.

It is not the purpose of the literature circle to reach some predetermined interpretation of the book. Rather, it is for each child to create a meaning and then develop that meaning in collaboration with the other readers. And it is not about learning about literary elements; instead, it serves a wider purpose. As Short (1995) argued, the literature circle provides a context for the children 'to learn about life and to make sense of the world' (p. x), especially within the context of an inquiry-based curriculum. Subsequently, other teachers and writers have provided examples of what those ideas might mean in primary classroom practice (Campbell Hill *et al.* 1995). For instance, Clausen (1995) relates how she used literature circles as part of daily literacy activities with a Year 1 class.

In that Year 1 class, *shared reading, story reading, sustained silent reading* and *writing*, as well as literature circles, were daily features. The literature circle was used to create an 'enthusiasm for reading and a love of literature' (Clausen 1995: 15) and to emphasize the import-ance of meaning making during reading. Clausen examines the prac-tical implications of working with several literature circles. Nevertheless, the responses from the children demonstrate how worthwhile it can be to stress the understanding of ideas and emotions within a book, rather than more frequently concentrating on print features.

At times, literature circles can be linked to author studies (Short 1999), as the children become interested in reading the books of one

author. At other times, the books being explored might relate to thematic or topic work that is interesting the children. On still other
occasions, the book selected will be free standing but one that has
captured the children's attention. Whatever the case, the literature
circle is a means of encouraging children to talk about their understanding of a book and to extend and develop that understanding in
collaboration with others.

Further reading

Chambers, A. (1993) *Tell Me: Children, Reading and Talk*. Stroud: Thimble Press.
This book does not state that it is about literature circles. However, it is about
'helping children to talk well about books they have read. And not only talk
well but listen well' (p. 9). In that sense, therefore, it is about literature circles
as it debates the classroom environment and the teacher support and questions
that enable children to 'tell' about the books they have read. A framework of
questions is provided for the teacher (pp. 87–91). However, this framework is
for guidance rather than strict use. The aim is to encourage the children to
talk and to generate their own questions about the books that they read.

miscue analysis

Almost inevitably during any reading of a text, children – or, indeed,
adults – will, from time to time, produce a miscue. So, instead of reading
the text word as expected, the reader miscues, or provides an observed
response, which is not in the text. The word used to describe that
deviation from the text is indeed a miscue, rather than a mistake or
error, because it indicates the strengths that the reader brings to the
reading rather than negatively referring to any failure. Kenneth Goodman (1969), a key figure in the development of miscue analysis, argued
for the use of the word miscue for that reason, but also to avoid the
implication that good reading does not include miscues.

Teachers who share books with young children know that miscues
will occur. The teacher, however knowledgeable about miscue analysis,
must consider the following: Why did the child read like that? What
information was being used to produce, for instance, 'horse' for 'house'?
Furthermore, because teachers ask these questions of themselves, the
basis for understanding miscue analysis is already in place. As Goodman

(1992: 194) suggested, 'Miscue analysis quite easily became a part of the repertoire of British teachers. For decades they'd been "hearing pupils read". Now they knew what they were listening for'.

Although most miscues (approximately 80 per cent) by children involve the substitution of one word for another, they also insert or omit words, repeat words, hesitate and self-correct. There six categories cover most miscues produced by children. Elsewhere, I describe these six types of miscue within one sentence (Campbell 1993):

In this sentence, the six miscues are:

1 Substitution	down (for the text word 'dry')
2 Insertion	in (added to the sentence after 'got')
3 Omission	and (left out during the reading)
4 Repetition	to-to (the word spoken more than once)
5 Hesitation	// (a pause longer than three seconds)
6 Self-correction	run-rub (initial attempt at the word is corrected)

Of these types of miscue, self-corrections often indicate children's positive attempts to check their own reading. As Marie Clay (1972) argued, self-corrections can be indicative of reading progress. Repetitions and hesitations are often used to give the reader more time to consider the next word and, in that sense, are positive; they might be viewed more negatively if they occur too frequently. An analysis of insertions and omissions often leads to the view that the readers are editing the text into their own dialect or level of understanding and, as such, they demonstrate a real involvement with the text. Occasionally, the omissions might, more negatively, be made to avoid a difficult word or phrase.

However, it is substitutions that are the most frequent and helpful miscues for teachers. They are helpful because teachers can analyse a substitution to consider the use that a child is making of the language *cue systems*. In other words, teachers can compare the observed response/spoken word with the expected response/text word for syntactic and semantic acceptability and graphophonic appropriateness.

In our earlier example, the reader had substituted 'down' for the text word 'dry'. We could ask of that substitution:

1 *Syntactically*, is the miscue acceptable structurally within the sentence – that is, does it still make a sentence?

2 *Semantically*, is the miscue acceptable meaningfully within the sentence – that is, does it make sense?

3 *Graphophonically*, is there a degree of similarity between the spoken word and the text word – for example, is there first letter similarity?

An analysis of this example suggests that all three language cue systems were being used. Occasionally, such an analysis will be made more difficult because of the need to look graphophonically at word endings, or word middles, rather than just first letters. Also, where the substitution is in the middle of a sentence, rather than the last word of the sentence, a judgement will have to be made as to whether syntactically and semantically the sentence was acceptable up to and including the miscue even if the complete sentence is not. Such complexities become less problematic the more frequently the teacher attempts a miscue analysis and, therefore, becomes more knowledgeable about it and more familiar with its use.

Of course, miscue analysis is not something that is attempted for its own sake. Miscue analysis might be conducted rather formally and very specifically to determine the reading strengths and weaknesses of the reader or, more informally, while the teacher is sharing a book with a child. Indeed, it could be argued that, once a teacher is familiar with miscue analysis, it is inevitable that every *sharing a book* or *hearing a child read* involves a miscue analysis because the teacher's knowledge now prompts him or her to ask: Why did the reader produce that miscue? Miscue analysis encourages teachers to become more diagnostic as listeners. But this diagnosis is not in itself sufficient; it is there because it enables us to move forward to consider literacy planning. We can use the information from the miscue analysis to assist us in determining what sort of literacy experiences the child now needs to develop further as a reader.

Many teachers of young children become familiar with miscue analysis not only through sharing books with children but also in a variety of other guises. For example, the *running records* that are a part of *reading recovery* involve the use of miscue analysis (or many of the principles of miscue analysis). Additionally, part of the standard assessment task test procedure for reading at Key Stage 1 (7 years of age) in England uses running records. All of this points to miscue analysis being useful as a means of finding out about young children's reading.

In the classroom

While sharing a book with a child, teachers have the opportunity to consider the miscues produced and, therefore, build a picture of the child as a reader. So when 5-year-old Richard read to his teacher, the miscues on the first few lines provided interesting insights into Richard's strengths:

> *Richard*: In the light of the moon
> the(a) little egg lay on a leaf.
> One Summers(Sunday) day(morning) the warm sun
> came out(up) and – pop – out of the egg
> a very(came-t) a tiny and very hungry caterpillar.
> He looked(started-t) to look for some food.
> (for the complete transcript, see Campbell 1992: 19–27)

Although he needed some support from his teacher (indicated by '-t'), nevertheless Richard maintained the sentence structure and, especially initially, the meaning of the text during the first six substitutions that he produced. And although there might have been less attention to the graphophonic features, his 'Summers' for 'Sunday' and 'out' for 'up', plus the verb ending -ed, suggested that that area was not neglected as he read. Richard was just 5 when this interaction took place, which serves to remind us of the strengths that he demonstrated as he read.

Further reading

Campbell, R. (1993) *Miscue Analysis in the Classroom*. Widnes: UK Reading Association.
Miscue analysis is widely recognized as a useful means of assessing children's development as readers and diagnosing current strengths and weaknesses. However, the procedures used may appear to be oriented more towards the researcher than the classroom teacher. This book provides a simple but concise description of miscue analysis for use by the classroom teacher. It includes, additionally, sections on more recent developments, such as retrospective miscue analysis.

Goodman, Y., Watson, D. and Burke, C. (1987) *Reading Miscue Inventory: Alternative Procedures*. New York: Richard C. Owen.
For teachers who require very detailed procedures for making a full miscue analysis of an oral reading, this book will suffice. The theory of miscue analysis is debated and practical procedures for collecting miscue data are provided. The procedures for miscue analysis are also considered, as are alternative procedures with varying intensities. In all, a very thorough text for reference purposes.

National Curriculum

A National Curriculum has been in place in England and Wales for over a decade. In the first edition of this handbook, I noted that it was developed by a working group that had been set up under the chairmanship of Brian Cox to produce a blueprint for the National Curriculum in English (DES 1988b). The report included the attainment targets that were to be set, separately for reading and writing, in the area of literacy. Subsequently, the English in the National Curriculum document (DES 1989) provided the fine details and statutory requirements for the teaching of English at Key Stage 1 for children in infant schools aged 5 to 7. In particular, the attainment targets for the testing at the end of Key Stage 1 at 7 years of age were indicated.

Since then, there have been various changes and several new documents leading to the current position. Now there is a foundation stage (QCA 2000) that begins when the children reach the age of 3 through to, and including, the reception class at 5 years of age. The foundation stage sets out the knowledge, skills, understanding and attitudes that children need to learn to achieve the early learning goals in several areas, including communication, language and literacy. The National Curriculum Key Stage 1 (QCA 1999a) provides for children in Years 1 and 2 at 6 and 7 years of age. There are levels of attainment for reading and writing with most 7-year-olds expected to reach Level 2 and most children expected to work at Levels 1–3 at this age. In addition, there is now the *literacy hour* as part of The National Literacy Strategy (DfEE 1998). It was put in place in an attempt to raise standards, in particular so that 80 per cent of 11-year-olds might achieve Level 4 at the end of the primary school. However, Hilton (2001) has questioned any apparent raising of standards, as the nature of the reading test was altered, and made easier, from 1998 to 2000 for that group.

The most positive feature of these documents might be the clarity with which each nursery setting or school can now approach reading and writing. Early learning goals are to be achieved and later attainment targets are to be reached. Furthermore, there is guidance on how that might be achieved. At the foundation stage, the document indicates the 'stepping stones' that children need to learn and 'what the practitioners need to do' to support that learning to achieve the goals. Then, at Key Stage 1, there are clear statements on what is to be taught in the *literacy hour*. So, for Year 1 children, for instance, in term one the word level work includes 'to practise and secure alphabetic letter knowledge and alphabetic order' and 'to discriminate and segment all three phonemes in CVC words' (DfEE 1998: 20). How this is to be taught and for how long each day is also indicated.

For some teachers, such detailed prescription is seen to be a problem rather than an advantage (Smith and Whiteley 2000). In particular, the *literacy hour*, which should help children to reach the attainment targets in the National Curriculum, has been perceived to be rigid and prescriptive. Whitehead (1999) was more wide-ranging in her critique of the early learning goals and the National Curriculum at Key Stage 1. For instance, although she recognized the goals (as they were in 1997) as being in part good sense, there was also she suggested 'excessive and insensitive detail' (p. 103). At Key Stage 1, she used as one of her examples the achievement of understanding and punctuating sentences. As she noted, understanding sentences is a complex linguistic issue and, for 6- and 7-year-olds, may be difficult and inappropriate.

In the foundation stage document (QCA 2000), the 'early learning goals for reading to the end of the foundation stage' are:

Explore and experiment with sounds, words and texts.
Retell narratives in the correct sequence, drawing on language patterns of stories.
Read a range of familiar and common words and simple sentences independently.
Know that print carries meaning and, in English, is read from left to right and top to bottom.
Show an understanding of the element of stories, such as main character, sequence of events, and openings, and how information can be found in non-fiction texts to answer questions about where, who, why and how.

(QCA 2000: 62)

In addition, there are goals for linking sounds and letters, writing and handwriting. The goals for sounds and letters are also developed with an emphasis on *phonics* here as well as at Key Stage 1. However, it is possible to use the guidance provided to develop children's knowledge of letters and sounds through play and context, rather than by direct teaching. In addition, encouraging writing, with an acceptance of *invented spellings*, is suggested as a means of helping children to think about letters and sounds.

At Key Stage 1, the Level 2 attainment in reading (QCA 1999a) can be seen to be developing further some of the above early learning goals. They are stated as:

Pupils' reading of simple texts shows an understanding and is generally accurate.

They express opinions about major events or ideas in stories, poems and non-fiction.

They use more than one strategy, such as phonic, graphic, syntactic and contextual, in reading unfamiliar words and establishing meanings.

(QCA 1999a: appendices, p. 5)

Of course, the programme of study to achieve Level 2 is more substantial and details are provided in the document (pp. 46–7). For instance, to support the children's reading for information, it suggests that they be taught 'to use the organisational features of non-fiction texts, including captions, illustrations, contents, index and chapters, to find information'. Although this is not developed further, it is possible to see how the use of *shared reading* with big non-fiction books would aid that teaching. (One of the interesting features of the National Curriculum documents is that they are worded consistently 'pupils should be taught' rather than 'pupils should learn', which may or may not be the same thing.)

The attainment targets for Level 2 reading when they were first offered (DES 1989) were:

Read aloud from familiar stories and poems fluently and with appropriate expression.

Demonstrate knowledge of the alphabet in using word books and simple dictionaries.

Use picture and context cues, words recognised on sight and phonic cues in reading.

Listen and respond to stories, poems and other material read aloud, expressing opinions informed by what has been read.

Read a range of material with some independence, fluency, accuracy and understanding.

(DES 1989: attainment targets, p. 5)

There have therefore been changes over time. From familiar stories to simple texts and from accuracy to generally accurate are two of the apparent changes. Nevertheless, the overall emphasis on reading with accuracy and understanding using a range of strategies has been maintained. However, looked at from the outside, it is difficult to determine what now constitutes a simple text, how accurate is generally accurate and how informed do the opinions have to be. Perhaps testing children using the standard assessment tasks will in part answer such questions.

The National Curriculum has created a great deal of debate. Many teachers saw the development as a vindication of the principles, beliefs and methods that they had been carrying through for some years. Others saw it as a means of restricting teachers, with its imposition of content and activities upon the early years curriculum. But there is now a generation of teachers who have taught for a decade or more without knowing anything other than a curriculum provided from outside. Whether a national curriculum increases or decreases the professional role of a teacher, raises their understanding or alters their role to that of technician is part of another discussion.

Further reading

QCA (2000) *Curriculum Guidance for the Foundation Stage*. London: Qualifications and Curriculum Authority with Department for Education and Employment.
QCA (1999a) *The National Curriculum Handbook for Primary Teachers in England, Key Stages 1 and 2*. London: Qualifications and Curriculum Authority with Department for Education and Employment.
These two documents provide all the details about the National Curriculum in the early years. The early learning goals and attainment targets are listed. Activities to encourage the achievement of those goals and targets are noted. A sequence of development in each aspect of speaking, listening, writing and reading is suggested. And there is also an indication of the underlying principles of teaching and learning in each stage.

non-fiction

Both at home and at school, young children have many opportunities to engage with stories. The initial story readings that children hear enable them to learn about books. Stories also inform children about the structure of the narrative or literary genre, which supports them in their own story writing. Such knowledge provides a good basis for them when they read storybooks either in the form of a *shared reading* or on their own. However, children also read other books that will be structured somewhat differently and use a vocabulary that is not typically found in stories. For teachers, the concern is how to help young children when reading non-fiction. At the very least, teachers will want to provide read-alouds with non-fiction, *shared readings*, *thematic work/topic work*, *shared writing* and other opportunities for *writing*.

In most readings aloud by the teacher, it will be *story readings* that are used. However, occasionally, the teacher might read a short extract from an information book – not as a replacement for the daily story reading, but in addition to it. These short readings from information books might take place, for instance, at the end of a period of *sustained silent reading*. Such readings may not be designed specifically to teach about the structure of non-fiction books. They are there because the class may have been exploring a particular topic and the teacher, having found an interesting item, reads it out to the class. Of course, the outcome of such readings is that the children will be informed not only about the subject matter but also indirectly about the organization, grammatical structure and flow of some information books. More directly, the teacher will refer to these features during *shared readings* with a variety of non-fiction. Big books are available on a variety of topics as well as big book dictionaries. Such texts provide the teacher with the materials to consider text features as well as content with a class. Phinn (2000) demonstrates this use of shared reading of non-fiction books as he explored the topic of dinosaurs with young children. At times, children will want to use an information book when *sharing a book* with their teacher. During these one-to-one interactions, the teacher is able to support the child's reading of the text and also to make comments about the nature of information books. Sometimes a non-fiction text might be explored during *guided reading*; this may be particularly the case with boys, as it has been reported that boys indicate a preference for non-fiction books (Browne 1996).

Involvement with information books occurs during other literacy activities. For example, when children are engaged in *thematic work/topic work*, they often need to consult a variety of books to find out more about their interests. The reading of these materials written in different registers needs to be supported by the teacher so as to avoid the simple copying of sections from the books. Demonstrations and guidance from the teacher are required, so that the children can make the best use of their reading skills in the context of reading differently arranged texts. This variety of reading by young children is now required as part of the National Curriculum in England and Wales (QCA 1999a) and mention is made of such reading at the foundation stage as well (QCA 2000).

Arranging for opportunities for the children to write can also facilitate the reading of non-narrative texts. For instance, when Alice was 5 years old, she produced unaided at home an 'ifmasn book' (information book) (Campbell 1999a: 130–1). Her book demonstrated an interest in writing about a topic and in setting that information out with headings and format just as in the non-fiction books that she had shared with adults.

Wray and Lewis (1997) demonstrated how the use of writing frames can assist young children to develop their writing of non-narrative forms. However, they also noted how the frame can become too formulaic and that children need to move on from using that support to writing without the use of the frame (Wray and Lewis 2001). Valerie Cherrington's (1990) example of children working together to write an information book is of 8- and 9-year-olds; nevertheless, it demonstrates some of the activities that are required to accomplish the task. The children had to locate information, use a variety of reading strategies including *scanning and skimming*, understand and extract information from the texts, record and store the information that was collected, and compose their own text collaboratively. All of this required substantial support from the teacher. The obvious outcome of the writing was that the children added to the information books available in their class library. Furthermore, the writing that had taken place was concerned with 'realistic tasks: with real reasons for inquiry, real reasons for writing and real audiences in mind' (p. 153). However, not only were the children learning to write in a non-narrative form, they were also able to take that learning to their subsequent reading of non-fiction.

Further reading

Neate, B. (1992) *Finding Out about Finding Out: A Practical Guide to Children's Information Books*. Sevenoaks: Hodder & Stoughton.
Bobbie Neate suggests initially that her book is for those who work with primary children. However, the subsequent emphasis in the text is on junior school children aged 7 to 11 rather than younger children. Nevertheless, there are many aspects of the book that will have applications for the teacher of younger children. The list comparing narrative and expository texts (pp. 49–51) has a general relevance for all teachers, which will raise questions about the provision of literacy activities in the classroom to support children's reading of information books.

Goodwin, P. and Redfern, A. (2000a) *Non-fiction in the Literacy Hour*. Reading: Reading and Language Information Centre, University of Reading.
As the title indicates, this book was developed primarily for teachers in England who were required to teach children about reading non-fiction books during the literacy hour. However, the book will be useful to a wider audience. It looks at a wide range of non-fiction, including *environmental print*, dictionaries and newspapers. The use of *shared reading* and *shared writing* to help the children is debated.

nursery rhymes

Traditionally, a part of children's early language development has been associated with the learning of nursery rhymes. Such learning often takes place as part of the rich exchange of language that occurs at home and at school as adults and children play with language. Some of this handing down of language culture also occurs between children, as one generation of children pass on to the next generation the rhymes and stories associated with certain games and activities (Opie and Opie 1959).

Although this section is entitled 'nursery rhymes', and nursery rhymes are a very important part of the language learnt by young children, the rhymes that children enjoy will lead us into other areas. For example, it is useful to think about finger plays, nursery songs and poems in addition to traditional nursery rhymes. Bernice Cullinan (1989) provides a comprehensive list of the various kinds of literature that young children enjoy and benefit from. As well as storybooks in various forms, and the value of *story readings* with those books, she also lists finger plays, nursery rhymes, songs and *poetry* as important early experiences for young children.

During the first year of a child's life, parents share events such as 'Round and round the garden, went the Teddy Bear. One step. Two steps. Tickly under there', as well as numerous other finger plays. Such games bring the adult and the child together in a shared enjoyment of language. And, even at 1 year of age, children are aware of sequence, memory and recall of the event, as well as anticipation of the final outcome, after just a few experiences of a particular game. Adults can also share nursery rhymes with children, at the same time engaging them in physical movements, as when Humpty Dumpty 'fell off the wall'.

Nursery rhymes are important because they are enjoyable and they provide a rich opportunity for sharing language. Dorothy White (1984), in her detailed diary account of her daughter's involvement with books before school age, frequently commented about Carol's love of rhyme and rhythm. She even suggested that Carol was offered poetry in a foreign language without destroying that enjoyment, because what intrigued Carol was the rhyme and the rhythm of the language. Chukovsky (1963) also demonstrated that children naturally enjoy playing with and making up rhymes. .

However, nursery rhymes are not only enjoyable, they also enable children to develop an understanding of language that contributes to their subsequent reading development (Meek 1990). Meek argued that, if we teach children nursery rhymes, then their awareness of phonology should follow naturally. We can see why if we look at part of the 'Hickory, dickory, dock' nursery rhyme. The first two lines end with 'dock' and 'clock'; a rhyming is created by the -ock rime endings. Children will recognize this link, and the 'd' and 'cl' onset units, without being taught about it directly. Such recognition, or phonological awareness, of *onset and rime* in the many rhymes that are heard, enjoyed and sung is an important part of children's subsequent reading development.

The link between early experiences with nursery rhymes and later reading development appears to be well established. Peter Bryant and his colleagues (e.g. Bryant and Bradley 1985; Goswami and Bryant 1990) have indicated that children with a knowledge of nursery rhymes at 3 years of age appear well disposed for acquiring *phonemic awareness* within the next year. And success at reading and spelling at 6 years of age is more likely. We need to remind ourselves that such success appears to be derived from the natural shared enjoyment of the language and laughter in nursery rhymes.

At play groups and nursery schools and in reception or kindergarten classes, teachers will want to replicate these experiences by making copious use of finger plays, nursery rhymes, songs and poems. Children can be encouraged to learn the rhymes, to present them in unison, to act them out and to represent them on paper. The latter is most likely to be in the form of drawings initially, but will soon include the children's writing, even if not presented conventionally.

As part of the learning of these various rhymes, the teacher will develop some of them as big books, or big sheets, during a *shared writing*, so that the children not only hear the words but also see them being constructed in print. Holdaway (1979), in his description of the development of big books, indicated that nursery rhymes, songs and poems were used for many of the big sheets that were produced for the children in his classroom. Those nursery rhymes on big sheets then become part of the *classroom print* to be used regularly for singing and talking about letters and words.

In classrooms where time is spent on nursery rhymes, the laughter and enjoyment initiated at home can be replicated in school. The learning that is derived from such experiences is of real benefit to the children both immediately and as a foundation for the future.

Further reading

Bryant, P. and Bradley, L. (1985) *Children's Reading Problems: Psychology and Education.* Oxford: Oxford University Press.
In part of this book, the authors describe the various studies that they have conducted that suggest a link between children's knowledge of nursery rhymes at 3 and 4 years of age and their subsequent sensitivity to rhyme. This sensitivity to rhyme and, therefore, phonological and phonemic awareness, supports the children in their development as readers. Such studies should provide further encouragement to parents, play group leaders and teachers to devote time to the enjoyable activities of finger plays, poems, songs and nursery rhymes.

Matterson, E. (1969) *This Little Puffin . . . Finger Plays and Nursery Games.* London: Puffin.
There are, of course, many books of nursery rhymes. This is but one example of that genre. However, it does also include many interesting finger plays, which the youngest children at home as well as those in the play group or nursery classroom will enjoy.

onset and rime

The terms 'onset' and 'rime' are debated by Goswami and Bryant (1990). However, put simply, the terms recognize the opening unit (onset) and end unit (rime) of a word. In the word 'mat', therefore, the onset is provided by the 'm' and the rime by the 'at'. It is the rime element that is used so extensively in nursery rhymes, while alliteration is developed by manipulating the onset unit of words. Children's awareness of onset and rime and their ability to manipulate them may be especially helpful for their developing literacy. It can be developed naturally with nursery rhymes and using books that place an emphasis upon rhyme and alliteration. Colin Harrison (1992) reminds us of the way in which some books can help with that process (e.g. *The Cat in the Hat* by Dr Seuss 1957).

Moustafa (1997) also suggests an emphasis on onset and rime with young children, which, she argues, are 'more comprehensible to children than instruction in letters and letter strings that represent phonemes' (p. 19). In her view of whole-to-parts-phonics, it is onset and rime that provides most help for children. After stories have been read with and enjoyed by children, she suggests creating an alphabet word wall in which *words* from the stories are displayed on separate pieces of paper. The onset and rime units of those words are highlighted and discussed with the children. Subsequently, the words can be grouped and regrouped to emphasize the onset or rime unit according to needs. So hat and cat might be grouped briefly from the Seuss story as the -at rime unit is emphasized.

Such experiences will also encourage children towards another advance in their reading, namely being able to read a word by analogy. Once cat and hat are known, it is possible to read rat by analogy. As Harrison (1992) indicated, the use of analogies might be more simple in the first instance, being no more than perhaps 'the word cat begins with a c, so perhaps this new word which begins with c is going to begin with the same sound' (p. 22). However, these readings by analogy can become more sophisticated as children read new words and do so by utilizing their recognition of onset and rime units. Therefore, words such as 'sight' and 'fight' can be determined because of a knowledge of 'light' and a recognition of the rime unit -ight.

The use of analogies is aided when the word is met in the context of meaningful reading. Then, reading the new word by analogy is supported by the confirmation that the word will fit in the sentence and will construct meaning. It is important, therefore, that children are able to select their reading from a wide range of interesting books, many of which have been selected by the teacher for the classroom because they contain rhymes, rhythms, alliterations and playful use of language.

Further reading

Goswami, U.C. and Bryant, P. (1990) *Phonological Skills and Learning to Read.* Hove: Lawrence Erlbaum Associates.
In this quite technical book, Usha Goswami and Peter Bryant debate the importance of phonological awareness, phonemic awareness, onset and rime, and analogies in children's early reading development. To support their debate, they use evidence from several experimental research studies in psychology, including many of their own or allied studies from Oxford. Among the features that emerge from those studies are the importance of nursery rhymes in children's earliest language experiences and the constructive way in which children infer some of the rules of language during the process of reading.

Moustafa, M. (1997) *Beyond Traditional Phonics: Research Discoveries and Reading Instruction.* Portsmouth, NH: Heinemann.
After considering aspects of how children have been taught to read and learn phonics, Margaret Moustafa discusses recent research that leads to alternative propositions. She argues for whole-to-parts-phonics instruction, in which the analysis of words follows the reading of predictable stories. It is then that

'explicit, systematic and extensive' (p. 93) phonics instruction occurs focused on onset and rime units.

Dombey, H., Moustafa, M. and CLPE (1998) *Whole to Part Phonics: How Children Learn to Read and Spell*. London: Centre for Language in Primary Education. A two-page summary of Margaret Moustafa's ideas are contained in this helpful edited text from the Centre for Language in Primary Education. In addition, there is the more extended debate by Henrietta Dombey on 'How phonics works in English' and the importance of onset and rime is part of that debate. There are also many practical classroom suggestions from CLPE staff that cover the early years from 4 to 8 years of age.

paired reading (and buddy reading)

The term 'paired reading' is used to describe at least three different forms of collaborative reading of a book. First, especially in early years classrooms, paired reading describes two children reading together from a book. The children might be matched for ability or a more competent reader might read alongside a beginner. Or this pairing may be a friendship pair. Second, an older child from a class a year or more older would share a book with younger child. This might be extended to an adult from within the school or a regular visitor to the school sharing a book with a child. In the USA, these two forms of paired reading are known as 'buddy reading' (e.g. Cunningham and Allington 1998). Third, there is a more formal paired reading between an adult and child as originally proposed by Roger Morgan (1976) in the USA. This paired reading is a relatively structured reading of a book that follows clear guidelines. It has been popularized and developed in the UK by Keith Topping (e.g. Topping and Lindsay 1992) and was a central feature of the very large Kirklees Project, another example of a *home–school* link.

Paired reading by two children from the same class is most easily organized. The children are easily paired or friendship pair themselves (Browne 1996). The sharing may be relatively equal as each child contributes to the reading. With the very youngest children, they may read the book from memory, but that is helpful because from time to time words in the print will be connected to the memory reading. So the children help each other to develop as readers. When a competent reader provides support to a less advanced reader when *sharing a book*, the competent reader might be told by the teacher to read a word for the other child when necessary. It is likely, however, that several different kinds of support will be given, drawn probably from that child's perception of what adults do when they share a book with a child. Teachers suggest that both children benefit from these paired readings and that the competent reader learns as much as the less advanced reader. Teachers should, of course, monitor such child–child interactions to assure themselves that it is proving worthwhile.

When an older child comes from another class to read with a younger child, there are benefits for both children. Cunningham and Allington (1998) suggest that, as the older readers are acting as reading models during buddy reading, they can be encouraged to read and reread easier books. They do so willingly because they want to be confident of reading the book well with a younger child. That practice helps them to become more confident with their own reading. The younger child also benefits from having another opportunity for *sharing a book*. *Gender* issues are also evident because younger boys get the opportunity to see a male role model as a competent reader. In the youngest classrooms, the teacher and other adult helpers are more typically female, so the opportunity to have a male as the teacher/helper is useful. In some schools, links are carefully established with the wider community so that adults can come and work alongside young children and provide a reading model for them within a paired reading.

When the more structured form of paired reading is adopted, the following structure is suggested:

- the children choosing their own books;
- devoting five to fifteen minutes each day of the week;
- a quiet and comfortable base is provided where both child and adult have a clear view of the book;
- before the reading, the book should be discussed;
- at natural pauses during the reading, discussions can take place to check on comprehension and prediction;
- when the child makes an error (miscue), the adult reads the word;
- the child repeats the word spoken by the adult;
- the child should not be asked to break up or sound out the word;
- praise should be given for the correct reading of difficult words, self-corrections and longer pieces of reading;
- with more difficult texts, both adult and child read all the words out aloud;
- finger pointing by the child, if required, is encouraged;
- when the child feels confident to read alone, a non-verbal signal is used by the child to silence the adult;

- the adult stops reading and praises the child for signalling;
- when reading alone, if the child struggles on a word for more than five seconds, or struggles and gets the word wrong, the word is read by the adult and the pair revert to reading together.

Although such guidance appears to be very prescriptive, there are links with *sharing a book*: the child and adult work together with a book; at times they read together; the adult supports the reader when miscues are produced and provides encouragement at appropriate moments; and the child takes over the reading when confident to do so. However, there are also differences. For example, when *sharing a book*, the child and the adult read together and the child is encouraged to read alone when it seems appropriate to do so. Then, meaningful miscues might be ignored. Telling children what a word is does not help them to develop their own strategies for reading and often does not help them when a word is next met; instead, other responses can be adopted (Campbell 1994). Furthermore, when *sharing a book*, the flow from the adult reading to the child reading is dictated by an awareness of what the child can do by both child and adult. For many teachers of young children, the strict interpretation of the 'rules' of paired reading might not tie in with the wish to develop a collaborative reading and enjoyment of a book.

In the classroom

In one Year 2 classroom, the children were regularly engaged in paired reading. For instance, Andrew acted as a tutor for Joanna the reader:

Joanna: The cat, the bird and the tree.
The cat. The bird. The bird is up in the tree.
The cat runs to the tree.
The cat// [// = hesitation]
Andrew: looks
Joanna: looks up. He sees the bird in a tree.
The little bird is singing, up in the tree.
The cat is near the tree.
The (He)// – He jumps up into the tree.
He climbs up//
Andrew
and
Joanna: and
Joanna: up and up.

As the cat climbs up the little bird looks down.
She – He (She)//

Andrew
and
Joanna: looks
Joanna: at the cat. The cat
Andrew: sits
Joanna: sits firmly (very)
Andrew
and
Joanna: still.
Joanna: He is on a branch.
The little bird is//
Andrew: afraid
Joanna: afraid of the cat.
The big cat jumps//
Andrew
and
Joanna: from
Joanna: the branch.
(for a complete transcript, see Campbell and Stott 1994)

Even in this short extract, it is evident that Andrew did not interrupt the flow of the text, although he did support Joanna most frequently by providing the word when Joanna hesitated. He also read in unison with Joanna to guide her reading. Furthermore, he did provide time for Joanna to lead the reading. Both children seemed to enjoy the reading session and both may have benefited from this experience of reading.

Further reading

Cunningham, P. and Allington, R. (1998) *Classrooms that Work: They can All Read and Write*. New York: Longman.
The authors describe buddy reading in kindergarten classrooms, as well as older primary classes, as one small part of the literacy curriculum. Nevertheless, they point to the advantages for the children. They note the way in which older readers can learn from the experience of working with younger children. However, it is the younger readers that buddy reading is designed to help and the authors suggest that, for boys in particular, there is an advantage of having a male reader role model.

Topping, K.J. and Lindsay, G.A. (1992) The structure and development of the paired reading technique. *Journal of Research in Reading*, **15**: 120–36.

This short article describes paired reading both as initiated by Roger Morgan and as developed by Keith Topping for the Kirklees Project. The summary flow chart presents at a glance the structure of the interaction. A brief review of research studies indicates the strengths of adult–child interactions centring on a book. Finally, there is a debate regarding the theoretical framework of this procedure. The authors claim that, although the procedure may have been developed from behavioural psychology, it can be seen to meet the needs of both real book approaches and more direct teaching methods.

phonemic awareness

When children read, they use cues from several different sources, including the contextual cues of syntax (how the words are strung together into sentences), semantics (the meaning element of the writing) and pragmatics (the recognition that particular words are normally expected to appear in particular kinds of writing). There are also cues that are linked more to the word itself, in particular the letters and associated sounds of those letters. Most writers would acknowledge that children make use of all these sources at various times. For instance, Kenneth Goodman, who might be regarded as emphasizing contextual cues, nevertheless recognizes the importance of the graphophonic cue system when children read. So if children are making use of the graphophonic or letter-sound cue system, then what knowledge do they need to succeed?

Goswami and Bryant (1990) use 'phonological awareness' as a blanket term to cover the general awareness of sounds that children might require for reading. One specific aspect of that generality is phonemic awareness. The phoneme is the smallest unit of sound and typically each alphabetic letter (grapheme) has an associated phoneme. So, in the word 'mat', there are three phonemes: m, a and t. Several writers, including Adams (1990), have stressed the importance of phonemic awareness for children to progress with reading. However, Adams also recognized the 'catch-22' – children who have acquired phonemic awareness have also learned to read. Such a view led Goswami and Bryant (1990: 26) to conclude that:

it is most unlikely that the progress that children make in reading is determined by their sensitivity to phonemes. On the contrary their progress in learning to read (or to read in an alphabetic script at any rate) is probably the most important cause of awareness of phonemes.

Such conclusions might leave teachers in a quandary as to what learning experiences to provide in the classroom. They need not worry, however. First, because the range of reading experiences such as *story reading, shared reading, sharing a book* and *sustained silent reading* all provide opportunities for children to learn about reading, to learn to read and to develop an awareness of phonemes. Second, the *alphabet* activities, opportunities for *writing* and enjoyment of *nursery rhymes* will more specifically encourage children to think about and develop an awareness of phonemes.

Nursery rhymes are particularly helpful because they encourage children to think about other aspects of phonological awareness, namely *onset and rime*, when concentrating on the initial and end phonemes in words. The alliteration in some rhymes, jingles and poems also encourages the children to consider the phonemes at the beginning of words. And playing simple games such as I-Spy, perhaps in those brief moments of transition from one part of the school day to another, also help children to think about phonemes. All of this is done playfully and with enjoyment and supports the children's phonemic awareness.

Further reading

Strickland, D. S. (1998) *Teaching Phonics Today: A Primer for Educators*. Newark, DE: International Reading Association.
Dorothy Strickland lists a number of worthwhile activities that support phonemic awareness (just as she suggests activities to help children with the *alphabet*). In addition to *shared reading* of nursery rhymes, poems and stories with rhyme or alliteration, she suggests encouraging children to fill in rhymes during the reading, memorize rhymes and create their own. Clapping syllables (which demonstrates the importance of music in developing reading) and playing with sounds are also noted.

Opitz, M. (2000) *Rhyme and Reason*. Portsmouth, NH: Heinemann.
In this book, Michael Opitz considers phonological awareness, phonemic awareness and phonics in a first brief chapter of sixteen pages. Subsequently, he provides an annotated listing of books that emphasize rhyming, alliteration or repetition as well as poetry and song texts. All of these, when used in the classroom as part of *story reading* or *shared reading*, help children to develop phonemic awareness.

phonics

There is general agreement that children's reading development is supported by their knowledge of letters and sounds. What is contentious is how children acquire that knowledge – that is, is it learnt during the process of learning to read or does it need to be taught in order to read? Goswami and Bryant (1990) concluded that progress in learning to read is probably the most important factor in becoming aware of phonemes. Thompson (1999: 33) also suggests that children learn 'by induction from reading experiences of words' (induced sub-lexical relations) the relations between many letters and sounds. And Alice, and other children, show us how phonic knowledge is developed as numerous literacy activities are enjoyed at home (Campbell 1999a). Therefore, a range of reading and writing activities is vital for children to be involved with language and thus actively construct their knowledge of letters and sounds.

A second area of contention concerns how teaching should take place if it is considered necessary to teach phonics, or at least ensure that knowledge of letters and sounds is being acquired. Three areas in particular are of concern: emphasis, timing and teaching (Campbell 1990b). First, a phonics teaching approach to early reading development would, of course, emphasize the direct teaching of phonics in some form. However, where a whole language or real books approach is adopted, then the emphasis should be upon authentic reading and writing, with some attention being given to letters and sounds. Second, if a phonics approach is being adopted, then phonics are taught almost immediately upon entering school; however, a whole language approach emphasizes the development of reading and monitoring that development for knowledge of letters and sounds. Inevitably, the teaching style would differ also, from the direct and systematic teaching of phonics in a phonics approach to the teaching in context that arises from the children's reading and writing (Dahl *et al.* 2001).

In addition to the major questions of emphasis, timing and teaching, teachers have to address the question of the nature of any teaching that takes place. Do we know what should be taught? Several suggestions have been made and, of course, in the *National Literacy Strategy* (DfEE 1998) for the literacy hour in England, there are clear guidelines as to what phonics is to be taught in each term during the early years. Such an arrangement ensures that there is sequential teaching; however, as Richard Allington reminded us, 'there is no scientifically determined sequence of instruction' (Cunningham and Allington 1998: 5).

A starting point is teaching the *alphabet*. Indeed, such an approach would be to follow a methodology used in the nineteenth century. Knowledge of the alphabet is often seen to be important because children who know the alphabet can usually be expected to succeed with reading. However, there are problems if it is only the letter names of the alphabet that are learnt, as it might not be especially helpful to children when deciphering words; for example, the letters see-ae-tee are joined together only with some difficulty to produce the word cat. Because of such difficulties, it has been argued that children need to learn the letter names and their usual sounds. An approach that emphasizes the consonants and short vowels might be most helpful to children. However, the letter sounds cannot be learnt easily in isolation from a word. In most circumstances, a neutral vowel (uh) is added when a single letter sound is uttered (e.g. ruh rather than /r/), which has consequences when the letters are combined to form a word: ruh-uh-nuh (run or runner?).

Reducing the amount of single letter learning and drawing the children's attention to such combinations as consonant blends (br) and consonant digraphs (ch), is a partial recognition of the single letter problem. Another approach might be to teach consonant–vowel combinations rather than single letters. The word cat could be taught as ca-t or c-at if the teacher wished to persist with this form of phonics teaching. As to which might be the preferred combination, the notions of *onset and rime* (Goswami and Bryant 1990) would indicate that c-at would be preferred because it links to children's knowledge of rhyme. But we also need to remind ourselves that such knowledge is probably derived from nursery rhymes and other language games, finger plays, songs and poems. Children 'develop phonological awareness through language play' (Goswami 1994: 36). In other words, children learn about letters and sounds through engaging with language in many different contexts.

There is another aspect of phonics teaching, namely phonic rules or generalizations, that needs to be considered. Although phonic rules are more truly expressed as phonic generalizations, in classrooms they are often stated as rules. Examples of such generalizations include the so-called magic 'e', which indicates that when a word ends with a silent 'e' the preceding vowel is long. However, when Clymer (1963) conducted a study of such generalizations, he found that the magic 'e' rule only applied in some 60 per cent of cases. In another example – when there are two vowels side by side, the long sound of the first is heard and the second is usually silent – Clymer noted that in only 45 per cent of cases did the generalization apply. Lefevre (1964) summed it up when he suggested of the rule, when two vowels go walking, the first one does the talking, 'There is no place here (or anywhere else) for that nonsensical "rule" of phonics' (p. 179). Perhaps it is easier to teach reading than it is to teach phonics.

However, even though children might be expected to learn about letters and sounds through many language and literacy activities, teachers should take the opportunity to draw the children's attention explicitly to aspects of letters and sounds. Redfern (1996) suggested that it was best to 'embed phonics teaching in a context of reading and writing for pleasure' (p. 6) so that learning comes naturally out of the materials being read to the child. Some teachers take the opportunity to extend such incidental teaching into displays that might emphasize objects that all begin with the same letter. Or they can use language games, such as I-Spy.

Whole language teachers are likely to operate in a manner similar to this. As Kenneth Goodman (1986: 38) noted: 'Whole language programs and whole language teachers do not ignore phonics. Rather they keep it in the perspective of real reading and real writing'. So just because whole language teachers argue for meaningful reading and writing, with an emphasis upon the whole rather than the parts, it does not, or should not, mean that they are unwilling to talk about letters and sounds with the children. As Goodman (1993) indicated in a later text, whole language teachers assess their pupils' development as they read and write and then support and help as needed. More directly, Mills *et al.* (1992) demonstrated how, within a whole language class-room, attention is given to letter–sound relationships as a natural part of language and literacy learning. Geekie *et al.* (1999: 137) emphasized involving 'children in writing from the very beginning of formal school-ing, [then] explicit teaching of phonemic awareness and word decoding would not be needed'.

Additionally, *nursery rhymes*, songs, demonstrations of reading during a *shared reading* and *classroom print*, which includes *alphabet* wall charts, all help children to construct their knowledge of letters and sounds. Furthermore, teachers in such classrooms will monitor the children's development in those areas through the use of miscue analysis and a careful reading of the children's invented spellings. Teachers will do so because they will want to ensure that the children are making good progress with an important aspect of the reading process.

Further reading

Adams, M.J. (1990) *Beginning to Read: Thinking and Learning about Print*. Cam-bridge, MA: MIT Press.

This book created quite a stir when it was published. It was suggested by those who wished to argue for phonics teaching that here was the case that indicated the need for explicit and substantial phonics teaching in classrooms. Yet, in reality, Adams was somewhat more circumspect in her conclusions. For instance, she indicated that 'to be most productive it [phonics instruction] may best be conceived as a support activity, carefully covered but largely subordinated to the reading and writing of connected text' (p. 416).

Among the concerns that were registered by those who might follow a whole language approach were: that the book was largely based upon a psychological perspective with an emphasis upon studies of word recognition, and that many of the references used by ethnographic studies of linguistics and pedagogy were ignored. Indeed, two advisers to the Centre for the Study of the Teaching of Reading, Dorothy Strickland and Bernice Cullinan, felt it necessary to write an afterword to the book that presented some of those emergent literacy perspectives.

An issue of *The Reading Teacher* (Vol. 44, No. 6, February 1991) devoted a large section to the debate about the book. The contributors, and the response from Adams, demonstrated the political dimension to the debate and that there were strongly held views on the subject of phonics teaching.

Campbell, R. (1999a) *Literacy from Home to School: Reading with Alice.* Stoke-on-Trent: Trentham Books.

As noted in *books for babies*, this book details a five-year longitudinal study of a child from birth to 5 years of age. It demonstrates how Alice became a reader and writer before starting school at 5. Although it was not the purpose of the study to explore phonics, Alice's knowledge of letters and sounds is made evident. She used that knowledge both as she read and as she wrote with *invented spellings*. Furthermore, this knowledge was not the result of any direct teaching of phonics – it occurred as Alice learned about phonics from all the literacy activities that she explored. This study and others like it (e.g. Martens 1996) have important messages for early years teachers.

play activities

Most nursery and infant classrooms will have a play area or home corner conveniently situated so that the children can engage in play activities during the course of the school day. They will want to do so even though *National Curriculum* and *literacy hour* initiatives might appear to be pushing staff in another direction (Miller 1998). The need for an emphasis on play remains because there are well-established views on the benefits that can accrue from such activity. The social and emotional benefits might appear to be obvious, but there is also recognition of the foundation that is provided for cognitive learning and literacy development through play: 'discovery, reasoning and thought grow out of children's spontaneous activity' (Manning and Sharp 1977: 12). Of course, teachers recognize that it is insufficient simply to designate an area for play. Materials and equipment are made available so that the structured play enhances learning. More recently, there has been wider recognition of the ways in which the play area can be developed to encourage literacy learning.

The inclusion in the play area of literacy materials is a starting point for the encouragement of literacy learning. Such materials include books, magazines, brochures, telephone directories, notices and instructions for reading, together with paper, notepads, envelopes, letter pads and blank forms with a variety of pencils, crayons, coloured pencils and felt-tip pens for writing. These materials will encourage children to become involved in literacy behaviours during play. Not only can the teacher extend this involvement by reminding the children about the materials and suggesting possible uses for them, but also by providing demonstrations of these suggestions during brief visits to the play area. To promote literacy learning, the teacher can also, in discussion with the children, develop the play area setting so that it becomes more specific (e.g. a restaurant, a dentist's waiting room, a post office). The designation of the area will have to be changed from time to time as the role-playing becomes static and the children's enthusiasm begins to wane. Several authors have written about the ways in which the play area can be developed and we shall look at some of these in a moment.

Inevitably, in making the area more specific, it becomes obvious what reading and writing materials to provide. The specific designation of the area can also help the children in providing a purpose for their writing. In her account of developing the play area in her classroom into a hairdresser's, then an optician's and, finally, a restaurant, Helen Dutton (1991) noted that there were six main categories of writing produced by her 6-year-olds: letters, messages, personal notes, instructions, factual descriptions and stories. This list is indicative of the literacy learning and purposeful writing that can be generated by structured play where the opportunities for literacy are organized and encouraged.

So what are some of the play area adaptations that can be used to encourage literacy? The list is almost never-ending. However, several authors have offered suggestions and descriptions of these suggestions as they were put into practice. Morrow and Rand (1991) suggested several possibilities, the first of which they described in detail.

Veterinarians' offices: A number of rooms, or areas, might be developed, including a waiting room which could include magazines, books and pamphlets about pet care. Notices, similar in kind to those found in waiting rooms, including examples of *environmental print*, and posters could be provided. There would be a link to the nurse's desk that would have a telephone, address book, appointment cards and patient forms. Then there would be the office itself with prescription pads and patient files. And Morrow and Rand suggest the children could be reminded to read to their pets while waiting their turn. All of this provides opportunities for literacy behaviours. Wray and Medwell (1991) described a similar arrangement with a class of 4- and 5-year-olds. They described how a dentist's surgery had been developed and the wide range of literacy-like behaviours that was evident.

Restaurant: The children can develop menus according to the type of restaurant or fast-food establishment. Order pads and cash registers would encourage child–child interactions. Also, the children could model fish, chips, muffins, etc., with dough, which when baked hard and painted could be used as part of the activity. Fiona MacLeod (1991) described such craft activities by the children in her description of a fish and chip shop.

Newspaper office: The very nature of this adaptation demands literacy. There would be a telephone for the reporters plus writing pads and typewriters or a computer. There would need to be reference texts of various kinds to help with the general news, sports, weather, travel, fashion, etc. And the children could make a newspaper for the class or, according to the children's age, perhaps for other classes in the school.

Supermarket or grocery shop: One of the advantages of this play area is that the cartons, packets, plastic bottles, and adverts from magazines and newspapers, can all be used to provide a wide range of literacy messages. The youngest children will be able to read some of these because they will recognize the examples of *environmental print*. Labels and prices on the shelves can add to the learning of literacy and mathematics.

Post office: The immediately obvious links to literacy are with letters, envelopes and stamps. But there are also forms to be filled, pensions(!) to be obtained and the various posters on the walls to be considered. A development of this is to set up a letter service in the classroom or the school so that the children write to each other. If this can be organized and maintained, then the opportunities for writing for a real purpose and *audience* are enhanced.

Petrol station and garage: Such a play area would bring into the activity maps of the immediate local area as well as more widely. There would be the usual magazines associated with cars, repairs to be arranged for the toy cars and bills to be paid.

Travel agency: Holiday brochures provide a colourful source of literacy and the children will be able to relate some of the destinations to their own holidays. Passports, visas and travellers' cheques might all have to be produced by the children. Catherine Coleman (1991) noted that, in her classroom, this adaptation led to planning and problem solving as well as to literacy.

This list can be expanded to include a wide range of shops and services that exist in the community. In most cases, teachers will know what is the most appropriate, based on their knowledge of the locality. The creation of something familiar to the children might be most helpful for the youngest children in particular. In many instances, members of the local community are willing to help with supplying posters, old forms, and so on, and sometimes to visit the school briefly to speak and answer questions about their work.

It is obvious that teachers have a very important role in this wactivity, both in discussing with the children the area and finding materials to stimulate literacy, and in moving in and out of the activity to suggest and demonstrate literacy behaviours. The nature of the literacy interactions with the children is an important element that can support the children's learning. Additionally, some of the literacy produced by the children can be collected, which will be useful as a means of making *assessments* of the children's growth as literacy users.

In the classroom

The 3- and 4-year-olds in one nursery classroom used many props, clothes and furniture to develop their imaginative play when they visited the home corner. One of the props, the old telephone, was used frequently by them to have 'conversations'. However, when the teacher added a telephone messages pad, it encouraged the young children to write as well as to speak. Of course, at such a young age much of the writing was presented unconventionally. Nevertheless, the scribbles often contained the vertical and horizontal lines as well as circles that are used to construct letters. The shapes were increasingly presented in a line and letters began to appear (A R I Y L 4 P B). Later, invented spellings (e.g. mmy) and names (e.g. SAM) were written occasionally. So the introduction of a very simple pad and pencil into the play area had positive literacy outcomes. This is especially likely to be the case where the teacher models the literacy for the children initially.

Further reading

Hall, N. and Abbott, L. (eds) (1991) *Play in the Primary Curriculum*. London: Hodder & Stoughton.
This book contains nine chapters by different contributors on play in the primary curriculum, which are divided into two sections. The two chapters in the first section provide the theoretical background for socio-dramatic or structured play in the classroom. Part of the argument here is that play remains important and need not be constrained by the National Curriculum in the UK. The second section contains reports, from seven classroom teachers, on the development of the play area, or home corner, as a travel agency, hairdresser's, restaurant, and so on. These case studies provide fascinating evidence of the ways in which literacy can be developed from structured play.

Morrow, L.M. and Rand, M.K. (1991) Promoting literacy during play by designing early childhood classroom environments. *The Reading Teacher*, 44: 396–402.
In this short article, the authors argue that play in the early childhood classroom can be organized and developed to promote literacy learning. They set the scene by providing a brief theoretical statement about the value of play in young children's learning. This is followed by a review of a study carried out by one of the authors, Lesley Mandel Morrow. She indicates the benefits that accrue when teachers introduce literacy-related materials into the play area and model literacy behaviour for the children. Several different adaptations to the play area are suggested, some of which were noted above.

poetry

As noted in the section on *nursery rhymes*, young children enjoy playing with language, especially when there is rhythm, rhyme and repetition. In the child's first few years at home and in the pre-school setting, finger plays, nursery rhymes, songs and simple poems are all part of the play with language (Whitehead 1999). We know that language play can be important to young children as well as enjoyable. They learn about *words, onset and rime* and aspects of *phonics*. As Opitz (2000) indicates, poetry helps 'children to better understand the sound structure of their language' (p. 104). However, such learning occurs not because these sound features have been taught directly, but because they are a part of the many rhymes and poems that children love to hear and to use for themselves. Furthermore, many of the picture books that children enjoy are also written with a strong rhyme element, which makes them into something akin to an extended poem, such as *Hairy Maclary from Donaldson's Dairy* (Dodd 1983) and *Green Eggs and Ham* (Seuss 1960). There are many other stories like those that can be enjoyed by young children and there are many poems that create the same interest and fun. Cookson (2000), in his anthology of poems for the literacy hour, provides many useful poems for early years teachers to use and, of course, for teachers in England, using poetry is part of the literacy strategy (DfEE 1998).

For the early years teacher, Phinn (2000) provides a list of strategies to heighten young children's awareness of poetry. These include reading a wide selection of poems during the year, with one poem a day just to be enjoyed rather than analysed; choosing a poem to write out, decorate and then to be included as part of a class anthology – such an anthology could be placed in the *library corner*; enlarging some poems for display that could be used during *shared reading* – with younger children it can be useful if the poem is written together during a *shared writing*. When the computer is not being used, he suggests that the screen saver might be organized to display a poem. No opportunity should be missed to encourage children to think about poems and, therefore, about literacy. His final point is to integrate poetry into *thematic work/topic work*.

Graves (1994) also suggests the regular reading of poems to young children. Such readings serve to provide the children with a model of what poetry sounds like and, when displayed, what it looks like. The model of poetry then replicates the models of stories that children will have acquired as they listen to stories. And having that model helps them when they begin to write poetry themselves. Riley and Reedy (2000) suggest that the sight and sound of poetry, as well as the structure (the organization of the poem including the repeated patterns) and the sense of the poem, are the distinctive features of poetry that are learned in part through hearing and seeing poetry. Children learn still more about poetry as they recite favourites together and when they are involved in constructing their own poems, initially during a *shared writing* as a group led by the teacher.

Although devoted more to older children, Brownjohn (1998) provides ideas that are helpful. One of her first suggestions for getting children to write poetry is producing alliterations. This can be done as a *shared writing* with the youngest children or individually with some of the older children in early years classes. Haiku poetry, with its three lines of five syllables, seven syllables and five syllables, is also suggested. As Brownjohn indicates, because these poems are short, the children are able to attempt them, be successful and get enjoyment from the writing. And young children are able to cope well with the syllable requirement. Furthermore, it creates an emphasis upon every word being important in the poem. Although alliteration and haiku are very useful, the teacher need not be restricted to these when working with young children. Other poetic forms when heard, seen and enjoyed by the children become the models for the children's own efforts.

In the classroom

In a Year 1 classroom, the teacher had read-aloud from the big book version of *Walking Through the Jungle* (Lacome 1993). Among the various activities that were generated from that *story reading*, the teacher encouraged the children to write alliterations about an animal of their own choosing. One of the children wrote about:

An creeping crawling crocodile crunching its tea.

(Campbell 2001a: 49)

Although there was a substitution of 'An' for 'A', more importantly the child took great delight in producing the alliteration using the 'cr' consonant cluster. Another one of the children wrote about flamingos:

A fluffy flmego fluffying its feathers.

(Campbell 2001a: 49)

The child's invented spelling for 'flamingo' demonstrated a developing knowledge of letters and sounds. She also invented the word 'fluffying'. Nevertheless, we can see how well that fitted within her alliteration. Importantly, the children were very involved with letters, sounds and words as they worked and they greatly enjoyed the poetic activity.

Further reading

Phinn, G. (2000) *Young Readers and their Books: Suggestions and Strategies for Using Texts in the Literacy Hour*. London: David Fulton.
This book considers how a variety of texts, including stories, non-fiction and poetry, might be used within the literacy hour. The suggestions and strategies that are provided could be used in a variety of contexts. There are two chapters on response to poetry. One chapter is devoted to Key Stage 1 (i.e. children of 6 and 7 years of age) and there is another on working with older children at Key Stage 2. The ideas on using poetry with young children are suitable for teachers not constrained by a literacy hour.

Riley, J. and Reedy, D. (2000) *Developing Writing for Different Purposes: Teaching about Genre in the Early Years*. London: Paul Chapman.
This book considers young children age 3–7 years writing in different genres and the ways in which teachers can support that writing. It is a useful book for writing in general with young children. More particularly for this section, there is a complete chapter devoted to 'Writing poetry' (pp. 85–112). Reading and reciting poetry and the shared writing of poetry with the teacher as a guide are all seen and debated as ways of supporting young children to write their own poetry.

punctuation

As children develop as writers, their scribbles become linear as first letter-like marks and eventually letters are written. Subsequently, as noted in the section on *invented spellings*, the children's writing, if constructed freely, will be governed by the sounds of oral language; it is then easier to decipher their writing. Eventually, the children will write with many of the words written conventionally. However, that writing is unlikely to be marked with punctuation, at least initially. Most frequently, the children will use 'and' to connect the meaning units that are written rather than making use of commas and full stops. Indeed, when children read, it is likely to be speech marks, question marks and exclamation marks, rather than commas and full stops, that are noted first. In Lester Laminack's (1991) record of Zachary's literacy learning, the exclamation mark was the first punctuation that Zachary commented upon when he was 4 years and 10 months old. Teachers can support such learning, for instance when reading a big book, by commenting upon the punctuation marks.

Graves (1994) noted that curriculum guides (including those for the National Curriculum in England and Wales) suggest that the full stop is one of the first punctuation marks to be taught. Yet it 'is one of the most difficult forms of punctuation for children to add to their repertoire of conventions. They often have trouble understanding when one idea ends and the next one begins' (p. 201). Hall (1998) also notes the difficulty that young children have with full stops and, when they do appear, they may be used as graphic punctuation. So the end of every line, rather than the end of sentences, may have a full stop.

Nevertheless, for many teachers of young children, it may be the demarcation of the sentence, with the use of capital letters and full stops, which is encouraged when the children are writing. The development of the National Curriculum in England and Wales has placed an emphasis on this aspect of punctuation because the assessment of the children's writing at seven years of age, Key Stage 1, places great importance upon the use of capital letters and full stops to signal a sentence. The emphasis on the punctuation of sentences has increased as the National Curriculum has been refined. However, the expectation that children need to demarcate their sentences to achieve success has caused concern that this will lead to more attention being paid to conventions rather than to content and flow of writing (Anderson 1993). In particular, such an emphasis might encourage teachers to teach the demarcation of sentences directly. However, there is no evidence to suggest that such a strategy would be effective. So what can teachers do to encourage the use of punctuation marks?

As with much of literacy learning, a good starting point in the promotion of an understanding of punctuation is to ensure that children have many opportunities for reading and writing. During this reading and writing, the teacher will support the child's efforts, respond to the child's questions and draw attention to aspects of the print. Also, when appropriate, the teacher will comment upon aspects of punctuation; importantly, this is done in the context of the child's current experiences with print. When the teacher or child is reading from a book, the teacher might comment on the use of speech marks by indicating: 'Those speech marks tell us when the boy is talking, don't they?' In the same way, when a child is editing a piece of writing, for inclusion in a book or for a display, the teacher might guide the child's attention to aspects of punctuation by suggesting: 'Should we put a full stop here at the end of your sentence?' Such comments during reading and writing, just like parental support when oral language is being developed, will guide the child towards an understanding of punctuation.

Teacher demonstrations of reading and writing provide useful opportunities to talk about, or refer to, punctuation in a meaningful context. *Shared reading* with big books enables teachers to demonstrate conventions of print as they model the reading of the book. And, during or after a reading of a big book, teachers can comment on the use of capital letters and full stops as well as other aspects of punctuation so that the children are made aware of those conventions. Similarly, during teacher demonstrations of *shared writing* in front of a group or the whole class, teachers can comment upon that writing, supported and guided now by the children. While writing in front of the children, teachers can think aloud such as, 'Now, what's that first sentence again?' Cambourne (1988) suggested that such think-aloud comments bring concepts and aspects of punctuation to the children's attention. Demonstrations of literacy used in this way help the children to an understanding of the use of punctuation.

Further reading

Ferreiro, E. and Teberosky, A. (1982) *Literacy before Schooling*. Portsmouth, NH: Heinemann Educational.
Emilia Ferreiro and Ana Teberosky present some evidence of children's progress, between the ages of 4 and 6, in their understanding of punctuation marks. As we might expect initially, children assume that there is no distinction between punctuation marks and letters. When children begin to differentiate between them, it is the dots (e.g. full stops and colons) which are noted to be different, whereas question marks and commas continue to be confused with similar letters or numbers (e.g. ? and 2 or 8; or the comma and 9). By 6 years of age, many children recognize that punctuation marks serve a different purpose to letters, although they may not yet be able to use the marks themselves in their writing.

Hall, N. (1998) *Punctuation in the Primary School*. Reading: Reading and Language Information Centre, University of Reading.
Hall uses evidence from research studies to debate the issue of young children's punctuation. This 18-page booklet provides the key ideas that are derived from that work. He notes the difficulty that many of the youngest children have with full stops, especially when they produce limited amounts of writing. He suggests that encouraging children to produce meaningful writing, which can be shared and discussed, provides the opportunity to explain why punctuation is needed. In many instances, it is teaching explicitly to children at the right moment that can help them move forward. Nigel Hall has also debated punctuation in the primary school in other texts, including:

Hall, N. and Robinson, A. (eds) (1996) *Learning about Punctuation*. Clevedon: Multilingual Matters.
Hall, N. (2001) Developing understanding of punctuation with young readers and writers, in J. Evans (ed.) *The Writing Classroom: Aspects of Writing and the Primary Child 3–11*. London: David Fulton.

reading drive

When introducing the idea of reading drive, as part of a formula for beginning reading, Vera Southgate (1968) suggested that of the factors which she had explored this was, in her view, the most important: 'I think that the most decisive factor influencing children's reading progress is the beliefs and attitudes of the staff about the importance of reading' (p. 26). So reading drive was considered to be important and the rest of the quotation indicated that reading drive was concerned with the attitudes and beliefs of the staff. She further indicated that it was in schools where reading was given prime importance, that a reading drive was likely to be in place and most children would learn to read 'early and well' (p. 26). Furthermore, in a statement that would be reflected subsequently by Frank Smith (1992; see section on the *teacher's role*), Southgate suggested that the progress made by children in learning to read would be 'almost regardless of the media, methods, materials or procedures adopted' (p. 26).

Reading drive, therefore, is linked very closely to some other areas that are explored in this handbook, including the *literacy hour, school policy* and the *teacher's role*. What the *literacy hour* achieves is a clear focus upon reading and writing. There is a clearly designated *time for literacy*, the children are made aware of the importance of reading and writing, and the daily emphasis upon literacy presents a reading drive that serves to support learning whatever strategies are adopted within the hour. Elsewhere, the views of the teachers in the school about reading and writing will be reflected in the *school policy*, which will indicate the ways in which practices derived from those views might be implemented in the classroom. When that policy suggests the prime importance of literacy, and the teachers are committed to an implementation of the policy in a dynamic manner, then it is likely that a reading drive will permeate the school. From such a starting point, the *role of the teacher* in the classroom will take over and the beliefs, actions and enthusiasm for literacy can then be conveyed to the children. Where the children are immersed in a sub-culture of an emphasis on, and enthusiasm for, literacy, then there is every chance that they will be facilitated in their literacy learning. Similar sentiments were recorded by HMI (1991) in their evaluation of the teaching and learning of reading in primary schools in England. They suggested that 'a major determinant of that [reading] success is what the teacher and the school bring to the situation' (p. 51).

In part, the reading drive will be derived from the positive perceptions that the teachers have about the children's ability as active learners to be competent literacy learners and to become literacy users. Several reports have stressed the need for teachers to have positive expectations about what the children can achieve (e.g. Alexander 1992). These high but realistic expectations, which lead to a range of literacy activities being provided in the classroom by teachers enthusiastic about literacy, will help to create a reading drive that benefits the children.

Teachers have to think about planning, organization, literacy learning and worthwhile interactions. But the knowledge that teachers need about reading, writing and children has to be matched by a drive to make it happen in the school and the classroom. In many respects, this dual requirement can be seen in books that provide insights into particular ideas or methods. For instance, in Sylvia Ashton-Warner's book, *Teacher* (1963), there are several interesting insights regarding important *words*, which she refers to as an organic vocabulary and a *language experience approach.* Yet the book also tells us about an enthusiastic and knowledgeable teacher who demonstrated great concern and empathy for the children she taught. We are left with a feeling that, despite any constraints that might have been imposed upon her, here was a teacher who would have overcome the odds and provided a drive and enthusiasm in the classroom that would have helped the children as literacy learners. And there are other books and articles that describe classrooms and schools in which a similar picture is presented. From such writing, we note that teachers and schools should create a drive for literacy and that reading drive has to remain in place throughout each school day to support children's literacy learning.

Further reading

Southgate, V. (1968) Formulae for beginning reading tuition. *Educational Research*, 11: 23–30.
This short article explores the areas that need to be considered when literacy research reports are read. Among the various aspects explored, it emphasizes reading drive as a vital part of any consideration. And although only a few lines are devoted to the exploration of reading drive, the suggestion that it is the most important factor leading to children's reading progress reminds us that we need to give attention to that enthusiasm for literacy in early years classrooms.

Goodman, K., Bird, L.B. and Goodman, Y. (eds) (1991) *The Whole Language Catalog.* Santa Rosa, CA: American School Publishers.
In this book, there are many reports of 'great teachers' written by colleagues who have witnessed particular teachers at work and have then described them

and the children in the classroom. These teachers, of course, work in a variety of contexts and with different styles. But each of the reports is suggestive of teachers who have created a reading (or literacy) drive in their classrooms. The children are left in little doubt about the importance and enjoyment of reading and writing, because everything that these teachers do seems to emphasize literacy. And, in such circumstances, the children are likely to develop as literacy users. Although not specifically about literacy, Woods (1995) also writes about successful and creative teachers in the primary school:

Woods, P. (1995) *Creative Teachers in Primary Schools*. Buckingham: Open University Press.

reading recovery

Most teachers of young children recognize literacy to be the main area for emphasis within their classrooms. A wide range of literacy activities is provided by the teacher within an organized classroom so as to encourage each child's growth as a literacy user. Yet in every infant class there are some children who do not progress as well as the teacher would like and may be achieving at a level well below their peers. In such circumstances, teachers normally consider ways in which the classroom, or the teacher's time, can be reorganized to provide more support for these children. Developing a firm foundation for children as literacy users is crucial for the subsequent learning in other subjects through literacy. Reading recovery is a programme that bears these concerns in mind, but which has developed towards a system of support for these children beyond, and additional to, that which could be provided in the classroom.

Reading recovery was developed in New Zealand (Clay 1985), but has subsequently been used widely in the USA as well as other English-speaking countries. It is regarded as an early intervention programme, for children at risk, rather than a remedial programme. In New Zealand, the programme is adopted with those children who, after a range of diagnostic tests, are regarded as being in need of support after their first year in school, usually when they are close to their sixth birthday. A key part of the diagnosis is the *running records* of the children reading from what Marie Clay (1985: 17) refers to as 'an easy text, an instructional text and a hard text'. From such records, the teacher is able to determine the 'error rate' and the strategies adopted by the children. But Clay suggests that no one mode of assessment is sufficient on its own to provide a detailed picture of the child as a reader. Therefore, other procedures are used as well, including letter identification (both upper- and lower-case letters), the Concepts about Print test – which indicates children's knowledge of the use of print in books (i.e. it suggests whether the children know about how a book works) – and word tests and writing tasks (either writing down all the words that the children know or writing a story). With all this information, the teacher is able to compile a detailed picture of the children's literacy development. This is important, because the reading recovery programme tries to build on that which is known.

The children selected for reading recovery are given thirty minutes extra intensive individual teaching each day. Because reading and writing are seen to be interwoven and supportive of each other, both are part of that extra teaching. The programme starts with 'roaming around the known', where the teacher and child get to know each other, working with the literacy that the child has demonstrated to be confident with in the diagnostic assessment. When the teaching programme starts, it typically includes reading and writing each day. This teaching usually has a format as follows (Clay 1985: 56):

- re-reading of two or more familiar books,
- re-reading yesterday's new book and taking a running record,
- letter identification (plastic letters on a magnetic board),
- writing a story (including hearing sounds in words),
- cut-up story to be rearranged,
- new book introduced,
- new book attempted.

Most of these activities, especially the emphasis on reading short story books and writing stories or a sentence, are likely to be part of the infant teacher's normal provision within the classroom. However, very detailed instructions are given for each of these activities and this is why an extensive training programme is suggested for reading recovery teachers.

Reading recovery is discontinued when it appears, from the reading and writing on the programme, that the child is able to cope with the normal activities of the rest of the class without regular individual guidance. As a guide, this is usually after fifteen to twenty weeks of reading recovery. Marie Clay (1985) provides evidence to suggest that children make considerable gains during their period of intensive individual instruction. Ted Glynn and his colleagues (1989), in their independent evaluation of reading recovery for the New Zealand Department of Education, also found that children who had attended reading recovery programmes made substantially more progress than comparable children who did not attend such sessions. However, as with several other support programmes, there was some indication that these children failed to progress further once reading recovery was discontinued. This serves to remind us of the need to monitor each child's literacy development and to ensure that progress is continued through the provision of appropriate literacy activities. Nevertheless, Smith and Elley (1994) suggested that reading recovery is possibly the most successful reading assistance programme because of its sound theoretical base, individual teaching and the intensive training and monitoring of its teachers. Furthermore, they consider that the organizational pattern keeps it within the framework of an inclusive education.

Although in the normal classroom intensive individual attention is difficult to provide without support from other adults, there are likely to be elements of reading recovery that teachers of young children will wish to use. Such provision is likely to be for the whole year, rather than for the short but intensive period suggested by reading recovery. Even without the resources required by reading recovery, some of its principles are likely to be utilized, including diagnosing the children's strengths and weaknesses, ensuring that the children read and write each day, and giving individual support as often as possible – which implies careful organization of the classroom.

Further reading

Clay, M. (1985) *The Early Detection of Reading Difficulties*. Auckland: Heinemann Educational.

Clay, M. (1993) *Reading Recovery: A Guidebook for Teachers in Training*. London: Heinemann Educational.

For any teacher wishing to consider reading recovery in greater detail, one of these texts is essential. For instance, the diagnostic procedures noted above are provided in great detail, allowing the teacher to carry out the assessments in an appropriate manner. These texts also demonstrate what information can be gained from the assessments. From such knowledge of the child as a reader and writer, Marie Clay then proceeds to describe the details of the programme.

reading schemes

A reading scheme might simply be described as a collection of books written with the express purpose of helping children to learn to read. In the USA, they are referred to as basal readers and comprise workbooks and ancillary materials, which suggest a tighter control of the teaching. In the UK, reading schemes more typically contain the central collection of books focused on a small group of characters. However, there are schemes in the UK that grade a collection of stories by difficulty, so that the children are reading *real books* by a variety of authors.

Teachers of young children have a similar goal to that of reading schemes (i.e. helping children to learn to read), so many schools use such materials. The HMI (1991) survey of 470 primary classes in 120 schools indicated that more than 95 per cent of the classes used reading schemes to some extent, albeit 'usually supplemented by other fiction or non-fiction books' (p. 7). Teachers who use reading schemes can point to the perceived advantages of such materials and, in particular, that they provide a structure to the teaching of reading. In 1988, Kenneth Goodman and his colleagues suggested that the tight organization and sequence of basal readers was the main strength of graded reading materials. However, they also suggested that such a structure was a major weakness, as it did not allow for easy modification and adaptation by the teacher. The provision of such a structure might nevertheless be important, especially when large classes are to be taught. Furthermore, the children's reading progress can be monitored by teachers and parents (and perhaps the children themselves) using the books of the scheme.

There are some key features of reading schemes. First, a controlled increase in vocabulary may lessen the demands placed upon the child. Second, a frequent repetition of vocabulary helps to reinforce the learning process. Third, the use of simplified short sentences may match the child's own repertoire of relatively short sentences. Fourth, if the reading scheme is phonic-based, then there is a systematic inclusion of particular letters and letter combinations.

Yet the use of reading schemes has been a contentious issue for more than a century (Burt 1893). The arguments in support of real books emphasized that debate (Browne 1996). Initially, the concern about graded reading schemes could be linked to the two different philosophies underpinning the production of texts. Some reading schemes were based on a strict look-and-say principle, where a controlled vocabulary and a high repetition rate were evident. On the negative side, that led to some schemes of the 'look, look, look' type that seemed to be divorced from the world of natural language. Other schemes were based on simple *phonics* teaching and, in some texts, this has led to the pedestrian 'cat sat on the mat' type of material for the children to read. In neither of these types of reading schemes was there a flow of language with a forward-moving narrative and cohesive links between the sentences. However, in recent years, publishers have largely met those criticisms and have produced schemes, sets or boxes with a greater reliance upon stories that make use of natural language.

Schools in the UK, having considered the structure that is provided by the reading schemes and the adequacy of the books in such schemes, have moved towards a policy with several different possibilities. First, a few schools use just one major reading scheme to teach their children to read. Often the school will develop themes based upon the characters or events from the scheme to consolidate or extend the learning. Of course, where there is a reliance upon one scheme, then it will need to be selected carefully by considering in detail the stories, illustrations and teacher's manual, which will indicate the philosophy behind the scheme, as well as determining whether the books will meet the interests of the children. Second, because it will be difficult to find a scheme that meets all the needs of the school, more than one reading scheme might be used, and a new structure can be created based on the texts from the different schemes. Third, although the intention is to encourage the children on to storybooks after using a reading scheme, some schools make it their policy to use a scheme for a short period only and then use story or real books to facilitate the children's reading growth. Fourth, because of the concerns about the language in some reading schemes, schools might use the natural language books in some of the recent reading schemes together with *real books*. Those books are then graded into a colour sequence, often using the helpful suggestions provided by Moon (2000 – and revised annually) to grade the texts for readability. Fifth, some schools use *real books* throughout the school to encourage reading development. In such circumstances, the careful selection of each book is important to ensure that there is a worthwhile story written in a natural language and which will be both interesting and meaningful to the children.

Although, as noted earlier, 95 per cent of classes in the UK use a reading scheme, the proportion using a single reading scheme is very much smaller. Nevertheless, whatever use is made of carefully selected reading schemes, decisions will need to be made about the organization of the classroom and the provision of the various literacy activities that are discussed in this handbook.

Further reading

Donaldson, M. (1989) *Sense and Sensibility*. Reading: Reading and Language Information Centre, University of Reading School of Education.
Reading schemes have been criticized for their lack of meaningful stories written in a natural language in a forward-moving narrative. Margaret Donaldson explores the real books/reading scheme issue, together with several other debates, and suggests that a general condemnation of reading schemes is inappropriate. In conclusion, she argues for 'the reading of text which is very simple, but which is not stilted in its sentence forms and is linked to familiar and interesting themes' (p. 33). Such a conclusion reminds us that what is required is a careful consideration of the quality of all the texts that we provide for children as they develop as readers and beyond.

real books

Real books is a term used to describe two different notions. First, as we shall deal with it here, 'real books' describes the materials that might be used in a classroom to encourage children's early reading development. It is used in this way to indicate those books that are written for the purpose of telling a story. This can be contrasted with those books that are written for the purpose of teaching children to read and which might be referred to as reading scheme books (or 'basals' in the USA). Second, as we will see in the following section, the *real books approach* refers not only to the books to be read, but also to a philosophy about the teaching and learning of reading.

The impetus towards the use of real books, as the materials by which young children's reading development is encouraged, emanates from a concern about many *reading schemes*. Many reading schemes are now based on collections of short stories, thus reflecting real books. Nevertheless, reading schemes have typically been based on short sentences, a simple vocabulary and the repetition of words. This often leads to uninteresting texts that restrain children's learning, although several key words are likely to be learnt and mastered. Barrie Wade (1990) has been very critical of reading schemes. He demonstrated that concern by presenting a text back to front, as well as in the appropriate order, where the ordering did not appear to influence the meaning of the text. We would normally expect stories to have a forward-moving plot and children would share that expectation. Indeed, children's implicit understanding of story structure may mean that they are well placed to use real books from the earliest moments in their contact with print, as many children do at home.

Although the emphasis on real books, and the benefits that they can bring, may appear to be a recent innovation, teachers have expressed concern for many years about books written especially for teaching reading (i.e. reading schemes, basals or reading books). As an example of this concern, let us consider Mary Burt's strong words from 1893:

At the end of the year we had proved that the reading-book was of no earthly use – unless to make good materials for bonfires. We had satisfied ourselves that reading-books made children timid towards real books, and thwarted the intention of the schools to teach 'the essentials' – or at least one of the essentials, namely 'readin'.

(p. 172)

So what are the qualities that one would expect to find in real books? I touched briefly upon the qualities of real books when dealing with predictable books in the *children's books* section. Real books are written with natural language, and they are predictable and meaningful. As Liz Waterland (1988: 46) indicated, this means that 'the story, however simple, [can] be read aloud by an adult in a natural, interested manner and without sounding lunatic'. Most frequently, these books are written about people, animals and events, which are a reflection of the real world and, therefore, children are able to contextualize many of the stories and to learn from them. Jill Bennett (1991: 7) developed this view and suggested that it might be the 'intrinsic humour of nearly all the books [which] seems to be what attracts children to them'. The illustrations in real books are there to support the text and, as Graham (1991) has argued, illustrations can extend the meanings of the story and also help children to understand the story. In addition, real books are often written in a way that produces a rhythm or flow to the words. So in Eric Carle's (1969) *The Very Hungry Caterpillar*, there was 'On Monday he ate through . . . On Tuesday he ate through . . .', etc., which produces a predictability but also a rhythm to that part of the story. And then there is repetition. Real books often contain aspects of repetition, but the repetition is based on units of language rather than single words (which might be evident in a reading scheme). Staying with *The Very Hungry Caterpillar*, despite the variety of eating 'he was still hungry' at the end of each day, and children appear to enjoy the repetition of that sentence with its predictability and rhythm.

Overall, as Barrie Wade (1990) argued, real books with their forward-moving narrative and logical connections and consequences give emotional and intellectual sustenance to a child. Of course, just because a book is not part of a reading scheme and has been written by an author (rather than a publisher) does not necessarily make it a worthwhile real book. Nevertheless, there are now hundreds of books that children find interesting and which provide sustenance in the sense noted above. And several texts have lists to help us make a start with our own selections. Both Wade (1990) and Slaughter (1992) provided a list of books for children, each with a brief description or comment; Bennett (1991) did the same but in greater detail. Our reading of some of these stories to and with children and the children's responses to them will help us to determine the quality of these real books.

Further reading

Bennett, J. (1991) *Learning to Read with Picture Books*, 4th edn. Stroud: Thimble Press.
Jill Bennett's book was first published in 1979 and its popularity is indicated by the continuing interest in revised editions. In addition to arguing the case for real books, and demonstrating how she has used such books in her classroom, she notes the qualities she would expect to find in them. However, for many teachers it is the very detailed list of real books and Jill Bennett's sensitive comments on them that are the great attraction of this booklet.

Meek, M. (1988) *How Texts Teach What Readers Learn*. Stroud: Thimble Press.
The title of this short booklet clearly conveys its message. Through a detailed consideration of some *children's books*, Margaret Meek shows us how the quality of real books not only helps children to learn to read but also how those stories teach about language, discourse and writing. And reading these multi-layered texts, as a reflective reader, assists in learning about life.

Wade, B. (ed.) (1990) *Reading for Real*. Buckingham: Open University Press.
Teachers and educators are the authors of the ten chapters in this book. Much of the book is devoted to real books as materials. Reading schemes, the power of stories and the attributes of real books are considered, together with lists of real books. These sections provide a useful and detailed extension to the comments made above on real books. The text goes beyond real books as the reading material to be used and also considers teaching and learning within classrooms when a *real books approach* is adopted.

real books approach

A starting point for the real books approach is the book to be read. As noted in the previous section, such books are *real books* in the sense that they are *children's books*, most frequently, which are written to tell a story rather than to teach a child to read, at least directly. However, some of the key features of storybooks – natural language, predictability, repetition and rhythm, illustrations, characters and humour, forward-moving narrative with logical connections and consequences – do facilitate children in their development as readers. Furthermore, teachers provide extra support by working alongside individuals in a one-to-one *sharing a book*. Such readings are an important feature of a real books approach, where the quality of the book, the efforts of the child as an active learner, and the sophisticated and changing role of the teacher all contribute to the making of a successful interaction.

Margaret Meek (1982) and Frank Smith (1978) have both argued the importance of the book, the child and the teacher to encourage reading development. *Sharing a book* within a real books approach provides these elements. However, the approach extends far beyond real books and adult–child readings and includes many other literacy activities within a careful *classroom organization and management*. Furthermore, the approach implies working with a view of teaching and learning that emphasizes the whole rather than the parts, and learning experiences rather than frequent direct teaching. Teachers who try to follow a real books approach would argue that it involves a complex teaching role requiring a sound knowledge both of children and of reading. It differs from the more prescriptive and teacher-led *literacy hour* that is used currently in Years 1 and 2 in England, although many teachers adapt that hour to suit a real books approach and teachers of younger children are not constrained by having to teach the literacy hour.

In practical terms, teachers working with a real books approach make a careful selection of books for the children and organize the classroom so that uninterrupted one-to-one readings can occur. However, the organization of the classroom encompasses more than this, because teachers will want to ensure that there are areas for literacy activities to occur. So the room will usually contain a *library corner*, listening area and *writing centre*. These areas will be developed to attract the children to them. The furniture will be arranged so as to support carefully managed movement and interaction in the classroom. Part of classroom management will be to ensure that there is sufficient *time for literacy*.

In some respects, it could be argued that the *classroom print* should be so great that the children are always engaged in literacy. However, it is important for teachers to ensure that not only is print available in the classroom, but that that print is used with the children as a class, a group or as individuals.

A real books approach also recognizes the importance of the home in supporting literacy development; therefore, *home–school links* will be a feature of a school adopting this approach. The wider environment should also be used to form a foundation for some of the *language experience approach* activities in the classroom, which enable links to be made between reading and writing as one supports the other. The above indicates that a real books approach is not a non-teaching approach. Furthermore, the teacher is constantly engaged in the *assessment* of the children so as to ensure that needs can be ascertained and subsequently met.

The real books approach does involve far more than just the books to be read and reading with a child. Nevertheless, the books are important as are the interactions between the teacher and the child or children. Therefore, teachers using a real books approach will use other opportunities to share books to encourage reading development. *Story readings, shared reading* with big books, *hearing children read* and *sustained silent reading* are all fundamental aspects of a real books approach, activities that provide a context for considering *phonics* meaningfully. They also provide the opportunity for teachers and children to interact with worthwhile and meaningful books, when learning to read and the enjoyment of reading can be brought together.

Further reading

Campbell, R. (1992) *Reading Real Books*. Buckingham: Open University Press. This book describes the principles and practices of a real books approach. It was written at a time when critics of real books were describing the approach as a simplistic non-teaching movement involving just real books and repeated readings of them. Although the text does note the importance of the books to be read and the use of *sharing a book*, it suggests that the real books approach involves far more. The book debates *classroom organization and management*, together with other literacy activities. Classroom examples are provided in many of the chapters.

Harrison, C. and Coles, M. (eds) (1992) *The Reading for Real Handbook*. London: Routledge. Colin Harrison and Martin Coles have gathered together several articles that emphasize literature-based approaches to early reading. The articles are arranged into three broad sections concerned with theories about learning to read, the books to be used and, finally, the organization and practices required to encourage children to be readers. The text argues that teachers need to have a sound understanding of the theory and principles that provide the rationale for the practice, so that at times of debate a strong defence can be made for the real books approach. The authors outline these theories and principles and, in each chapter, provide the reader with some questions to reflect upon.

record-keeping

Teachers of young children will want to keep a record of the literacy developments of each child in the class. This is because having a systematic and detailed account of each child's literacy growth enables the teacher to reflect upon the activities that might be provided to build upon that child's current strengths and support the child's needs. Of course, the records serve other purposes as well, as they can form the basis for discussions with parents about a child's progress and can be passed on to other teachers who teach the child subsequently. In England, the teacher is expected to maintain a record of achievement for each child in relation to the targets of the National Curriculum as a guide to setting targets for the class and children (QCA 1999c). What the teacher in the busy classroom will want to compile are records on each child that are informative yet do not take too long to complete.

The records that are kept will be based upon the observations, inter-actions and analyses that will be part of the *assessment* procedures in the classroom. These occur throughout the school day, although there are particular times when information can be collected in greater detail. *Sharing a book* provides a good opportunity for the teacher to learn about the child as a reader. During such interactions, a *miscue analysis* or *running record* can take place and a discussion with the child can add to the information. The Primary Language Record (CLPE 1988) includes a pro forma, 'Reading Sample Form', for providing a description of the reading by the child during such an interaction. Used on occasions as an informal observation of the child's reading, it can add other details to the miscue analysis or running record. The form includes:

- the title of the book;
- whether it is a known or unknown text;
- overall impression of the child's reading;

- strategies used by the child when reading aloud (which implies some reference by the teacher to miscue analysis);
- the child's response to the book; and
- a reflection by the teacher about the child's development as a reader and the support now needed for further development.

This sample of the child's reading could be added to the regular record that is kept when the child shares a book with an adult. Such reading diaries might include:

- the date;
- the book read;
- the teacher's comments on what are perceived to be significant features of the child's reading;
- comments from the parents and child about the child's reading;
- responses to the reading; and
- the extent of any teacher support.

Such a diary, over a period of time, provides interesting insights into the child's progress as a reader, as Browne (1996: 225) demonstrates. All of this information provides an extended narrative or description of each child as a reader. From that description, particular aspects can be extracted as necessary. In some schools, a record sheet is used in an attempt to provide an immediate visual impression of what a child has achieved. Liz Waterland (1988) provides a reading wheel on which certain reading behaviours can be noted. The use of the wheel to record the information is indicative of the non-linear development of literacy growth. The Sheffield Early Literacy Development Project used a jigsaw, for similar reasons, to enable parents to see their children's development with *environmental print, writing* and *sharing a book* (Weinberger *et al.* 1990).

The obvious way to maintain a record of a child's *writing* is to retain samples, or photocopies, of that writing, often chosen in collaboration with the child. These samples can be kept in a scrapbook or portfolio; over a year they build up to a very complete record of the child's progress. And over a three-year period, these samples provide not only a detailed picture of the child as a writer, but also provide a wealth of information to help teachers evaluate the literacy policy of the school. The sample of writing requires some additional comment by the teacher to contextualize the writing product. For instance, any support the child might have received can be recognized. Typically, the teacher needs to date the work and provide information about the stimulus for the writing, the extent of teacher support, whether the work was independent or collaborative, whether invented spellings were used, whether a word book/dictionary was used, and so on. All of this information is important so that the writing can be analysed in the most informative way. The sample of writing should be sufficient to demonstrate the child's growing knowledge of story structure, ability to organize and structure the writing according to purpose and audience, writing in different *genres*, as well as indicating knowledge of conventions, such as spelling and *punctuation*.

Although each school is likely to develop somewhat different record-keeping practices, certain principles will underpin that practice. Myra Barrs and Gillian Johnson (1993) suggest that observation-based records should be based upon:

- regular, frequent and systematic recording (some recording takes place daily);
- the recording of normal behaviour in favourable contexts (the children are assessed in normal classroom circumstances rather than in special and artificial contexts);
- an emphasis on positive recording (focusing on the child's strengths);
- records that includes evidence from home (thus emphasizing the home–school link);
- records that stress the links between different aspects of language (so that reading and writing growth can be looked at together);
- records that view non-conventional reading and writing as information (miscues and invented spellings are good examples of such information);
- records that include contributions from children (which might develop from small beginnings where the child helps with the selection of writing for the portfolio);
- helpful structures for recording (an open structure that suggests areas for information but which encourages observations and comment rather than checklists);
- recording in different contexts and in different formats (so that we are not reliant upon just one type of record to judge a child's literacy progress).

This extensive list of principles can be used to judge the earlier suggestions for record-keeping in this section. It is also helpful to teachers as a means of evaluating their own record-keeping practice.

Further reading

Barrs, M. and Johnson, G. (1993) *Record-keeping in the Primary School*. London: Hodder & Stoughton.

This short book provides a very readable and practical introduction to record-keeping. The examples are drawn from primary schools but they are of particular relevance to infant school teachers. As Myra Barrs was associated with the development and use of the Primary Language Record, the discussion of that language record is well informed. For teachers who need to consider record-keeping in the context of the National Curriculum, there are many helpful links.

responding to miscues

During the literacy interaction of *hearing children read*, children spend part of the time reading aloud to their teacher. This is also the case, at least in part, with younger children when *sharing a book*. During such oral readings, the reader inevitably produces some miscues. The teacher has to consider how to respond to those miscues using a variety of strategies to support the child at that time.

A starting point for many teachers and parents is to consider the pause–prompt–praise continuum (Glynn 1980). These three 'p's' remind us to pause before mediating in a child's reading, thus giving the child time to think about his or her own reading, to provide some response or prompt if it is required and, subsequently, to praise the child's efforts.

But what should be the format of the teacher's response or prompt? Elsewhere I have suggested that teachers working in the normal classroom environment use several different responses to support a child's reading (Campbell 1992). Using the example of 5-year-old Richard reading from Eric Carle's (1969) *The Very Hungry Caterpillar*, I was able to demonstrate five main strategies that teachers adopt and suggest the reasons for the use of those responses (pp. 57–9).

First, teachers may use the strategy of non-response:

Richard: In the light of the moon
          the (a) little egg lay on a leaf
Teacher: —

In this example, Richard miscued the text word 'a' and read 'the', although later on the same line he read the word 'a' accurately. This miscue did not alter substantially the meaning of the book and the teacher, working to the notion that meaning is the essential feature of reading, decided not to mediate.

Second, teachers may use a word-cueing strategy, which involves the teacher in reading the part of the sentence that leads up to the miscued word and to do so with a rising intonation, which draws the child back into the interaction as the reader:

Richard: one cupcake and
one slice of salami (watermelon)
Teacher: one slice
Richard: one slice of watermelon

Importantly, this strategy often seems to work (Campbell 1994). Perhaps it does so because it does not draw the child's attention away from the text, it informs the reader of the need to reconsider a word and it does so by reminding the reader of some of the semantic and syntactic cues. Additionally, as Marie Clay (1972) has shown, children who can read well often use the strategy of restarting a sentence to help them with a word that is creating a problem. Therefore, by using this response, teachers help children to develop strategies that they will be able to use themselves later.

Third, teachers may use a soft, non-punitive 'no' as a means of informing the reader that a miscue has been produced:

Richard: He looked (started)
Teacher: No.
Richard: He starts (started)
Teacher: Yes.
Richard: He started

Without a great deal of disruption of Richard's reading, the teacher was able to help him read the verb correctly, if not completely accurately. It would appear that many teachers use this response especially where the miscued word is at the beginning of the sentence and, therefore, where the teacher cannot use the word-cueing strategy.

Fourth, the teacher might very simply provide the word for the reader:

Richard: out of the egg
a very (came)
Teacher: came
Richard: came a tiny and very hungry caterpillar

This response by the teacher is predictably successful. The child hears the word and can echo the word in the reading. However, although it may provide for immediate success, this teacher response may not help the child in the long term. The child has not been involved with the word and, therefore, teachers often find that after telling a child a word the same word can be miscued two or three lines later. The response does not encourage the child to be an active learner or encourage the child towards independent reading. For these reasons, teachers will wish to use this response sparingly.

It was, in part, because Southgate *et al.* (1981) found this response being used so frequently that they were critical of teachers spending substantial periods hearing children read. But many teachers will, of course, use a range of responses. Nevertheless, they will provide the word on occasion to maintain the flow of reading, or because they are working with a very young beginning reader and they wish to give extra support in the early stages.

Fifth, the teacher will occasionally use a response that draws attention to the letters and associated sounds in words:

Richard: he ate through
            two peppers (pears) //
Teacher: They do look a bit like peppers.
            And they do begin with a 'p'.
            But they might be something else do you think?
Richard: pineapples – eh –

Following Richard's miscue of the word 'pear', the teacher's response includes an emphasis on the initial letter 'p' in the text word and Richard's miscue. Although this strategy did not help in this instance, it did remind Richard of the graphophonic cue system. This might be another response that the teacher would wish to use sparingly because it takes the reader away from a meaningful reading of a book. However, its occasional use will draw attention to the importance of letters and sounds in reading.

The teacher needs to respond to the reader's miscues with care. In particular, the teacher will want to keep the child involved with the book as an active reader. The teacher will also wish to provide responses that create minimal disruption to the reading and to help the reader not only with the immediate reading, but to help the child to develop strategies for the future.

In the classroom

In the section above, we looked at the various responses that a teacher made when sharing a book with 5-year-old Richard. However, these responses were drawn from various parts of the book and it might create more coherence if we look briefly at the beginning of that reading, with the various comments and discussion removed and just the reading by Richard and the response by the teacher left in place. Your familiarity with this piece of reading by Richard might also support you in your consideration of the teacher's responses:

Richard: In the light of the moon
the – the (a) little egg lay on a leaf
One summer's (Sunday) day (morning) the warm sun
came out (up) and – pop! – //
Teacher: out
Richard: of the egg
a very (came)
Teacher: came
Richard: came a tiny and very hungry caterpillar

An interesting feature of this opening is that the teacher did not respond to the first four substitutions. This non-response seems appropriate for this 5-year-old reader. After all, each of the miscues did not alter substantially the nature or meaning of the story that Richard read. Later, the teacher did provide two words when it seemed necessary to keep Richard on track with his reading. We know that the teacher in this example continued to use a variety of responses. But even this short example from the beginning of the reading serves to demonstrate how, in the context of a busy classroom, the teacher can support a reader and respond to the miscues in a way that helps the reader rather than distracting him or her from the book.

Further reading

Campbell, R. (1992) *Reading Real Books*. Buckingham: Open University Press.
The examples of Richard's miscues and the teacher response to them are debated more extensively in this book. Furthermore, the complete *sharing a book* between the teacher and Richard is provided. Therefore, it is possible to consider the miscues and the teacher response to them within the complete reading of the book.

Campbell, R. (1994) The teacher response to children's miscues of substitution. *Journal of Research in Reading*, 17: 147–54.
This article considers the various teacher responses that are used following children's miscues of substitution. Using data from a research study, it explores the teacher responses to almost 3000 cases of substitution. The analysis indicates the particular usefulness of the word-cueing strategy to help readers immediately and to support them in subsequent readings.

Guppy, P. and Hughes, M. (1999) *The Development of Independent Reading: Reading Support Explained.* Buckingham: Open University Press.
This text explores the one-to-one interaction of adult and child reading a book. In doing so, it presents a reading continuum of five overlapping stages, which includes *sharing a book* and *hearing children read*, although not named in that way. The fourth stage they refer to as 'assisted reading' as the child takes on the role of reader to a greater extent. Then the adult has to consider how to respond to miscues of the child. Guppy and Hughes present 'ten supportive actions for a problem word' (pp. 92–107). Some of those are similar to the responses to miscues presented above; for example, 'take another run at it' is similar to the word-cueing strategy. This book adds to the debate on responding to miscues.

running records

In early years classrooms in England and Wales, there will be some knowledge of running records as it is one of the modes of *assessment* used as part of the testing arrangements for Key Stage 1 of the *National Curriculum* (QCA 1999c). However, a knowledge of running records will also have come from other sources. First, where teachers have used *miscue analysis* at some stage, then the concept and practice of running records is readily understood, because of the similarities between these two modes of diagnosis and assessment. Second, even where miscue analysis is unknown, most infant teachers as they are *sharing a book* will have kept some form of record of the child's progress and that *record-keeping* may well have included some reference to words that the child was unable to read. So normal classroom literacy activities provide a basis for an acceptance of running records as the ideas are already implicit in the teacher's everyday working.

The running record is a simple means of recording the oral reading of a child. It is simple because it does not require a duplicate of the pages being read and the reading is not tape-recorded. Because the teacher codes the oral reading of the child on to a plain sheet of paper, a running record can therefore be taken at any time. Indeed, the development of the running record was to meet these very needs of the teacher for the day-to-day activities of the classroom with young children (Clay 1985). It is similar in concept to the more detailed *miscue analysis* developed in the USA (see Goodman *et al.* 1987). So how is a running record coded?

Each child reads aloud from the book he or she has selected. This reading to the teacher isrecorded on to a plain sheet of paper. Each word read accurately is recorded with a tick and miscues (or errors as Marie Clay, 1985, refers to them) are noted using several conventional marks:

/	word read correctly
T	word told by the teacher
the	substituted word
it-the	substitution sequence
O	omission of word
SC	self-correction of word by the child

For example:

The boy saw a dog.   / / / it-the /

It can be seen at a glance that the reader read four of the five words accurately and substituted the word 'a' first with 'it' and then 'the'. Marie Clay (1985) suggests that the text word might be written under the miscue so that the nature of the substitution can be seen at a glance. However, many teachers of young children are able to record the reading and recognize the coding in relation to the text (providing the title of the short book is noted at the top of the sheet) because of their familiarity with the books in the classroom. There are other miscues that are produced by children, so the teacher might have to represent repetitions using an 'R' for example. However, as a starting point, the short list of conventions above will account for much of the child's reading of a book. In the busy classroom, some teachers abbreviate the running record even further. They might place only one tick on a line when the child has read that line without a miscue (QCA 1999c: 17).

Once the reading is completed, then, as with a *miscue analysis*, the teacher may ask, 'Why that miscue?' This raises the issue of which language *cue system*, or systems, the child was using to produce the miscue. Marie Clay suggests that the letters M, S and V might be inserted on to the coding, these letters representing the meaning, structure and visual cues being used. Such an analysis is not dissimilar to a miscue analysis, because meaning (M) will be indicative of the child using the semantic language cues, structure (S) will suggest the use of the syntactic cues and visual (V) will indicate some use of the graphophonic cue system. When an analysis is undertaken, it will be noted that the child may apparently have used one, two or all three of the cue systems; it is seldom the case that children use just one of the cues throughout a reading. However, we need to recognize that, when we undertake an analysis of the child's reading and miscues, we are making our best judgement of what the child might have done. We can never be totally sure because we cannot get fully into the mind of the reader, although the miscue analysis or running record enables us to get close to achieving that goal. Nevertheless, such analyses can be used to help to determine the literacy activities that might be provided to support the child in the classroom.

Although the running record is a development from *miscue analysis*, it is important to remember that it is a simplification of that mode of diagnosis and that some information might be lost in that simplification. As an example, it is well known that when a child's oral reading is audio-recorded for subsequent miscue analysis, there are many points where the listener has to listen two, three or more times to be sure that the coding of the miscues is accurate. Coding straight on to a plain sheet of paper will include some errors by the teacher, or there will be some coding that on reflection after further hearings of the reading might be interpreted differently. Therefore, it might be the more complete miscue analysis that teachers will use, especially with children who may require extra attention. Nevertheless, the use of a running record can be helpful in a busy classroom for gaining some insight into the reading strategies being adopted by the children, and the teacher can use that information to evaluate the range of literacy activities provided in the classroom.

Further reading

Clay, M. (1985) *The Early Detection of Reading Difficulties*. Auckland: Heinemann Educational.
Part of this text, which is largely about reading recovery, describes running records. This description of running records is comprehensive and provides sufficient information to enable us to understand the process. For those teachers in the UK who have been involved with SATs and therefore have carried out a running record in a more limited way, this text will provide greater insights into this mode of assessment.

Campbell, R. (1993) *Miscue Analysis in the Classroom*. Widnes: UK Reading Association.
This short book provides a simple but concise description of miscue analysis for use by the busy classroom teacher. Inevitably, given that the emphasis is upon the classroom, there is also a section on the use of running records in which the coding used is described. The link to miscue analysis is more firmly

established by using the same short passage and the oral reading of a child for both a miscue analysis and a running record.

scanning and skimming

Scanning and skimming are two reading techniques, or styles, which are often regarded as part of the repertoire of older readers. For instance, in their study of secondary school reading, Lunzer and Gardner (1979) referred to four styles of reading. They indicated the need for children from ten to fifteen years to be able make flexible use of scanning, skimming, receptive reading and reflective reading, according to the demands of the text and the purposes of the child. They defined skimming and scanning as follows:

> Skim reading is a rapid style used mainly to establish what the text is about before deciding whether and where to read . . .
> Scanning is a kind of skimming to see if a particular point is present in the text – or to locate it.
>
> (pp. 26–7)

Many teachers of young children might react initially to these definitions by suggesting that such skills can be left until later. Their priority will be to get children to read and to be interested in books, so that there is a good foundation for a subsequent variety of reading and reading to learn. Nevertheless, helping children to scan and skim is part of the National Literacy Strategy at Year 2 (DfEE 1998). Furthermore, a closer analysis suggests that, although teachers of young children might not necessarily introduce the terminology, or teach scanning and skimming directly, they will appear as part of the interactions between the teacher and child centred on a book.

When teachers use big books, in a *shared reading* with the children, that literacy activity teaches the children about how to use storybooks. The youngest children quickly learn about front-to-back and left-to-right directionality, and the reading of the complete text assists children with meaning and with knowledge of words. However, not all the books that are used are likely to be read in that most normal of ways. There will be occasions when the youngest of readers need to use scanning. A simple example is when children start to consult a dictionary to find the spelling of a word. At that point, the normal strategy of front-to-back reading will not be very helpful. So young children will have to be encouraged to scan the text to find the initial letter and, subsequently, the actual word that is required. To facilitate such learning, some guidance from the teacher will be required.

Guidance will also be required when children begin to consult information books while engaged on *thematic* or *topic work*. Of course, much of this work will be based on the experiences of the children and the teacher will attempt to extend those experiences and knowledge by arranging visits and bringing artefacts into the classroom. It will also include using information and reference books. The teacher will want to avoid this degenerating into low-level learning (Alexander 1992) where the children might, for instance, copy large chunks of the book. Instead, the teacher will want to encourage the children to use the books to locate, and extract, specific information that will be useful to them. This suggests that the teacher will talk with the children individually, in groups and as a class about the process of scanning.

A similar argument can be put forward in relation to skimming. Take, for instance, the task of selecting a book to read. The child will use several strategies to help him or her in that endeavour. The illustrations might be used as a guide to selection and a growing knowledge of authors can also be helpful. However, at some stage, the child will want to glance through the book and get a feel for what the story is about and to decide on the basis of that skim read whether to select the book or not. Children can be helped to develop such a strategy by the demonstrations that the teacher might give in the *library corner* or when introducing a book before a *story reading*.

It is not the aim of this section to suggest that scanning and skimming are major areas for teachers of young children to consider. However, they are reading styles which the teacher is bound to introduce and demonstrate as the children begin to approach books for a variety of purposes. It is important that the teacher provides these introductions and demonstrations because it enables the children to gain flexibility in their reading.

Further reading

Southgate, V., Arnold, H. and Johnson, S. (1981) *Extending Beginning Reading.* London: Heinemann Educational.
This book is the report of the Extending Beginning Reading Project, which studied in depth the literacy practices in many schools and which concen-

trated upon 8- and 9-year-old children in their Year 3 and 4 classes. The extensive study looked at the wide range of literacy practices in classrooms for these age groups. The report contained many recommendations, including that there should be support for 'a gradual transition to the realization that skimming and scanning are as legitimate for certain purposes as reading every word' (p. 291). There is no particular section on these reading strategies, but throughout the book there are ideas to encourage children to become sophisticated and reflective readers. Part of that sophistication is that children should have flexible strategies for dealing with print.

school policy

Throughout this book, there are suggestions about literacy activities and practices for use in the early years settings. In the main, the activities are set within the classroom where the teacher works together with a number of children. But, of course, most teachers work in schools, or other settings, alongside colleagues. It would be strange if each teacher worked in isolation from the other teachers in the school. So a school policy is required and there is evidence to suggest that schools that are successful in helping children with literacy learning typically have a school policy on language.

The members of the Bullock Committee (DES 1975) argued the case for a school policy very emphatically when they suggested that 'a coherent strategy, understood and agreed by the staff, is the best instrument for improving standards of reading and language' (p. 212). This view was reinforced by HMI (1991) when the teaching of reading was evaluated during visits to many schools in England in 1989 and 1990: 'clear well-formulated policies for reading were strongly associated with good standards' (p. 13).

Why should the existence of a clearly written and comprehensive school policy on language and literacy be helpful in encouraging standards of literacy in the school? At the simplest level, of course, it will mean that there are plans for *classroom organization and management*, as well as the monitoring and *assessment* of reading and writing to meet the literacy aims of the school. There are also very specific issues to be addressed, including the school policy on *gender* (Baxter 2001). All teachers will recognize these needs, namely to have planned for the literacy teaching and learning that will take place in the classroom.

And that need for planning includes whole language teachers (Goodman 1986), even though occasionally they are accused, falsely, of just allowing learning to happen.

For many teachers, there are now the dictates from central government (David *et al.* 2000). For teachers in England, there is the foundation stage document (QCA 2000) for 3- to 5-year-olds and the Key Stage 1 National Curriculum document (QCA 1999a) for 6- and 7-year-olds. There is also the very detailed National Literacy Strategy (DfEE 1998). Nevertheless, despite all the detail, it is still important for teachers to work together on a school policy that places all of that detail into context.

It is not just the existence of the school policy that is important. The means by which the policy is established is also important. In particular, where the staff have taken time to debate the development of the school policy, there is a better chance of that policy being offered in each classroom. Robin Alexander (1992), in reporting upon the evaluation of the Primary Needs Programme in Leeds, indicated the value of such a debate:

> equally important was dialogue on matters of purpose and policy within each school, especially between head and staff. Without such dialogue, and the associated openness in management and decision making, there could be a substantial gap between a school's espoused philosophy and its classroom practice.
>
> (p. 149)

So debate reduces the likelihood of a gap between the policy and the practice. However, it does more than that; debate encourages collaboration between staff and becomes part of the continuous learning process for all the teachers in the school. The roles of the headteacher and the language coordinator in providing leadership and guidance for other colleagues during such a debate and, subsequently, in supporting the teachers in the classroom, whenever possible, can also be helpful.

The policy then sets the framework for the literacy teaching and learning in the school. But it is useful to think of it as a framework within which teachers can work flexibly. This does not mean that each teacher is at liberty to ignore the policy, but it does allow each teacher to develop his or her particular strengths in the classroom, consistent with the policy agreed in collaboration with colleagues. No two teachers are exactly alike and, therefore, it would be unreasonable to expect all classrooms to be exactly alike. So there is flexibility, but it is a flexibility within the framework of the school policy.

Of course, the policy is always being developed, so that in one sense it is never finalized. In England, there have been constant developments as the various initiatives from government have been published. But the school policy on literacy has to be revised constantly for other reasons. Teachers new to a particular school can only acquire a real feel for the policy if they are able to take part in debates with colleagues about that literacy policy. The policy has to be revised regularly for that reason, but teachers should also be developing their knowledge of literacy; regular debates about aspects of school policy will help in that development. Such regular debates should also ensure that the policy remains appropriate.

Although the school policy may have to be a relatively short and succinct statement of plans and practices, the debates that take place will have to address very minute details of classroom practice. For instance, during a staff discussion on the school policy, the practice of *shared reading* using big books might be debated. Is that best practised as a group or class activity? How is it best fitted in during the school day? Does the literacy hour provide the best time for using this activity? What might the children be expected to learn during that activity? What variety of strategies might the teacher employ to encourage that learning? Not all of the responses to such questions will be a part of the school policy document, but having been a part of the debate about such issues can be helpful to the teacher in the daily task of teaching literacy in the classroom. And that can have a beneficial effect upon the literacy learning experiences of the children.

Further reading

QCA (1999a) *The National Curriculum Handbook for Primary Teachers in England Key Stages 1 and 2*. London: Qualifications and Curriculum Authority with Department for Education and Employment.

QCA (2000) *Curriculum Guidance for the Foundation Stage*. London: Qualifications and Curriculum Authority with Department for Education and Employment.

DfEE (1998) *The National Literacy Strategy: Framework for Teaching*. London: Department for Education and Employment.

As noted in the section on the *National Curriculum*, the first two of these documents provide a wealth of information on the teaching of literacy from 3 to 5 years of age and for Key Stage 1 for 6- and 7-year-olds. The learning that is expected of the children and the strategies to achieve that learning is indicated. The National Literacy Strategy gives even more detail of the sequence of teaching and the activities to be used. Although this does not necessarily create a school policy, in England it does provide the basis for such a policy.

Whitehead, M. (1999) *Supporting Language and Literacy Development in the Early Years*. Buckingham: Open University Press.
Although Marian Whitehead does not debate school policy as such, she does consider four essential strategies to support children's language and literacy learning. These four strategies suggest a broad range of important features that we might expect to be evident in a school policy. The first of these is talk, play and representation and she considers how these might be given a central position in the curriculum. Then she notes the importance of rhyme, rhythm and language patterns. Stories and narrative as a means of thinking and as a way into literacy are suggested. Finally, environmental print and messages to help children learn about writing is debated. These four strategies could inform discussions about school policy.

shared reading

A shared reading occurs as a teacher uses a big book with a group or class of young children. Most frequently, the big book is a storybook and the print is large enough to be visible to the children from a distance of fifteen to twenty feet. So not only do the children hear the story as it is read, they can also see the print. Such shared readings are an important part of the literacy hour in England (DfEE 1998). Although shared reading is now considered an activity with a big book, that was not always the case. When developed by Holdaway (1979), he referred to it as shared book experience (or even more simply working with big books), whereas shared reading denoted a teacher *sharing a book* with a child (e.g. Davis and Stubbs 1988).

Initially, classroom teachers developed shared readings with big books so that the story reading experiences of home could be replicated in the classroom. Of course, teachers of young children also have *story readings* daily with normal-sized books, but, as Holdaway (1979) argued, in such story readings the children cannot see the print in the same way that they can at home in one-to-one interactions with one of their parents. Big books were developed, therefore, so that a teacher could model the reading process in front of the class. By pointing to the words during the reading, the teacher enables the children to both hear the reading and to follow the print. In doing so, the children can learn incidentally about the left-to-right and top-to-bottom orientation of print, the separation of one word from another by a space and other conventions of print. The print is large, therefore, not only so that it can be seen, but also so that it can be shared and discussed.

As noted by Holdaway, it was the teachers who initially constructed the big books. Subsequently, however, many publishers began to produce big books and a large selection is now available. But, importantly, because teachers want the children to join in with the reading, the books that are made, or purchased, are often predictable books. *Children's books* are helpful if they contain patterns of repetition (phrases and sentences rather than single words), which the children can recognize, learn and repeat. The books are also helpful if they have a rhythm that supports the children in the reading of the text (Rhodes 1981). In addition, predictable books are written in a natural language (that is, they sound sensible and real when read aloud), with pictures that support the text and with stories that reflect happenings in the real world.

Such books allow the teacher to provide support initially by reading the whole story, but subsequently, during re-readings – an important feature Parkes (2000) reminds us – the teacher can read in a way that encourages the children to join in with a reading of key words or repeated phrases and sentences. So the use of big books provides the opportunity for a shared reading.

Although stories will form a major part of the big books in the classroom, there are other possibilities. Holdaway (1979) also constructed big sheets of *nursery rhymes*, songs and poems. These were used as part of the extended shared experience, with the children joining in as the rhymes and songs were recited or sung. As the children's knowledge of the sheets increased, so they were able to anticipate the language and join in more frequently. At other times, non-fiction can be used to support children's understanding of how books work.

Teachers working with very young children will find big books and shared reading a useful activity to get children involved with, and interested in, books. That may be especially the case for those children who may not have experienced frequent story readings at home (Combs 1987). Shared reading also provides important learning experiences about the conventions of print, the structures of stories and the nature of books and authorship. Children who have had many experiences of story reading will begin to use elements of the stories, that were used during shared reading, in their writing. So children's learning during big book interactions forms a basis for learning about reading, learning to read and as a support for writing.

It is important to heed the concerns, however, of Marian Whitehead (1999). She reminds us that shared reading has been used for many years now in early years settings. In those readings, the emphasis has been on the nature of the literary experience, how narrative works and how a reader creates meaning. This is different to the greater emphasis on aspects of print 'and teaching word level skills' (DfEE 1998: 11) that is suggested for the literacy hour. A teacher needs to think carefully about the nature of shared readings in the classroom.

Further reading

Holdaway, D. (1979) *The Foundations of Literacy*. London: Ashton Scholastic.
This book is widely regarded as having introduced the idea of big books and shared reading. Holdaway wanted to replicate in the primary classroom context the individual book experiences of story reading at home. He felt that story reading in the classroom denied children the opportunity to see the print and join in with the story, so he developed his own big books for group and class readings. In the *Foundations of Literacy*, there is a vivid account of his initial attempts to develop big books and to use them in the classroom.

Slaughter, J.P. (1992) *Beyond Storybooks: Young Children and Shared Book Experience*. Newark, DE: International Reading Association.
This book develops in considerable detail the ideas first suggested by Don Holdaway. Judith Slaughter writes on organizational features, such as selecting and making big books, and displaying them by means of an easel. She debates possible features of a shared reading, including a discussion of aspects of the story before it is read to develop a background knowledge, and using the title and the cover picture to encourage the children to make predictions about the story. Additionally, there are questions after the reading to extend the children's understanding of the story; encouraging choral reading of part of the story (or more frequently with poems and songs); and discussing the illustrations and thinking about authorship. She also considers the way in which the use of big books and shared reading (or shared book experience as she called it) can be extended. Follow-up work, including writing, is debated through the use of some classroom examples. An appendix provides a list of predictable books with comments on each of them.

Parkes, B. (2000) *Read it Again! Revisiting Shared Reading*. Portland, ME: Stenhouse.
As the title suggests, repeated re-readings of worthwhile *children's books* are a useful feature of shared readings. It is during those re-readings that children are able to extend their meaning making. Of course, this text is about far more than the re-readings of favourite books. It provides helpful and practical details about the organization and structure of shared readings in primary classrooms, including the use of *non-fiction* books.

shared writing (and interactive writing)

Shared writing has become an important literacy activity within early years classrooms. It provides an opportunity for the teacher to demonstrate the process of writing, as well as to involve the children in the construction and refinement of the writing. Donald Graves (1994) indicated that, initially, he did not demonstrate the process of writing in his classroom. However, he now sees that activity as a very important means of helping children to develop their own writing. In the demonstration of shared writing, the teacher uses a bold marker pen on a large sheet of paper, a whiteboard or overhead projector, so that the children are able to see the print with ease. Then, together, the teacher and children construct some writing. Typically, it is the teacher who constructs the writing using the comments from the children. However, McCarrier *et al.* (1999) suggest that it can be useful for the children to share the pen, as they term it, and contribute to the actual writing; this form of shared writing they refer to as interactive writing. In both cases, it is the construction of writing in front of the children that is important.

Whitehead (1999) suggests that the very youngest children can be helped to identify the marks that are made and that letters and spellings are required. The writing is, of course, derived from the children's interests and experiences; the teacher can write down the spoken contributions from the children. In the early stages, there will be talk about the words to be used, where to place the word, what letter might it start with, and so on. With older children, the interaction will be different, as the text is extended and other issues, such as speech marks and where they are placed, are debated. Indeed, it is possible to see how shared writing can be used right through to much older students as different purposes and more complex issues are featured.

What is evident is that shared writing is about both composition and transcription. This is emphasized in the *literacy hour*, where shared writing is an important part of the first fifteen minutes. It has been suggested that 'teachers should use texts to provide ideas and structures for writing and, in collaboration with the class compose texts, teaching how they are planned and how ideas are sequenced and clarified and structured' (DfEE 1998: 11). These aspects of composition will require many shared writing sessions where different texts are composed and ideas exchanged. However, the transcription features are also demanding, as the shared writing is used to consider 'grammar and spelling skills, to demonstrate features of layout and presentation and to focus on editing and refining work' (DfEE 1998: 11). In the early years classroom, Browne (1996: 45) noted a variety of topics for writing that could be demonstrated. These included retelling a familiar story, making a new version of a known story, making up a new story and using other *genres*, including writing letters, recording information, writing instructions and making a list. She also indicated a variety of teaching points that might be emphasized relating to transcription, including spellings, grammar, the choice of *words*, punctuation and patterns in words. Exploring the patterns in words provides a context for considering *onset and rime* and other features of *phonics*.

Shared writing, then, demonstrates both composition and transcription. However, its purpose is to enable children to write independently. Geekie *et al.* (1999), in what they describe as 'blackboard stories', suggest that these demonstrations help to build confidence and competence so that children are able to write something personal on their own. In the classroom, the teacher will need to ensure that there is a balance between the shared writing demonstrations and discussions, with opportunities for the children to write independently and to have sufficient time so that they can engage in extended *writing*.

In the classroom

In one nursery classroom, the teacher had been singing *nursery rhymes* with the children during the term. She developed this further by showing the children how they might be written during a shared writing:

> *Teacher:* So if I write
> *Humpty Dumpty*
> Now what comes next?
> *Children:* *sat on a wall*
> *Teacher:* I'll write
> *sat on a . . .*
> *Children:* *wall*
> *Teacher:* *wall.*
>
> (Campbell 1996: 34–5)

Initially, the emphasis here was on the children remembering the rhyme and the teacher demonstrating how that might be written. Nevertheless, the 3-year-olds were seeing writing being constructed and would be considering the way in which the teacher used letters to make up the words. The teacher then became more specific:

Teacher: Who can help me with wall?
What letter do I need to start?
Wendy: w
Teacher: Yes it is a w.
I think it is like your name isn't it Wendy?

As so often happens with young children, it is the first letter of a forename that is provided. Nevertheless, these 3-year-olds had heard the teacher use words such as 'write, letter and start' as well as hearing her name the letter 'w'; they had also seen her writing the words in a way that many of them had yet to master. Furthermore, the writing when it was completed would provide print to be used in a *shared reading*. When that was read together, the teacher might draw attention to rhyming words of wall and fall and, perhaps (without naming it as such), the rime unit of -all and the first letter differences of 'w and f'. For the 3-year-olds, this would be an enjoyable activity. However, a considerable amount of literacy learning is likely to occur as well.

Further reading

McCarrier, A., Pinnell, G. and Fountas, I. (1999) *Interactive Writing*. Portsmouth, NH: Heinemann.
This is a very substantial text. Fifteen chapters are divided into five sections exploring aspects of interactive writing. It provides many practical details and classroom examples of interactive writing. The key use of sharing the pen as a development from both the *language experience approach* and *shared writing* is debated. There are also links to other aspects of literacy provision, including the use of word walls and other *classroom print* to help young children to find *words* to include in their writing.

Hall, N. (1999) *Interactive Writing in the Primary School*. Reading: Reading and Language Information Centre, University of Reading.
Nigel Hall uses the term 'interactive writing' in a quite different way. For him, 'interactive writing is essentially about two people writing to each other for an extended period of time. It is about achieving a strong personal relationship between the writers that reflects friendship rather than power' (p. 5). As he indicates, interactive writing has different forms, all of which are variants of letter writing. So this book is not about shared writing or interactive writing in the sense used in the above section. However, we need to be aware of what others might be referring to when debating interactive writing.

sharing a book

Sharing a book involves a child and a teacher or other adult reading together, in a one-to-one interaction, from a book. It is a practice used frequently in early years classrooms (Reception, Years 1 and 2 in the UK, or K-2 in the USA). It is also a practice commonly used by many parents at home (see *books for babies*). Often the *home–school link* is emphasized, as schools produce small booklets for the parents that describe the main features of the interaction.

Sharing a book is a practice that places importance upon each of the three elements of the interaction – the child, the book and the adult – as well as the interaction itself. Frank Smith (1978) and Margaret Meek (1982) have argued that the interaction between child, book and adult is an important basis for reading success. The principle underpinning this literacy event is that, to learn to read, the child needs to read, just as there is a need to practise to learn to play a piano. Sharing a book enables the child to learn to read naturally. The child is perceived to be an active learner trying to make sense of the print. And the book will usually be selected for its natural language (*real books*), which is meaningful and of interest to the child and in which the flow of language and predictability facilitates the child's reading.

Although the active role of the child and the quality of the book are important, so too is the role of the teacher. The teacher will model the reading as well as supporting, guiding and encouraging the child during the reading of the text, responding to the perceived needs of the child. The teacher will also try to develop a discussion of the book and encourage the child to initiate questions about it.

Sharing a book covers a variety of interactions. This is because, as the child develops as a reader, he or she will take more control over the reading of the book. The role of the adult as reader will be reduced, but that as guide and supporter will be increased.

There appears to be a way in which sharing a book develops. First, the teacher might read the book to the child, during which the teacher and child make comments about the story, the characters and illustrations or make connections from the text to life experiences. Occasionally, the child might be drawn into the reading of the story where the flow of words allows the child to predict the language with some ease. In Pat Hutchin's (1972) *Good-Night Owl!*, the repetition of 'and owl tried to sleep' quickly enables young children to contribute to the sharing.

Guppy and Hughes (1999) refer to this stage of sharing a book as book-binding. At the end of the reading by the teacher, the child might retell the story in his or her own words. Such retellings may be a useful growth point for the child as well as providing insights to the teacher about the child's understanding of that book in particular and reading more generally.

Second, the teacher might again lead with a reading of the story, during which a similar sort of discussion to that noted above takes place. However, after this reading, the child is encouraged to provide an emergent reading of the story. It will be an emergent reading because, although the child might convey the general structure and meaning of the story, the precise wording of the story will not be maintained. There will be places where the child reads a word, phrase or sentence from the text but it will not be a fully conventional reading. Such emergent readings, with some limited attention to the conventional print, requires careful listening by the teacher. The teacher needs to identify the strengths that the child displays as the story is recalled and as he or she begins to insert some of the text words into the reading.

Third, the reading of the book starts to resemble the teacher and child reading alongside each other, but not always in unison. At times, therefore, the adult will read and the child will be fractionally behind and echo the words. At other points, the teacher will recognize the growing confidence and ability of the reader and so will encourage the child to lead the reading, the teacher now echoing the child's reading. This drawing back by the teacher will, on occasions, mean that the teacher drops out of the reading altogether. The child therefore reads alone, although the adult is always listening to the reading and ready to support as necessary. During this form of sharing a book, the teacher encourages the child to read or leads the child in the reading, not in any mechanical way, but because the teacher is in tune with the child's intentions and ability with the book being read.

Fourth, the child will have reached a level of attainment that allows him or her to produce a more conventional reading of the book. However, although the child may be more confident and independent as a reader, the teacher will still need to provide support by listening to the child (*hearing children read*). Also, the teacher will note the miscues (*miscue analysis*) that are produced and consider how to respond to them to provide support and encouragement for the reader. A complete section is devoted to *hearing children read*, as it plays such an important part in teacher–child classroom interactions.

During each of these forms of sharing a book, the teacher will discuss with the child aspects of the story, the characters, plot, setting and illustrations. These discussions usually occur before but also after a reading. And as Margaret Meek (1988) demonstrated in her book *How Texts Teach What Readers Learn*, these sometimes include a discussion of the cover, author and publisher. With more fluent readers, the discussion may become the main part of an interaction, with any reading of the text being only a small part of the time spent with a book.

Sharing a book as described in this section is a one-to-one interaction. However, Don Holdaway (1979) debated the use of *shared readings* with big books in the context of a group of children working together. Such a strategy is important for teachers, particularly with younger children. However, many teachers find it useful to progress from group readings with a big book to one-to-one interactions of sharing a book.

Teachers place an emphasis upon sharing a book because it provides an opportunity to support each child's reading to help them develop as readers. Furthermore, it enables the teacher to analyse the reader's developing strategies, strengths and needs.

In the classroom

When 5-year-old Kirsty shared her book *Dizzy Dog* with the teacher in a reception class, there was first a reading of the book by the teacher to Kirsty. Furthermore, during the reading by the teacher, there was a discussion about the story, often using the illustrations, and at appropriate moments during the reading Kirsty was brought into the reading in a natural way:

> *Teacher:* It's fallen all the way down the stairs – bump, bump, bump.
> Now.
>   The dog gets out of the box
>   And what does he try to do?
> *Kirsty:* Stand up.
> *Teacher:* Yes.
>   The dog falls . . .
> *Kirsty:*   . . . over.
> *Teacher:* . . . over.
>   Yes.

Such readings by the teacher with discussions about the text provide the support that enables young children like Kirsty to provide an emergent reading, and later a conventional reading, of the book. The use of a rising intonation as the teacher read 'The dog falls' led Kirsty to provide the completion to the sentence, 'over'. So, although the teacher was reading, Kirsty was being helped to read by being given an opportunity to take part.

Further reading

Campbell, R. (1992) *Reading Real Books*. Buckingham: Open University Press.
As part of a consideration of the real books approach to reading, there is a chapter on sharing a book (although noted at that time as shared reading). Here, too, there is a transcript of a child reading to his teacher, but interestingly the example indicates that, although a sequence of development may be the case with sharing a book, each sharing a book may be more complex than that sequence suggests.

Guppy, P. and Hughes, M. (1999) *The Development of Independent Reading: Reading Support Explained*. Buckingham: Open University Press.
The one-to-one interaction of an adult and a child sharing a book is explored. A reading continuum of five overlapping stages is suggested, with one stage merging with the next as the child develops as a reader. The continuum presented ranges from bookbinding, chiming in, cue talk, assisted reading through to branching out. The balance of responsibility for reading changes as the child gradually takes over the reading of the book.

speaking and listening

Speaking and listening, oracy, oral language, language and talk are descriptors that have been used when discussing this very important aspect of communication in the early years classroom. Speaking and listening are important, as any visitor to a pre-school, nursery or infant classroom would attest: children talking to one another, conversations and imaginary talk in the play area, asking questions, making comments, responding to stories, talking about experiences and interests, expressing opinions, voicing requests and all the time extending knowledge and understanding across a range of areas including literacy. For Whitehead (1999: 120), 'spoken language remains central to the curriculum because it shapes all our thinking'.

To achieve high levels of language, the *role of the teacher* and of other adults in the setting is very important. The *classroom organization and management* will set the scene for worthwhile discourse because the rooms are organized for appropriate activities and planned to encourage the young children to talk with their peers and with adults. The way the teacher actually uses language can encourage and extend the talk of the young children as well as enabling them to develop their thinking. Furthermore, when the more structured *literacy hour* is used with 6- and 7-year-olds in the way it was first suggested (DfEE 1998), then it is expected to be discursive and 'characterised by high quality oral work' (p. 8). Any reduction to simple transmission teaching is not what was originally put forward for this mode of literacy organization; instead, the teacher is advised to use language to encourage and extend the contribution from the children.

Supporting play with language is especially important for young children in various pre-school settings. Whitehead (1999) suggests that introducing 'rhymes, songs, music and dance steps, sayings and proverbs, chants, advertising jingles, poems, jokes, puns and tongue twisters, and so on' (p. 24) is intellectually important for children and extends their language learning. However, these activities are not given as a ten-minute session, but are integrated into the structure of the day. Play with language is inserted into the working of the day whenever it is appropriate as a means of adding to and extending the activities of the children. This is the foundation for literacy learning. When children play with language in this way, they develop *phonemic awareness* knowledge of *onset and rime* and an understanding of aspects of *phonics*. Such learning is achieved not because of any direct teaching, but through the involvement of the children in the playful and subtle use of language.

Many of the literacy activities in the home and the classroom have language discourse as an integral and natural feature. For instance, when *sharing a book* with a young child, the adult will ask questions, encourage comments and questions from the child, respond to the child's comments and talk with the child about the book, characters, setting, plot, author and features of the print. However, the way in which that discourse takes place will be crucial. The children have to be supported in a way that enables them to extend their language and thinking. The adult uses *sharing a book* to encourage an enjoyment of the book, develop a more general interest in books, support literacy development and facilitate the child's use of language.

Each of the story-based literacy activities that have such a central role in early years education include an oral language element that requires careful language strategies by the teacher and supports young children's language development. *Story reading* can be seen simplistically as the adult reading a book to the children. However, it is far more than that because, with young children, it is an interactive reading. The children comment on the story, join in with repetitions that occur, ask questions about aspects of it and take part in a discussion. This helps them to extract meaning from the book, develop thinking and extend their language. *Shared reading* more explicitly requires the teacher to talk with the children about the book, the contents and the print features. However, the nature of the teacher talk is important, as it will influence the children's contributions within the discourse. The same is true of *literature circles*. Although the emphasis here is upon the children expressing feelings towards a story and their understanding of it, this can be supported or hindered by the teacher's own use of language. The teacher needs to provide the support that facilitates the children's use of language. When that happens, the children can use language to extend their understanding and develop their thinking.

Further reading

Corden, R. (2000) *Literacy and Learning Through Talk: Strategies for the Primary Classroom.* Buckingham: Open University Press.
Although this book is concerned with the primary classroom through to 11 years of age, there is much that is useful for the early years settings. Both theory and practice are presented in some detail and many examples of classroom talk are explored. The analysis raises questions for teachers and adults to consider as they work alongside and engage in 'interactive discourse' with young children. Throughout the text, there is an emphasis on teachers who model, demonstrate and scaffold the learning. In particular, there are examples of speaking and listening that lead to reading and writing.

story grammar

Many children have the advantage of having stories read to them at home. Additionally, they may have heard nursery rhymes, played finger games and perhaps witnessed or played other games that involved language stories. And they may have heard events described by adults as well as beginning to tell their own stories about things that have happened to them. All of this enables the children to develop their language. One aspect of this development is that the children will begin to acquire, intuitively, knowledge about story grammar or story structure. They will not have been taught this grammar directly, but their own telling of stories will indicate that knowledge of story grammar is being acquired. Indeed, evidence of such knowledge, albeit limited, is apparent among some 2-year-olds as they tell stories (Applebee 1978).

So what is the story grammar that is being learnt? There are several ways of describing it, although most descriptions include key elements, including the characters, setting (indicating time and/or place) and a plot with a problem or wish leading to some resolution (the plot might contain a number of events or episodes). Stories are also expected to have a beginning, middle and end with the use of a consistent past tense. Applebee (1978) debates the way in which children from 2 to 5 years of age gradually demonstrate greater control over the use of a formal opening phrase ('Once upon a time'), a formal closing ('happily ever after') and the use of a consistent past tense when asked to tell a story. In more sophisticated story structures, description and dialogue might be included.

In most circumstances in the classroom, the structures suggested above would be more than adequate for the teacher to analyse the children's development as storywriters. However, Applebee (1978) extends his analysis to consider how complexities in children's stories are accommodated. Using ideas from Vygotsky (1962), he suggests a series of stages in story development: heaps with unconnected sentences; sequences and primitive narratives in which events are linked to a central core of the story; chains in which there are links between incidents; and, finally, narrative in which there are complex links between events.

Most teachers of young children will not be familiar with such sophisticated analyses of children's stories. However, teachers will be aware that, as children develop as storywriters, they are able to distance themselves from the story. The stories, told or written, are less likely to be about home and family. The stories will also be decreasingly concerned with reality and will be noticeably more complex. And this complexity can be detected in the use of characters, setting and plot.

Some knowledge of story grammar will therefore help the teacher to analyse the children's development as storywriters and to provide support, where necessary, to extend the children's knowledge. In England, the national testing procedures at 7 years of age – the *standard assessment tasks* (*SATs*) – utilize the children's written stories to assess progress in writing. However, beyond the regime of testing, developing the implicit knowledge of story grammar among children is important. Not only does it help children in their own writing, but it also enables them to understand more thoroughly the stories they hear read to them and which they read themselves. This is important because stories have a role in the socialization of children. Stories can pass on the cultural heritage of society, inform about ways of behaving and moral values, and help children to come to terms with fears. More succinctly, Trelease (1995) suggested that the purpose of literature is to provide meaning in our lives.

If the development of a story grammar is important for each child, how can it be encouraged? In part, this question has already been answered because, as noted in the introduction to this section, hearing stories read aloud is instrumental in enabling children to acquire a story grammar. The work of Carol Fox (1993) indicated the extent of that knowledge among pre-school children where they had enjoyed many story readings at home. Therefore, *story reading* in the classroom by the teacher and opportunities for the children to read stories will be used to support their learning of story structure. The provision of a wide variety of *children's books* in the classroom will underpin these readings. *Writing* stories frequently, with encouragement and feedback from the teacher and a real *audience* for the output, will also help children to develop story grammar knowledge.

The use of direct instruction is more problematic. The concern about the direct teaching of a story grammar – as suggested by the National Literacy Strategy (DfEE 1998) in England – is that children might begin to check off the use of characters, setting and plot in their stories, rather than concentrating on the story to be written. Nevertheless, Temple *et al.* (1988) suggested that mini-lessons might have a part to play. These might simply involve the use of appropriate language when, for instance, discussing the cover of a book. So the teacher might ask, 'Who do you think are going to be the main characters in this story?' while showing the children the book cover. This introduces to the young children the term 'characters' and requires them to make explicit their partial understanding of story grammar. Similar discussions while looking at stories written by a child also make explicit the child's knowledge. We need to recall that 2-year-olds demonstrate that story grammar can be learnt incidentally through engagement with stories. It is this provision of *story readings*, and other engagements with stories, that should be emphasized in the classroom.

Further reading

Applebee, A.N. (1978) *The Child's Concept of Story*. Chicago, IL: Chicago University Press.
This book has been very influential in the many debates on story grammar. It is derived from the author's doctoral dissertation, although modified by 'reflection

and reformulation'. It is quite technical and contains a substantial amount of theory. However, there are detailed and informative chapters devoted to young children's developing awareness of story grammar. This analysis is extended subsequently to a chapter on the response of the adolescent to literature.

Fox, C. (1993) *At the Very Edge of the Forest: The Influence of Literature on Storytelling by Children.* London: Cassell.

Carol Fox carries through a detailed study of the stories of five children who each related many stories into a tape-recorder at approximately 4 to 5 years of age. These stories indicated that the children had acquired an understanding of story grammar, as well as many other complex aspects of language. This knowledge appeared to have been acquired because the children had heard many hundreds of stories read to them at home during their pre-school years. Her analysis of the children's story structure in part utilizes ideas from the work of Labov. Such an analysis considers: abstract, the opening remark; orientation, character, setting, time; complicating action, what happened; resolution/result, the outcome of events and coda, the closing of the story. But, Fox argued, such an analysis also includes evaluation, the narrator's stance to what happened.

Temple, C., Nathan, R., Temple, F. and Burris, N.A. (1988) *The Beginnings of Writing.* London: Allyn & Bacon.

This text presents story grammar as part of a more general book on writing in the early years. Chapter nine, entitled 'Writing in the poetic mode', explores children's story writing and utilizes story grammar as a means of doing so. There are many examples of children's stories in this practical book and the authors acknowledge Applebee's ideas. Chapter nine considers suggestions for classroom practice; space is also given over to debate the dilemma of how far the direct teaching of story grammar, if at all, should be utilized.

story readings

The reading of a story by the teacher to the children is a very important part of the school day. In pre-school settings before 5 years of age and in infant classrooms between 5 and 7 years of age, teachers will want to ensure that there is time available each and every day for stories to be read to the children. Indeed, the teacher will want to read more than once a day to the very youngest children. This attention to story reading in school will, in many instances, be a reflection of the time spent on this literacy activity at home, where parents will have read to their children on a regular and frequent basis. But it is not enough to say that this is a very important literacy activity. We need to consider why it is thought to be so important and what the benefits are to the children and what is the nature of the activity.

The results of the longitudinal Children Learning to Read Project in Bristol, directed by Gordon Wells, suggested that story readings by parents had a positive influence upon the literacy development of their children (Wells 1986). Listening to the stories, watching the parent handle the book and being involved in discussions about the stories were all regarded as being important for the child. But we are not just reliant upon the data from that study to inform us of the importance of story readings. Teale (1984), in his survey of studies into home and school story readings, demonstrated the considerable evidence that exists to indicate the positive effects of this literacy activity. Furthermore, many articles and books by Margaret Meek (1982, 1988) have provided us with a detailed analysis and argument to sustain the view that these story readings are fundamental in helping children to learn about reading and to learn to read. Additionally, there have been longitudinal studies of young children at home that have shown the benefits from daily story readings and *sharing a book* (e.g. Campbell 1999a).

An important first part of the benefits to be gained from story reading relates to the enjoyment that children get from this activity. This enjoyment comes from at least two sources. First, there is enjoyment of the stories that are read, which indicates the need for the adult to think carefully about the books that are selected for reading. Second, there is enjoyment of the sharing of the book with the parent at home and the teacher at school; this enjoyment is important because it can motivate children to learn to read. Furthermore, we do not just want to teach children to read, but hope that they will find the contact with books so interesting, worthwhile and enjoyable that they will want to continue reading once their independence as readers has been established.

There are many other benefits to be gained from story reading. Most fundamentally, stories are a way of thinking, as experiences are organized into stories (Bruner 1968). So children are familiar with that form of language structure. There are also very specific concepts about books and print that are learnt. How do you know how to hold and use a book unless you have seen books used by others? Children are very quickly made aware of front-to-back and left-to-right directionality, which are fundamental to reading books written in English, while listening to story readings (Strickland and Morrow 1989b). If the reading allows the child to see the book, then the print features, including the separation of one word from another by a space and the fact that each word is spoken, can also be noted.

During story readings, children will also learn about authorship, especially where the adult reading the story takes time to comment about the writer. In most circumstances, at least initially, it will be stories that are read rather than other book genres. This has the advantage for children that they will come to the story with some notion of story structure. They will do so because they will have heard stories told by others, made up stories themselves and heard stories as part of the rhymes associated with some of the games that they will have played. This background places the children in a good position for developing an implicit knowledge of *story grammar*. By listening to many story readings, their awareness of character, setting and plot, beginning, middle and end, episodes, problem and resolution with consistent use of past tense will be developed. As Carol Fox (1993) demonstrated, children who have heard many story readings develop an awareness of story structure as well as other aspects of language. Such an awareness helps young emerging readers not only to understand the stories that are heard, but it also helps them with their own attempts to write, often in story format. Story readings, then, help children to learn patterns of discourse as well as new words, new syntactic forms and new meanings (Dombey 1988).

If this learning is to take place, then story reading becomes a very important part of the school day. Teachers who recognize its importance will want to avoid it becoming the last thing on the agenda of each school day, or for it to be regarded as a low status activity (Goodwin and Redfern 2000b). Indeed, many teachers find that so much can be developed from, as well as learnt during, story readings that the beginning of the day is a more appropriate time for the readings to take place. Many teachers of very young children read at both the start and end of the day and often in between too.

The selection of the *children's books* to be read is an obvious first step for the teacher. Will a particular story read well? Do the illustrations add to the telling? Will the children enjoy it? Does the story relate to others that have been read? Have several books by the same author been read? Will the children be able to make connections from the stories to their own lives? Is the story more complex than some others that have been read? Trelease (1995) suggested that it is useful occasionally to read above the children's intellectual level and challenge their minds. Of course, not all these questions apply for each book, but they are among the questions that the teacher might consider as books are selected for reading. Because the book selected will have been read by the teacher before reading it to the class, this will enable the teacher to read with enthusiasm, pacing and emphasis, often with eye contact with the children.

Before the reading of the book, the teacher might discuss the cover with the class and note the author; Meek (1988) provides an example of such an introduction with one child. Beyond the cover and the author, part of the discussion might be to make text-to-life connections derived from the characters and setting of the story to the world that is known by the children. All of this gives the children some prior knowledge before the reading begins and helps them with their understanding of the story. The background knowledge also helps the children to make predictions as to the events and the outcomes of the story.

During the reading itself, teachers will probably have several goals. In the pre-school setting, and the reception or kindergarten class, teachers will expect interruptions as the children predict events, ask questions, relate the text to their own experiences and make comments. As a means of facilitating the children's involvement with, and learning from, the story, the teacher might encourage such interruptions. The teacher does so by breaking off the reading to respond to the children, then gradually moving the discussion back to the reading. Later, with older children, the teacher might want to concentrate on the reading of the story and emphasize the discussion at the end of the read. In any discussion after the story has been read, the teacher will not only ask 'what' questions, but also 'why' questions and queries about the children's feelings towards the story.

All of these possibilities indicate not only the importance of the story readings for the children, but also the subtlety of the *teacher's role* during the literacy activity. In particular, teachers recognize that achieving a worthwhile interaction during the story reading, while maintaining the story line, requires considerable skill.

It is clear that there is some discrepancy between the one-to-one interaction of parent and child story reading at home and the teacher and class at school. Can the children all benefit at school? How will they be able to consider aspects of the print if the teacher has the book? One answer is provided by *shared reading* with big books, which can be used to demonstrate print features with younger children while the story is being read. The more general question of whether the children will benefit or not may be in the hands of the teacher. The careful selection of books, the timing and setting of the story reading, and the skilful reading of the story are demonstrated daily by many teachers in schools. The evidence is that children learn about reading, and in part to read, from such organized and well-managed story readings.

In the classroom

When a reception class teacher read the story of *Bertie at the Dentist's* (Bourma 1987) to a class of 5-year-olds, there was inevitably much conversation around the story. Inevitably because very young children always want to comment about the story, ask questions, make predictions and link the story to their own experiences. This can be demonstrated by a brief extract:

> *Teacher*: Bertie nearly fell off.
> *Katrina*: He didn't though.
> *Teacher*: No, he didn't. Why do you think he nearly fell off?
> *Katrina*: Because he's on the edge of the arm.
> *Teacher*: He nearly fell over the edge of the arm, yes.
> 'You sit here, Bertie', said the dentist.
> He began to wash his hands.
> Why do you think he washes his hands? Why does he?
> *Helen*: So you don't get germs.
> *Teacher*: So you don't get germs, that's right. He has to be all lovely and clean. And as Claire said he washes with the soap. Bertie was fascinated. He had never seen soap in a bottle before.
> *Robert*: I have.

Interestingly, the teacher appears to be able to encourage the children to be involved in the story by asking questions and accepting and using comments from them. However, she also maintains the story line by returning to a reading of the book wherever the discussion allows for it to occur naturally.

Further reading

Campbell, R. (2001a) *Read-Alouds with Young Children*. Newark, DE: International Reading Association.
This book starts with an example of a read-aloud, or story reading, from a reception (kindergarten) classroom. The transcript, like others that have been reported (e.g. Dombey 1988), provides opportunities for the reader to gain insights into the way teachers read stories with children interactively. The importance of this activity for young children is debated. The way in which the story reading can lead to other curriculum areas and a range of activities, including aspects of phonics, is then explored.

Teale, W. (1984) Reading to young children: its significance for literacy development, in H. Goelman, A. Oberg and F. Smith (eds) *Awakening to Literacy*. London: Heinemann.

In the chapter by Bill Teale, there is an exploration of the evidence for the use of story reading, the benefits to the children and the nature of the interaction. There are many references to the research that had been conducted on this literacy activity at the time of writing. This review of the literature led Teale to conclude that the 'results from research consistently indicate that being read to is one type of experience that delightfully and effectively ushers a child into the world of literacy' (p. 120).

Trelease, T. (1995) *The New Read-Aloud Handbook*. London: Penguin.

This is a very practical book. After the initial chapter on why reading aloud is so important, there are chapters entitled 'When to begin to read-aloud', 'The stages of read-aloud' and 'The do's and don'ts of read-aloud'. The seven pages of do's and don'ts will appear very simple to experienced and successful teachers, although the comment that the most common mistake in reading aloud is reading too fast remains an important reminder. A large part of the book is devoted to a list of books that might be used for story readings; in the description of these books, Trelease makes links with other similar texts or books by the same author.

sustained silent reading

The idea of a period set aside for the whole class to read silently to themselves appears to be derived from the suggestions of Hunt (1970), although the practice would probably have already been in place. Initially, the abbreviation USSR (uninterrupted sustained silent reading) was used. However, perhaps for historical and cultural reasons, that soon became SSR (sustained silent reading) in the USA. McCracken (1971) was using the abbreviation a year after Hunt's article appeared. So what is sustained silent reading and why is it considered an important school practice?

Stated in its simplest form, sustained silent reading is a period of time set aside each day in the classroom (or even throughout the school) for the children to engage in personal reading. In many classrooms, this reading time is associated with the rule that there is silence or quiet (for the youngest children). Nevertheless, the aim is that noise, or movement around the room, is minimized. If there is to be no movement, then it is a prerequisite that the teacher has organized the classroom to ensure that each child has a personally selected book to read and perhaps another book to hand if the current book is nearly finished. Typically, the teacher should also spend the same time reading, as this provides a model for the children. The children should be informed as to how much time they have for their reading; this is usually about ten minutes, although it can be extended for older children to as much as twenty-five minutes. Teachers of very young children might initially devote less time to this activity, say five minutes, with the intention of increasing it in due course. We shall see later that there are other variations that might be required for teachers with the very youngest of children in school.

The time devoted to sustained silent reading is important because teachers want not only to teach children to read but, having done so, also encourage them to read. Teachers wish to encourage children to read for enjoyment, as well as to read for information. However, there is evidence (e.g. Southgate *et al.* 1981, in their study of 8- and 9-year-olds) that in primary classrooms children do not often have the opportunity to read for any sustained period of time. This led Southgate *et al.* to argue that more opportunities for personal reading should be given to children in the classroom. Now, within the National Literacy Strategy (DfEE 1998), there is still the suggestion that outside of the *literacy hour* time might need to be found for the pupil's own reading for interest and pleasure. It would be strange if teachers, who devote so much time to the teaching of reading, then deny the children any opportunity to engage in that activity.

In terms of organization within the classroom, many teachers find that placing sustained silent reading alongside a natural break in the day (e.g. lunch time) can be useful. After all, the whole class is usually brought together before and after such natural breaks in the day and it is relatively easy to link this with a quiet time spent reading. At the end of the reading, it is useful to spend a short time sharing some of the reading experiences. The teacher can demonstrate this sharing by reading a short section of their own book or telling the children about an interesting phrase or word that was in the story. Children will begin to recognize that teachers have been reflecting on their reading and will want to make a similar contribution to the sharing. However, as McCracken (1971) indicated, there is no formal writing of reports or records kept about the books read; it is a time to enjoy books and to share some of that enjoyment with others in the class.

In many classrooms, sustained silent reading might be referred to using a different term. The acronyms used include DEAR (Drop Everything And Read), ERIC (Everyone or Enjoy Reading In Class) and BEAR (Be A Reader). These may be preferable with younger children, as the word silent no longer appears. This could be important, because although it might be reasonable to have a quiet class engaged with books, it may be difficult to have a silent class. Some young children may mouth the words of a book, even when they believe they are reading silently. In such circumstances, it might be sensible for the teacher to encourage quietness rather than attempting to insist on silence.

When working with very young children, many of whom will not be able to read, at least in the conventional sense, it might be asked whether sustained silent reading is possible, at least in some recognizable form. The answer would appear to be 'yes', although adaptations might need to be considered. For instance, rather than thinking of the children reading, it might be necessary to ask instead whether the children are demonstrating reading-like behaviours – looking through a book, turning the pages, building up the story from the pictures, and so on. And, rather than engaging the whole class on the activity, it might be appropriate to work with a group from the class initially, so that the teacher can demonstrate the activity on a more individual basis. Later, it might be possible to combine the groups so that the whole class is engaged on sustained silent reading.

Many children do appear to get a good deal of enjoyment from this activity, in part because it gives them time to read a book undisturbed by other events. 11-year-old Stephen reflected on his experience with this reading time and commented:

> I enjoy ERIC very much and I look forward to it every day. ERIC was a brilliant idea and I wish someone could have thought of it earlier, then I could of had 10 minutes silent reading for 4 years if it had been thought of when I was in the first year. ERIC has encouraged me to read more at home because it shows how much fun reading can bring.
>
> (Campbell 1990a: 66)

Not all children are as positive, but if it does encourage children like Stephen to read at home and at school, then sustained silent reading will have served its purpose.

In my description of this literacy activity at the beginning of the section, I suggested that it might include the teacher reading at the same time as the children to serve as a role model. The importance of the teacher as a model for reading has often been stressed and there is some research evidence to substantiate it (Wheldall and Entwistle 1988). However, what may be more important is the overall ethos towards literacy, the *reading drive* in the classroom perhaps (Campbell and Scrivens 1995). And what this seems to suggest is that where reading is not given a high priority, then the teacher as a reading model may be vital, but even that might not be successful. However, if there is a strong *reading drive* and the teacher conveys a real interest in, and an enthusiasm for, reading, then acting as a role model may not be essential. In such circumstances, sustained silent reading becomes one of many important literacy activities that can contribute to the children's reading development.

Further reading

Campbell, R. (1990a) *Reading Together*. Milton Keynes: Open University Press.
One of the chapters in this book is devoted to sustained silent reading. There is a discussion of the origins of the activity and guidelines for it in practice are debated. The chapter also includes case studies of two schools in which ERIC and SQUIRT (Sustained Quiet Uninterrupted Reading Time) were part of the daily school routine. The role of the teacher is also considered in a final section on sustained silent reading.

Edelsky, C., Altwerger, B. and Flores, B. (1991) *Whole Language: What's the Difference!* Portsmouth, NH: Heinemann Educational.
This book is about the philosophy and practice of whole language. One part of the book considers 'What whole language looks like in the classroom'. Several scenes are depicted, one of which, scene four (pp. 92–5), explores a classroom where DEAR is in operation. The authors have conveyed the sense of involvement of the children with their books, and teachers will find the description of a classroom in action very useful.

Fenwick, G. (1997) *Sustained Silent Reading in Theory and Practice*. Liverpool: Liverpool John Moores University.
This thirty-page booklet provides a wider debate on sustained silent reading. For those wishing to pursue this topic, there is also a list of references. Of course, sustained silent reading is considered here across all the age ranges, including secondary school. There is, therefore, only a limited focus on the early years. Nevertheless the general issues such as 'What is SSR?' suggested strategies, evaluation, and so on, are useful.

teacher's role

Whenever a debate takes place on the teaching of reading in the early years of primary education, it often focuses on the methods of teaching – or a linked issue of standards of reading. In the early 1990s, the methodology debate focused on phonics teaching and real book approaches. This is an important debate because we do need to think carefully about the ways in which the literacy learning experiences of the children are structured in the classroom. Unfortunately, such is the intensity of the debate that, on occasions, it appears that 'debate' is not the appropriate word to use; Nicholson (1992) goes so far as to suggest that a 'reading war' might more correctly indicate the intensity of the beliefs and arguments. However, in one important sense, such involvement in the debate could mean that a crucial issue risks becoming minimized. This issue concerns the role of the teachers and the importance of their role in enabling children to develop as readers and writers. This importance, especially in relation to the methodology debate, was expressed very succinctly by Frank Smith (1992): 'Methods can never ensure that children learn to read. Children must learn from people' (p. 34).

This emphasis on children learning from people, which sees parents at home and teachers at school as the main contributors to children's reading development, is indicative of current thinking and theory. For instance, Teale and Sulzby (1989) refer to literacy as a complex sociopsycholinguistic activity. The use of this term emphasizes literacy not only as a cognitive and language skill, but one with a social learning dimension. Children need to learn from people and the role of teachers is, therefore, vitally important. More recently, the introduction of the *literacy hour* in England demonstrates the complexity of roles required by the teacher (DfEE 1998), as they are expected to direct, demonstrate, model, scaffold, explain, question, initiate and guide explorations, discuss, investigate ideas, listen to and respond.

Throughout much of this handbook, the importance of teachers is recognized. During the prior planning and leading on to *classroom organization and management*, it is teachers who are responsible for ensuring that the arrangements are satisfactory. The time that is devoted to literacy and the progress of the children is monitored and recorded by the teachers. Furthermore, within most literacy activities, it is teachers who facilitate the children's learning by guiding, supporting, instructing and encouraging. In such circumstances, the knowledge, skills and enthusiasm of teachers are vital.

Teachers need to have knowledge of reading, children and pedagogy. This knowledge is required so that when an unusual circumstance is met, the teacher is able to think the problem through based on information that will help in the analysis and evaluation of the situation. Although it is useful to know the various activities and strategies that might be used to encourage literacy development, teachers also need to have the background knowledge 'about reading in general and about [those] children in particular' (Smith 1978: 3). Such knowledge will provide the basis for the teachers to become more skilful in their practice. And the roles of the teacher as an organizer, manager and teacher are important, because these skills set the scene and provide the background to the children's learning. Finally, teachers need to be enthusiastic about books, reading, writing, learning and teaching, and be able to convey that enthusiasm and vitality to the children.

The need for teachers with knowledge, skills and enthusiasm can be demonstrated more clearly if we briefly consider one of the literacy activities of the classroom. *Story reading* provides a good example, because whichever methodology is argued for, story reading is an important part of the literacy activities that are provided (Campbell 2001a). For the story readings to be successful, the teacher needs to know about the *children's books* that are available. In part, this knowledge will be gleaned from colleagues and from the experience of story readings over the years. The teacher will also know why story readings are important and that knowledge will influence the nature of the story reading. Because the teacher knows about books, and will have read a particular book before presenting it to the children, the actual story reading will demonstrate the skill of the teacher as the book is read. Therefore, the story reading will be delivered in a positive, enthusiastic and skilful manner – the pace of the reading, the intonation and emphasis, the involvement of the children, the eye contact with the class. This will capture the children's attention, interest, thoughts and feelings. In contrast, story readings in the hands of an adult or teacher without such knowledge, skill and enthusiasm are unlikely to be successful and the learning opportunities for the children will consequently be reduced.

Although there have been a few reports of children who appear to have discovered how to read without adult support, in the main it is the quality of the teaching that will determine the success of children's literacy learning. And this teaching quality, although it must be concerned with literacy activities that are appropriate for the child, will be dependent upon the knowledge, skills and enthusiasm of the teacher. The teacher's role is very important.

Further reading

Campbell, R. (1992) *Reading Real Books*. Buckingham: Open University Press.
In this book, I consider the various aspects of a real books approach to reading.
An exploration of the various activities that make up the approach was necessary
because critics were suggesting, incorrectly, either that the approach consisted
merely of real books and shared readings (sharing a book) or that it was a non-
teaching approach. Neither of these views is correct; first, the approach is about
far more than real books and shared readings, although they are important, and,
far from being a non-teaching approach, 'it requires subtle and sophisticated teaching' (p. 81). Throughout the book, the requirement for skilful teaching is emphasized and the final short chapter is devoted to the importance of the teacher.

thematic work/topic work

Many teachers of young children find that a *language experience approach*
helps children to express their thoughts and feelings about objects and
events related to their personal experiences. These thoughts and feelings
can be expressed orally and then written down for themselves and
others to read. Almost inevitably, the children and the teacher together
gradually move from that interest, on the immediate and personal, to
a wider range of interests and questions. Arising out of these interests
and questions are likely to be themes or topics which become important
for the child, a group of children or the whole class. Topic studies are
useful for several reasons. Holdaway (1979: 145) suggested that they
are a 'source of strong motivation to produce various forms of writing'.
This is one of the main reasons for the popularity of this approach with
teachers of young children. Reading and writing for authentic reasons
and which serve a variety of purposes are almost guaranteed when
topic work is used in the classroom.

How should the topics for study be selected? Many teachers are
concerned that if the children always select the topics, they could be
rather restrictive and limiting in the way that they incorporate other
subject areas naturally. Conversely, if the teacher always selects the
topics, then are they really derived from the children's interests? There
might be advantages if the teacher and children can together discuss
and agree the subject of the topic and the path along which that topic
might be developed. Alternatively, in some classes there may be class
themes that the teacher and children develop together, while at other

times the children might be engaged on individual topics. In the topics, the impetus comes from each child with the teacher acting more as a guide and support to help the children in their endeavours. What is important about this work is that it is sustained over a period of time. Judith Slaughter (1992) demonstrates how some teachers achieve sustained involvement in themes derived from the *shared readings* with the class. Very often the use of the *story reading* to develop a theme will be apparent in the early years classroom (Campbell 2001a). We noted in the section on *story reading* how a reading at the beginning of the day can be used to support learning based on a real interest in the story and developing into a theme. Don Holdaway (1979) also provides a case study of a class in which the reading of Eric Carle's *The Very Hungry Caterpillar* was used as the interest and stimulus for the development of a theme on caterpillars and other insects. The sustaining of interest over time is important because it allows for a deep exploration of the subject and extended *writing*. Holdaway suggests that worthwhile written expression can be developed from a subject when the children have a depth of experience and adequate time for reflection. Teachers do have an important role to play in providing the opportunities for that sustained involvement with a theme, rather than allowing superficial attention to be given to a theme before the children move on to another area of interest.

So themes encourage children to read and write for authentic purposes, especially where adequate time is allowed for the children to become intensely involved with the theme. Often, the theme will also require the children to begin to explore other areas of the curriculum as a natural outcome of pursuing the questions generated by the theme (e.g. Hoodless 1998). This extension into other areas of the curriculum is a welcome by-product of thematic work. The Plowden Report (DES 1967) welcomed such flexibility in the curriculum and debated the value of topics, projects or centres of interest as means of integrating the curriculum and stimulating the reading and writing experiences of children. Furthermore, the advent of the National Curriculum in England and Wales (DES 1989) did not halt the use of thematic work, especially with younger children, although initially there were fears that that might have been one outcome of the changes. However, the use of cross-curricular elements was suggested in those initial documents.

Perhaps of greater concern is the recognition that not all topic work facilitates children's literacy development. Robin Alexander (1992) noted that topic work could result in low-level learning, especially if the children merely copied from information books. This was a timely reminder of the teacher's role in monitoring the activities of the children to ensure that worthwhile learning takes place. The issue had been debated by the Bullock Report (DES 1975). It was recognized that when the children were following their own interests, it was important for the teacher to monitor the literacy experiences that were being generated by the topic and to keep a check on the direction of the work. However, here as with most aspects of classroom life, the careful and skilful *classroom organization and management* by the teacher can facilitate the learning opportunities of the children.

Using themes or topics with young children means a range of interests can be covered. This is because children have so many questions to ask based on their curiosity about the wider environment. Teachers need to support such interests by helping with the planning, supporting the inquiry when it is under way, and providing many opportunities for reading and writing (as well as other forms of expression) as the children seek explanations and answers to their questions.

Further reading

Hoodless, P. (ed.) (1998) *History and English in the Primary School: Exploiting the Links*. London: Routledge.
This book deals just with history and its links with English. Furthermore, it extends the ideas right across the primary years. Nevertheless, there are chapters on work with nursery children and later at Key Stage 1. In each of these examples, the extensive learning by the children is made clear. And the involvement of the children in writing about what they had experienced is demonstrated. Those case studies also imply what might be possible as themes and topics from other subject areas are explored.

time for literacy

It might be regarded as self-evident that, for children to develop their understanding and use of literacy, they need to spend time engaged with reading and writing. Harris (1979) suggests that the single most important characteristic of successful reading teaching is the amount of time spent on reading. Additionally Frank Smith (1978: 5) stated that 'to learn to read children need to read', and he made a somewhat similar statement about writing: 'writing is learned by writing' (Smith 1982: 199). These statements emphasize that children need to spend time reading and writing to become proficient readers and writers. An analogy is often made to learning to ride a bicycle or play a piano; to become proficient, many hours have to be devoted specifically to those tasks. The same could be said for literacy. But as Smith (1978: 5) recognized, 'the issue is as simple and as difficult as that'. And the difficult part is that it still requires the teacher to organize and manage the time for the many literacy activities that enable children to develop as literacy users.

In the classroom, there are perhaps three elements that the teacher needs to consider. First, what will be the *classroom organization and management* to ensure that literacy activities are predominant? Second, how much time should the teacher devote to providing and supporting literacy activities for the children? Third, how much time should each child devote to literacy activities? These questions are important because, although we all recognize the need to devote time to literacy to help children to develop as literacy users, as teachers with pressures from many sources, we need constantly to remind ourselves of that fact in the classroom. There is a need to think about, and plan for, time for literacy.

The beginning of such thinking and planning is the classroom organization and classroom management for literacy. In England, the *literacy hour* ensures that one hour a day is devoted to literacy by the teacher; although the children may not be involved in learning throughout that one hour. There is evidence to suggest that a high level of teacher involvement is not always matched by equal literacy involvement by the children (Southgate *et al.* 1981). Nevertheless, the positive feature of the arrangement is that it ensures one hour for literacy every day. However, an hour a day may be inadequate to devote to such an important aspect of learning (Campbell 1998, 1999b). Other literacy activities need to occur beyond the one hour. There are also alternative suggestions to the literacy hour.

Cambourne (1988) recommended a practice that he had seen working effectively in Australian primary schools. This required the first two hours of the school day to be devoted to language. These two hours were divided into four main components. The first component is described as a whole-class focus time lasting approximately ten minutes. This time might be used to read to the class, write in front of the class or to demonstrate to the class some new language activity; the emphasis is on an open sharing of a process, a demonstration rather than direct teaching. Next, for up to twenty-five minutes, there is sustained silent reading; for reception or kindergarten classes, perhaps just ten minutes when the children are involved with a book if unable to read in a conventional sense. Then, for up to an hour there is a period of elective or compulsory activity time. In the former, the children are free to choose from a range of options; in the latter, the activity of the group is chosen by the teacher so as to emphasize or introduce an aspect of language learning. Once a compulsory activity has been organized, the teacher will move around the classroom to interact with the children and offer support where required. In the final part of the language session, there are twenty-five minutes of sharing time. This is a whole-class period when children report on their reading and writing and others listen and question. The teacher can help to develop the sharing time by providing a model of the kind of questions that might be useful.

Describing the practice in some classrooms in the USA, Cunningham and Allington (1998) argued for two and a half hours to be devoted to literacy each day. Here, too, there are four blocks, although these are arranged at various times throughout the day. The forty-minute guided reading block contains both *shared reading* of a big book and *guided reading* in small groups. However, the reading might also lead to other activities such as considering some key words or acting out the story. Thirty minutes is devoted to self-selected reading, which includes a *story reading* by the teacher and a time for *sustained silent reading*, during which the teacher will have a reading conference with a few children individually, perhaps *sharing a book*. Third, there is a thirty-five minute writing time. *Shared writing*, independent writing and reading one's own writing from the author's chair all occur. Finally, there is a thirty-minute word block, which includes considering patterns in words and attention to high-frequency words.

However, some teachers of young children might argue that none of the suggestions go far enough. They might argue that, throughout the school day, the arrangements for all the curriculum areas should be based on the need to encourage language and literacy. In this way, early years classrooms become literacy learning environments. Without a firm foundation in reading and writing, most subsequent learning could be restricted. Therefore, the classroom organization will be premised on the whole day being devoted to the development of literacy; other subjects will be studied in some depth within thematic work/ topic work. Within such a structure, teachers will spend a substantial part of the day facilitating, guiding and supporting the children's literacy. In some literacy sessions, the role of the teacher is obvious. So, in *story reading*, teachers will spend all of their time facilitating literacy. But when the children are engaged in other literacy activities (e.g. writing, thematic/topic work, play activities, etc.), the role of the teacher is to manage and monitor the activities and to extend beyond those roles. Time is given to one-to-one literacy interactions with children, conferences with the children about their writing, and discussions with groups on some aspect of their literacy. Teachers need constantly to be asking themselves how the children can be supported in their literacy development. The likely outcome is that teachers will spend substantial parts of the day – or the complete day – on literacy.

Whitehead (1999) argued that it might be best to think in terms of twenty-four hour literacy. Language and literacy are with us throughout the day and young children may not distinguish between home and various care and educational settings. For these young children, Whitehead suggests that the essential strategies for literacy include talk, play and representation; rhyme, rhythm and language patterns; stories and narrative; and environmental print and messages.

Because time for literacy is so obviously important, there is the danger that we take it for granted. That would be a mistake. It is useful for teachers to check, on a regular basis, the organization of the classroom for literacy, the time they spend themselves on literacy and, most important of all, the extent of the children's involvement and support with reading and writing each day.

Further reading

Cambourne, B. (1988) *The Whole Story: Natural Learning and the Acquisition of Literacy in the Classroom*. Auckland: Ashton Scholastic.
There are many practical points in this text. Cambourne's practical recommendation that the first two hours of the school day should be devoted to language activities serves to emphasize the need to ensure that sufficient time is spent on language and literacy. He gives details of the ways in which the two hours might be arranged to provide a variety of language and literacy experiences for the children.

Cunningham, P. and Allington, R. (1998) *Classrooms that Work: They can All Read and Write*. New York: Longman.
This book provides a considerable amount of practical detail on the four-block framework. For instance, many activities are suggested to support young children's learning during the *word* block. The word wall, and its use, is one of those activities as part of the *classroom print* that is explored in detail. The other three blocks also receive detailed attention.

whole language

Whole language is not a method of teaching reading and writing. It is a set of principles and beliefs about language, learning, teaching, curriculum and community that provide the framework for teachers to organize and manage the classroom to help children develop as literacy users. Kenneth Goodman (1986) has played a major part in furthering these ideas. However, he did not 'found whole language' (Goodman 1992); it was, as he has argued, a 'grassroots creation of professional educators, mostly classroom teachers' (p. 188). So teachers were developing their classroom practices and others were writing about those practices and the principles that lay behind them. Historically, that writing can be traced back to major figures such as Dewey (1916, 1938), although at that time the set of principles and beliefs would not have been described as whole language.

A basic feature of whole language is the view that language is indeed whole and it is best learnt as a whole with meaningful and relevant texts. The reading material, therefore, is *real books* written with a story to tell or something to say, rather than books that might have been written for other purposes, such as teaching phonics or systematically controlling the language in some way – often in reading schemes the controlled introduction of new words. The texts that are used should, therefore, be written typically in natural language. *Environmental print*, which provides an authentic and functional use of language, is used alongside the stories and other books which are meaningful to the children.

The learning experiences that are provided for the children should recognize the active and constructive role of children in the learning process. Therefore, contexts that the children might perceive to be important and which require the need to communicate should be provided, rather than the children being confronted by substantial periods of direct teaching. The learning should not be premised on the teaching of a sequence of skills, but should be based on learning to read by reading predictable texts, where the children are able to generate hypotheses as they transact with the text. [Reading as a transactional process, based on the ideas of Rosenblatt (1976), which expresses the complex relationship between readers and their unique interpretation of the text, is a feature of whole language.] And the children can learn to write by writing, especially where the writing is for a clear purpose.

The teaching that is provided in whole language classrooms does not follow *laissez-faire* principles. The teachers will analyse needs, plan

the teaching, develop the curriculum and monitor and evaluate progress. Therefore, although whole language teachers facilitate, guide,
support, encourage and monitor, rather than teach directly (although
such teaching does occur at appropriate moments), they also ensure that
learning takes place and, in that sense, they are teaching. Importantly
within their planning, they ensure that they have created the necessary
social settings for interactions – often teacher–child interactions – to
occur. Vygotsky's (1978) notion of the zone of proximal development
provides support for the importance of the teacher–child interaction,
in that the teacher can support the child in his or her learning so that,
once internalized, the child can work independently at similar activities.
Inevitably, this means that a whole language teacher does not work
merely as a technician following through the demands of a curriculum
set by a textbook or an externally imposed curriculum, but has to work
as a professional who knows about children and reading (as well as
other curriculum areas).

Teachers develop the curriculum by starting, whenever possible, from
where the children are in their learning and then building from there.
And there needs to be an integration of language with the content of
other subjects, so that finding out about some aspect of science leads
to authentic speech and literacy activities. Thematic units or topics, with
an emphasis on direct experiences in many instances, are common
features of whole language classrooms. Nevertheless, there are activities
in the classroom that most teachers recognize as being highly supportive
of literacy development. The use of *environmental* and *classroom print*, a
library corner, listening area and *writing centre, story reading, shared reading,
sharing a book* and *sustained silent reading*, will all be evident because
they provide many opportunities for reading and writing.

A whole language classroom attempts to create a community of learners
in which the children support each other in their endeavours and the
teacher is available to support and guide the learning and to learn
alongside the children. In a whole language classroom, the teachers may
not be immediately noticeable because, instead of being at the front of
the classroom teaching directly, they usually work alongside individual
children or groups of children. Of course, at certain times (e.g. *story
readings, shared reading*, etc.) they may well work with the whole class.
However, teachers still maintain order and there will be 'a set of rules,
and a structure in their classroom' (Goodman 1986: 74). And the community will extend beyond the classroom and the school because the
teachers like to ensure that there are productive *home–school* links.

Many British teachers who have worked within an integrated infant
classroom will have a feel for the principles and beliefs of whole

language. Indeed, as Kenneth Goodman (1992: 195) has stated, 'the basic concepts of whole language [largely without the term] have become institutionalized in British schools'. The guidance provided for teachers at the foundation stage in England (QCA 2000), which includes the reception aged children, is compatible with maintaining those principles. Nevertheless, teachers who work to whole language principles and beliefs will understand that no two whole language classrooms are alike, because the teachers and children will respond to their own social and cultural contexts. In contrast, two classrooms that appear similar (at least superficially with story readings, writing, topic work, etc.) may in one case have a whole language teacher while the other works more didactically. It will be the way in which the language learning is managed and developed, and the nature of the teacher–child interactions, that will help the observer to detect the whole language teacher.

Further reading

Goodman, K. (1986) *What's Whole in Whole Language?* Portsmouth, NH: Heinemann Educational.
This short text provides a very readable and succinct statement about the nature and process of a whole language approach and, therefore, provides a good introduction to the subject. However, it does more than that. It indicates how whole language might be translated into classroom practice with several very practical suggestions. And, despite being a short text, many teachers find that they return to it constantly for support and ideas.

Edelsky, C., Altwerger, B. and Flores, B. (1991) *Whole Language: What's the Difference?* Portsmouth, NH: Heinemann Educational.
Although Kenneth and Yetta Goodman's names are immediately associated with whole language, many other university staff and primary classroom teachers are developing whole language principles. And this inevitably means there are now many books on the subject. This book was developed from a 1987 article in *The Reading Teacher* by the same three authors. The sections in this text deal with: what whole language is; some misconceptions, including a warning about commercial programmes that have begun to appear in the USA under titles such as 'whole language basals' and 'whole language phonics programs'; historical perspectives; and some scenes of classroom life. The book does more than just provide practical examples, however, as it debates thoroughly the principles of whole language from a theoretical perspective. The authors argue that whole language teachers must have a theoretical base, 'a transactional, sociolinguistic model of language use and a social interactionist view of language acquisition' (p. 108), to be able to develop the practical classroom.

Turbill, J. and Cambourne, B. (eds) (1997) *The Changing Face of Whole Language.* Carlton South, Victoria: Australian Literacy Educators' Association.

This text consists of a collection of articles by educators from Australia, New Zealand, the United States and England. The articles explore the development of whole language philosophy and practice over the past twenty years. They refute some of the ill-informed descriptions and critiques of whole language that have been put forward by those wishing to espouse approaches with more direct teaching and frequent testing. The articles provide support for those teachers wishing to continue to develop their classrooms for whole language learning.

words

Words are an important and obvious part of reading and writing. Here I look at words from four perspectives: words as an organic vocabulary, a word wall in the classroom, key words and words in the National Literacy Strategy (DfEE 1998).

Sylvia Ashton-Warner (1963) indicated in her work with Maori children that an organic vocabulary consists of words of personal and intense meaning for each child. They include words of fear (e.g. ghost and tiger), sex words (e.g. kiss and love), words of locomotion for the boys (e.g. aeroplane and tractor), words of domesticity for the girls (e.g. house and mummy) and others (e.g. school and frog). Bettleheim and Zelan (1981) suggested also that words that have emotional significance for children are readily learnt. Therefore, words which come from children and which are intensely felt might provide a springboard to literacy development.

Ashton-Warner (1963) wrote on a card, for each child, the key organic word that he or she had stated each day. They were what she called 'one look' words; that is, they were intensely felt and, therefore, would be remembered after only one look. The children shared their words with each other, and these words came to be recognized and spoken because they were felt and known. The children's words could be used, Ashton-Warner argued, to develop dynamic material that could then be utilized to form the first reading material for each child. Of course, it was important that the Maori children moved eventually from their own organic reading, 'reaching further and further out to the inorganic and standard reading, [so that] there is a comfortable movement from the inner man outward, from the known to the unknown' (p. 62). So the children moved from their own self-constructed books with organic words, to those constructed by the teacher which reflected the children's words and writing and, finally, to books available from publishers.

When an alphabetic word wall is provided in the classroom, initially it is those organic words or the children's names that are among the first to be included. Typically, the word wall consists of an area of classroom wall where words are arranged alphabetically. Importantly, the word wall is at the children's height so that they can readily use that *classroom print* as they need it. When the youngest of children have their forename on the word wall, that involves talking about the word, creating an alphabetic order, considering names starting with the same letter and noting other features such as similar letters or letter endings. This encourages the children to think about words, letters and *alphabet*. Subsequently, in some settings, the characters or words of interest from stories might be added to the list. Then key words that might be needed for writing can also be included, perhaps in a different and bold colour so that they can be easily picked out from the growing collection of words. As Cunningham and Allington (1998) noted, it is not sufficient to have a word wall, it is important to 'do word walls' (p. 136). The word wall has to be talked about, words added gradually and those words discussed. The word wall is used also as the teacher develops a *shared writing*, for instance the children seek out a word from the wall to include in the writing. However, the words on the wall should to be reviewed from time to time and changed as needed to ensure that the word wall is a creative support for the children (Brabham and Villaume 2001).

Key words are among the words that might be added to a word wall. For instance, we know that ten words – a, and, in, is, it, of, that, the, to, you – make up 25% of all that is read. Therefore, it is useful if those words can become part of a young child's visual memory. The problem is, of course, that such words 'only make any kind of sense in context' (Whitehead 1999: 112). Therefore, the teacher will want to add such words to a word wall, probably in a bold colour, as the children require them. Fortunately, such words are seen by children in books, are noted during *shared readings* and *shared writing* and are used by them as they write. When Alice was 4 years and 5 months old, she decided to write a list of words at home that she knew. Those words were 'to, and, the, up, no, do' (Campbell 1999a: 105), including three of the key words listed above. Her list contained simple words that were part of her visual memory and she indicated as she talked about them that they were words from stories that she had shared with adults. So 'do' had come from the enjoyment of Eric Carle's (1988) book *Do You Want to be My Friend?* Noting and talking about the words in context helps children to acquire a visual memory of key words.

The National Literacy Strategy (DfEE 1998) addresses the idea of key words and word level work in a somewhat different way. There is a list of 'high frequency words to be taught as "sight recognition" words through reception year to year two' (pp. 60–1). The list includes forty-eight words to be taught to the 5-year-olds in the reception year and approximately 150 words to be learned between Years 1 and 2. Then there is the word level work that is part of the second fifteen minutes of the *literacy hour*. In that word level work, *phonics, spelling* and vocabulary are taught. The teaching sequence is set out clearly and it may be that some teachers will teach key words directly rather than considering them in context.

So words are important. Young children notice them during *story readings* at home, begin to learn about the nature of them as they explore the writing of their own name over a period of months and see them in *environmental print*. At school their attention is brought to words during *shared readings* and words are talked about during *shared writing*. They will also see words on the word wall and use them as they write, with conventional and *invented spellings*. And throughout all of these activities, adults will talk with the children about words and therefore support their learning.

Further reading

Ashton-Warner, S. (1963) *Teacher*. London: Secker & Warburg.
This book details the author's use of a key or organic vocabulary with Maori infant school children aged 4 to 6 years in New Zealand. Inevitably, literacy was just a part of her teaching and, therefore, the book is about more than just organic vocabulary. It tells about her teaching in various classrooms as she attempted to help build a bridge from one culture to another, from Maori to European. It was a process she described as 'creative teaching'; the extension of her teaching outside of the classroom where nature and number were learnt is vividly portrayed. The principles that Ashton-Warner put forward are regarded as being part of a *language experience approach* and, as Veatch (1991) argued, one of the antecedents to *whole language*.

Cunningham, P. and Allington, R. (1998) *Classrooms that Work: They Can All Read and Write*. New York: Longman.
One of the features of this practical book is the detailed discussion about word walls. As noted above, the authors indicate that it is insufficient to have word walls; teachers have to do word walls. They suggest limiting the words on the wall to common words in use and only adding five in any one week. Making sure each word can be seen, practising the words in a variety of ways, reviewing

the words that are on the wall and ensuring that wall words are being spelled correctly by the children are also suggested.

writing

Although this book's title is *Reading in the Early Years Handbook*, it is inevitable that writing will form part of the text, because the development of reading and writing are so closely linked. For instance, a child's writing of his or her own name is an important early indicator of literacy development (Campbell 1999a). Although most of the sections in this handbook have a title that suggests some aspect of reading, there are some, like this one, which are more specifically focused on writing. But the link extends beyond these few sections on writing or aspects of writing because several of the reading sections also make connections to writing. Perhaps we should remind ourselves of these connections.

We have noted that teachers who use a *language experience* approach emphasize the link between oral and written language and that children do, with teacher support, provide their own reading material by writing about that which has been experienced. For some teachers, these early attempts at writing can be facilitated, it is argued, by encouraging the children to use an organic vocabulary. The demonstration of writing during a *shared writing* time or support for a few children with *guided writing* have also been noted. But we can move away from the specific and recognize that teachers of young children will create a classroom organization to ensure that many opportunities for writing are made available. The *writing centre* is merely an obvious and named part of that provision; *play activities* are also organized to encourage writing by the children. However, the provision for writing can be encouraged before school is started and we have seen how one *home–school links* project emphasized writing, together with *environmental print* and *sharing a book*, as a means of facilitating *emerging literacy*. Some emphasis upon writing in a book that is about reading should not be a surprise, as a *real books approach* and *whole language* both argue for many opportunities for authentic writing to support children in their quest for meaning and an ability to communicate. Finally, writing is used within a *reading recovery* programme for those children perceived to need extra individual support, and it becomes a central part of *thematic work/topic work* where children are using writing as well as reading to assist their learning in other areas.

Writing, therefore, is very much a part of many of the literacy activities in the classroom. But the teacher will need to provide real purposes for writing and a variety of *audiences*. A starting point could be when children write about their experiences and that writing then forms part of a diary or journal. Additionally, writing letters can be employed usefully because there will be an obvious audience for the children. In the book *Writing with Reason* edited by Nigel Hall (1989), there are many interesting examples of children's letter writing in chapters very much based on classroom practices. Furthermore, because so much of the children's initial involvement with reading is centred on stories, that *genre* can also be used for some of their writing. Children can rewrite stories they have already heard as well as produce stories of their own; stories which can be shared with others in a number of ways. They can be included in the *library corner* as sheets on display, as book reviews, or new stories can be produced in a book format. Chris Burman (1990) includes sections on class and individual *book-making* in her writing about organizing for reading in the early years classroom.

Not all the writing will be in the expressive or poetic modes. The Bullock Report (DES 1975) made use of James Britton's model of writing, which suggested three main categories of writing: poetic, expressive and transactional. Children write in the transactional mode when they produce writing about observations that they have made – for example, a record of the birds which visit the bird table (SCDC 1989) or as a report of a scientific experiment. And they can prepare plans for building with bricks or making a model. In such writing, the children soon understand that a story structure does not apply and they respond to this form of writing with different conventions. The children may have already written shopping lists with their parents at home and they can work alongside their teacher to do the same as they prepare for cooking. They can conclude such sessions by writing up the recipe so that others can follow the instructions.

So the teacher will organize the classroom to provide for many opportunities for authentic writing for real audiences. And in the busy classroom, the teacher has to ensure that opportunities to engage in extended writing are made available. Occasionally, the pressures of the curriculum can restrict writing to short bursts. The teacher needs to encourage some extended writing and a variety of writing but what about the actual process of writing? The work of Donald Graves (1983) has been especially influential. In particular, he has popularized what has become known as 'process writing'. This suggests that writing involves a rehearsal (i.e. where ideas are sorted out), composing (i.e. where a first draft is prepared), redrafting (i.e. where the writing is developed and refined) and editing (i.e. where spelling, *punctuation* and presentation, which might include handwriting, are perfected). This complete process, however, may not always apply. A shopping list is an example where, although we might need to rehearse and compose the list, redrafting may or may not be required depending on whether items need to be added to or subtracted from the list, and an editing stage is most unlikely.

The number of stages to writing a letter may depend upon the audience and our relationship with that audience. But how do young children learn about such a process? First, the teacher can demonstrate the process during a *shared writing*. During such writing, the teacher is able to demonstrate that the first attempts at writing often have to be refined to achieve what the writer really wants. Second, conferencing on writing, between the teacher and an individual child, provides an opportunity for the teacher to bring to the child's attention the possibilities for redrafting and editing. Such teaching will enable the child to develop these writing strategies for use when writing independently.

Writing is a major part of the early years classroom because the ability to communicate to others is a crucial part of every child's learning. However, while writing, children have to attend very carefully to the letters, words, sentences, and so on. That attention to the written language will support them subsequently when they read. Reading and writing are very closely linked and the teacher of young children will want to ensure that there are many opportunities to engage with both.

In the classroom

Teachers who provide many opportunities for young children to write find that those children develop a confidence when putting their thoughts on to paper. Of course, this means that the very youngest children may produce a page of vertical lines (|||||) as their writing emerges from earlier scribbles. Later, the children may produce writing such as that produced by 4-year-old John: 'I c s u'. He told his teacher that it said 'I can see you'. Kevin's use of the first letter or dominant sound to produce his writing is typical of many young writers as they develop their *invented spellings*. Many teachers become extremely competent at deciphering such writing. For instance, the first letter of the words represented two of John's 'words', which is a common feature of children's writing initially. In addition, one word was written in a conventional form, 'I', and the last word was represented by a letter that is also the sound of the complete word. Being aware of the way in which young children construct their writing enables teachers to read much of what is written in the classroom. Furthermore, the children develop gradually towards more conventional representations of writing, which helps the teacher to read the writing and to support its further development.

Further reading

Graves, D. (1983) *Writing: Teachers and Children at Work*. Portsmouth, NH: Heinemann.

Graves, D. (1994) *A Fresh Look at Writing*. Portsmouth, NH: Heinemann.

Many books on the teaching of writing have been published since the early work of Donald Graves. Yet his work is still worth reading, as it sets out the details of process writing. The purpose of his first book was 'to assist classroom teachers with children's writing', and many teachers would attest that it did achieve that purpose. Aspects that are covered include starting to teach writing, making the writing conference work, helping children learn the skills they need, understanding how children develop as writers and documenting children's writing development. In his later book, Graves refines some of his ideas and develops them further.

Evans, J. (ed.) (2001) *The Writing Classroom: Aspects of Writing and the Primary Child 3–11*. London: David Fulton.

The fifteen chapters in this book deal with writing throughout the primary age group. Nevertheless, the range of topics covered makes it a useful text not only for that wider age group, but also for the early years. Using nursery rhymes and other rhymes as a way into writing, punctuation, onset and rime, poetry and non-fiction are among the many areas covered. Therefore, many of the chapters can be linked directly to the sections in this handbook. And each of the chapters contains sufficient detail to add to the debates.

writing centre

As part of the setting or classroom organization, it is useful to have a writing centre. This is especially the case when the teacher utilizes some form of integrated day in the classroom in which the children move from activity to activity throughout much of the day. In such circumstances, the teacher will want to ensure that many of the activities that the children spend time on encourage an involvement with literacy. The writing centre will be one of those areas that encourages literacy and, at least initially, will require little in the way of space and resources for it to be established.

To begin with, the writing centre will require a table and some chairs. However, as Morrow (1989) suggested, the addition of a message board is useful, as it can be used to exchange messages between the teacher and the children, and the teacher can provide information for the class by posting notices. Importantly, the message/noticeboard can demonstrate the role of writing as a means of communication. The children can be attracted to the writing centre by the variety of writing materials that the teacher makes available. Therefore, adequate quantities of writing instruments (e.g. pencils, coloured pencils, crayons, felt-tipped pens and biros, as well as chalks and chalk boards) should be made available. Similarly, a range of materials to write on (e.g. lined and unlined paper in various sizes, shapes and colours) should be provided. It is also useful to introduce different materials from time to time to refresh the children's interest. The introduction of a typewriter, keyboard or word processor is likely to increase the children's interest in writing. Often, such equipment encourages discussion and collaborative writing. In addition to the materials used directly for writing, it is helpful to have scissors, glue and other materials available, close to the centre, so that the children can produce greetings cards, posters and books where the purpose of the writing suggests that to be appropriate.

Teachers and other adults need to spend some time at the writing centre to encourage the purposeful use of the area. So brief visits to demonstrate/model writing, observe, question and suggest might all be part of the teacher's role (Campbell 1996). For instance, if an adult visits a writing centre in a pre-school setting and talks aloud about writing a shopping list and writes a list, almost inevitably young children will try to do the same. The children will produce shopping lists. Indeed, a wide variety of writing might be produced at the writing centre – stories, poems, letters, greeting cards and messages. Other writing might include various lists, recipes, directions and notices, as well as personal writing by the children in their own diaries or journals, especially when used by older children at Key Stage 1.

The writing is encouraged by the teacher's presence and by the authenticity of the writing, which has a purpose and an *audience*. Sheila Taylor, a reception class teacher, in her description of a writing table (or centre), noted the importance of an audience for the children's writing and she indicated the range of audiences that she developed (SCDC 1989). She demonstrated the importance of the other children in the class as an audience for the writing, as well as other classes, the headteacher and parents. The inclusion of her daughter at university, as a recipient for letters, indicated the ingenuity to which teachers will stretch to obtain an authentic audience – the children apparently knew her daughter.

Like most other literacy provision, the writing centre requires an initial careful organization. That organization then needs to be sustained by a sensitive management of the literacy events that take place. The writing centre, like other areas and activities in the early years classroom, or as part of a *library corner* or literacy centre, requires support from the teacher. The teacher will act as a demonstrator of writing, but also as a guide and support for the children's own writing, which will facilitate the children's literacy development.

Further reading

SCDC (1989) *Becoming a Writer: The National Writing Project.* Walton on-Thames: Nelson.

Although there is reference to writing centres in many books on the teaching and learning of writing with young children, it is seldom backed up with substantial information about the centre at work. The description by Sheila Taylor of the writing table (centre) in her reception classroom is one example where we do have more details of what might be involved in the setting up and subsequent management of a centre to encourage children's writing.

your classroom

At the end of this book, it is appropriate to bring together some of the ideas from the various sections. However, before doing so we need to recognize that the sections contain a variety of topics. There are approaches or philosophies for the teaching and learning of literacy (e.g. *whole language*), aspects of *classroom organization and management* (e.g. *library corner*), specific activities to encourage literacy development (e.g. *story reading*) and more detailed aspects of literacy learning (e.g. *invented spelling*). Of course, from time to time in the educational and national press, a specific literacy activity might be offered as the answer to all literacy learning. And for teachers in England, there is the *literacy hour* to be followed with children in Years 1 and 2 (DfEE 1998) – but not to be followed literally step-by-step (Frater 2000). However, teachers recognize that a range of activities needs to be provided in the classroom to support children's literacy learning. Of course, these activities are selected because they meet the requirements of the approach that has been adopted by the teacher. But it is a selection of activities rather than reliance upon a single activity that is provided in the classroom.

However, as teachers we need to recognize that it is each one of us that is likely to be crucial in supporting children's learning. We need to be knowledgeable about children and about literacy, so that our decision-making in the classroom is informed decision-making. Undoubtedly, too, we need to be skilful when it comes to *classroom organization and management* of events within the room. And our enthusiasm for literacy should be such that it motivates the children and makes them enthusiastic for literacy.

Clearly, the classroom should be a hive of activity related to literacy. Reading and writing should feature prominently throughout the day as the children engage with interesting print materials and write with a purpose for an authentic audience. I shall refrain from listing again all the activities, features and aspects of literacy that should be commonplace in the classroom, as that is what this book has been about. But each classroom has to be an area for literacy learning. This book has attempted to highlight the importance of that learning and to provide suggestions that will enhance children's literacy.

Further reading

Minnis, P. (2000) Literacy in reception classes, in R. Drury, L. Miller and R. Campbell (eds) (2000) *Looking at Early Years Education and Care*. London: David Fulton.
Pauline Minnis shows in her chapter in this book the variety of literacy activities that were offered in one reception classroom. As she follows Kieran during his first year at school, we see how *story reading, shared reading, shared writing* and many others activities all support his learning. She provides an insight into the careful organization and management of a classroom to encourage literacy learning.

Campbell, R. (1999a) *Literacy from Home to School: Reading with Alice*. Stoke-on-Trent: Trentham Books.
This book is about the variety of activities that support literacy learning in the home: *story readings* and repeat readings of those stories, *sharing a book*, opportunities for *writing, nursery rhymes* and songs, *environmental print* and other activities that are seen to support a young child's literacy development. It is meaningful and enjoyable reading and writing, rather than the direct teaching of phonics or the prolific use of worksheets, that is evident. The story of Alice's reading development has implications for teachers of young children.

REFERENCES

Adams, M.J. (1990) *Beginning to Read: Thinking and Learning about Print*. Cambridge, MA: MIT Press.

Alexander, R. (1992) *Policy and Practice in Primary Education*. London: Routledge.

Anderson, H. (1993) Creative full stop. *Times Educational Supplement*, 18 June, pp. vi–vii.

Anderson, H. (1995) About as big as the library: using quality texts in the development of children as readers and writers, in E. Bearne (ed.) *Great Expectations*. London: Cassell.

Applebee, A.N. (1978) *The Child's Concept of Story*. Chicago, IL: Chicago University Press.

Arnold, H. (1982) *Listening to Children Reading*. Sevenoaks: Hodder & Stoughton.

Ashton-Warner, S. (1963) *Teacher*. London: Secker & Warburg.

Baghban, M. (1984) *Our Daughter Learns to Read and Write*. Newark, DE: International Reading Association.

Bain, R., Fitzgerald, B. and Taylor, M. (eds) (1992) *Looking into Language: Classroom Approaches to Knowledge about Language*. London: Hodder & Stoughton.

Barratt-Pugh, C. and Rohl, M. (2000) *Literacy Learning in the Early Years*. Buckingham: Open University Press.

Barrs, M. and Johnson, G. (1993) *Record-keeping in the Primary School*. London: Hodder & Stoughton.

Barrs, M. and Pidgeon, S. (eds) (1998) *Boys and Reading*. London: Centre for Language in Primary Education.

Baxter, J. (2001) *Making Gender Work*. Reading: Reading and Language Information Centre, University of Reading.

Beard, R. (1999) *National Literacy Strategy: Review of Research and other Related Evidence*. London: Department for Education and Employment.

Beard, R. and Oakhill, J. (1994) *Reading By Apprenticeship? A Critique of the Apprenticeship Approach to the Teaching of Reading*. Slough: NFER.

Bennett, J. (1991) *Learning to Read with Picture Books*, 4th edn. Stroud: Thimble Press.

Bettleheim, B. and Zelan, K. (1981) *On Learning to Read*. Harmondsworth: Penguin.

Beverton, S., Hunter-Carsch, M., Obrist, C. and Stuart, A. (1993) *Running Family Reading Groups*. Widnes: UK Reading Association.

Bissex, G. (1980) *GNYS AT WRK: A Child Learns to Read and Write*. Cambridge, MA: Harvard University Press.

Bloom, W. (1987) *Partnership with Parents in Reading*. Sevenoaks: Hodder & Stoughton.

Brabham, E. and Villaume, S. (2001) Building walls of words. *The Reading Teacher*, 54: 700–2.

➤Browne, A. (1996) *Developing Language and Literacy 3–8*. London: Paul Chapman.

Browne, A. (1998) *A Practical Guide to Teaching Reading in the Early Years*. London: Paul Chapman.

Brownjohn, S. (1998) *Does It Have to Rhyme?* Sevenoaks: Hodder & Stoughton (first published 1980).

Bruner, J. (1968) Two modes of thought, in J. Mercer (ed.) *Language and Literacy from an Educational Perspective. Vol. 1: Language Studies*. Milton Keynes: Open University Press.

Bryant, P. and Bradley, L. (1985) *Children's Reading Problems: Psychology and Education*. Oxford: Oxford University Press.

Burman, C. (1990) Organizing for reading 3–7, in B. Wade (ed.) *Reading for Real*. Buckingham: Open University Press.

Burt, M. (1893) Communications: experiments in the teaching of reading. *The Dial*, 16 March, pp. 172–3.

Butler, D. (1998) *Babies Need Books: Sharing the Joy of Books with Children from Birth to Six*. Portsmouth, NH: Heinemann.

Calkins, L. (1983) *Lessons from a Child: On the Teaching and Learning of Writing*. Portsmouth, NH: Heinemann.

Cambourne, B. (1988) *The Whole Story: Natural Learning and the Acquisition of Literacy in the Classroom*. Auckland: Ashton Scholastic.

Campbell, R. (1988) *Hearing Children Read*. London: Routledge.

Campbell, R. (1990a) *Reading Together*. Buckingham: Open University Press.

Campbell, R. (1990b) *Phonics, Standards and Real Books*. Exmouth: Rolle Faculty of Education, University of Plymouth.

Campbell, R. (1992) *Reading Real Books*. Buckingham: Open University Press.

Campbell, R. (1993) *Miscue Analysis in the Classroom*. Widnes: UK Reading Association.

Campbell, R. (1994) The teacher response to children's miscues of substitution. *Journal of Research in Reading*, 17: 147–54.

Campbell, R. (1996) *Literacy in Nursery Education*. Stoke-on-Trent: Trentham Books.

Campbell, R. (1998) A literacy hour is only part of the story. *Reading*, 32(1): 21–3.

Campbell, R. (1999a) *Literacy from Home to School: Reading with Alice.* Stoke-on-Trent: Trentham Books.

Campbell, R. (1999b) Four blocks for literacy. *Reading,* 33(1): 30–4.

Campbell, R. (2001a) *Read-Alouds with Young Children.* Newark, DE: International Reading Association.

Campbell, R. (2001b) 'I can write my name I can': looking at the importance of the writing of own name. *Education 3–13,* 29(1): 9–14.

Campbell, R. and Scrivens, G. (1995) The teacher role during sustained silent reading. *Reading,* 29(2): 2–4.

Campbell, R. and Stott, G. (1994) Children's experience of learning to read. *Reading,* 28(3): 8–13.

Campbell Hill, B., Johnson, N. and Schlick Noe, K. (eds) (1995) *Literature Circles and Response.* Norwood, MA: Christopher-Gordon.

Carter, R. (ed.) (1990) *Knowledge about Language and the Curriculum: The LINC Reader.* London: Hodder & Stoughton.

Chambers, A. (1993) *Tell Me: Children, Reading and Talk.* Stroud: Thimble Press.

Cherrington, V. (1990) Developing contexts for writing non-narrative, in B. Wade (ed.) *Reading for Real.* Buckingham: Open University Press.

Chukovsky, K. (1963) *From Two to Five.* Berkeley, CA: University of California Press.

Clausen, C. (1995) A delightful journey: literature circles in first grade, in B. Campbell Hill, N. Johnson and K. Schlick Noe (eds) *Literature Circles and Response.* Norwood, MA: Christopher-Gordon.

Clay, M. (1972) *Reading: The Patterning of Complex Behaviour.* London: Heinemann.

Clay, M. (1985) *The Early Detection of Reading Difficulties.* Auckland: Heinemann.

Clay, M. (1993) *Reading Recovery: A Guidebook for Teachers in Training.* London: Heinemann.

CLPE (1988) *The Primary Language Record.* London: Centre for Language in Primary Education.

CLPE (1999) *Learning to be Literate: Gaining Control Writing at KS1.* London: Centre for Language in Primary Education.

Clymer, T. (1963) The utility of phonic generalizations in the primary grades. *The Reading Teacher,* 16: 252–8.

Coleman, C. (1991) We're all going on a summer holiday, in N. Hall and L. Abbott (eds) *Play in the Primary Curriculum.* London: Hodder & Stoughton.

Coles, M. (1990) The 'real books' approach: is apprenticeship a weak analogy? *Reading,* 24(2): 50–6.

Combs, M. (1987) Modeling the reading process with enlarged texts. *The Reading Teacher,* 40: 422–6.

Cookson, P. (2000) *The Works: Every Kind of Poem You will Ever Need for the Literacy Hour.* London: Macmillan Children's Books.

Corden, R. (2000) *Literacy and Learning through Talk Strategies for the Primary Classroom.* Buckingham: Open University Press.

Cullinan, B. (1989) Literature for young children, in D. Strickland and L.M. Morrow (eds) *Emerging Literacy: Young Children Learn to Read and Write*. Newark, DE: International Reading Association.

Cunningham, P. and Allington, R. (1998) *Classrooms that Work: They Can All Read and Write*. New York: Longman.

Dahl, K., Scharer, P., Lawson, L. and Grogan, P. (2001) *Rethinking Phonics: Making the Best Teaching Decisions*. Portsmouth, NH: Heinemann.

David, T., Raban, B., Ure, C., Gouch, K., Jago, M., Barriere, I. and Lambirth, A. (2000) *Making Sense of Early Literacy: A Practitioner's Perspective*. Stoke-on-Trent: Trentham Books.

Davis, C. and Stubbs, R. (1988) *Shared Reading in Practice*. Milton Keynes: Open University Press.

Dearing, R. (1993) *The National Curriculum and its Assessment: An Interim Report*. London: National Curriculum Council.

DES (1967) *Children and their Primary Schools (The Plowden Report)*. London: HMSO.

DES (1975) *A Language for Life (The Bullock Report)*. London: HMSO.

DES (1988a) *Report of the Committee of Inquiry into the Teaching of English Language (The Kingman Report)*. London: HMSO.

DES (1988b) *English for Ages 5 to 11 (The Cox Report)*. London: HMSO.

DES (1989) *English in the National Curriculum*. London: HMSO.

Dewey, J. (1916) *Democracy and Education*. New York: Macmillan.

Dewey, J. (1938) *Experience and Education*. New York: Macmillan.

DfEE (1998) *The National Literacy Strategy: Framework for Teaching*. London: Department for Education and Employment.

DfEE (1999) *The National Curriculum Handbook for Primary Teachers in England Key Stages 1 and 2*. London: Department for Education and Employment.

Doake, D. (1988) *Reading Begins at Birth*. Richmond Hill, Ontario: Scholastic Canada.

Dombey, H. (1988) Partners in the telling, in M. Meek and C. Mills (eds) *Language and Literacy in the Primary School*. Lewes: Falmer Press.

Dombey, H., Moustafa, M. and CLPE (1998) *Whole to Part Phonics: How Children Learn to Read and Spell*. London: Centre for Language in Primary Education.

Donaldson, M. (1989) *Sense and Sensibility*. Reading: Reading and Language Information Centre, University of Reading.

Drury, R. (2000) Bilingual children in the pre-school years: different experiences of early learning, in R. Drury, L. Miller and R. Campbell (eds) *Looking at Early Years Education and Care*. London: David Fulton.

Dutton, H. (1991) Play and writing, in N. Hall and L. Abbott (eds) *Play in the Primary Curriculum*. London: Hodder & Stoughton.

Edelsky, C., Altwerger, B. and Flores, B. (1991) *Whole Language: What's the Difference?* Portsmouth, NH: Heinemann.

Evans, J. (ed.) (1998) *What's in the Picture? Responding to Illustrations in Picture Books*. London: Paul Chapman.

Evans, J. (ed.) (2001) *The Writing Classroom: Aspects of Writing and the Primary Child 3–11*. London: David Fulton.

Fenwick, G. (1997) *Sustained Silent Reading in Theory and Practice*. Liverpool: Liverpool John Moores University.

Ferreiro, E. and Teberosky, A. (1982) *Literacy before Schooling*. Portsmouth, NH: Heinemann.

Fisher, R. (ed.) (1998) *Hours of Literacy*. Teaching in Practice Series (TIPS) No. 4. Royston: UK Reading Association.

Fountas, I. and Pinnell, G. (1996) *Guided Reading: Good First Teaching for All Children*. Portsmouth, NH: Heinemann.

Fox, C. (1993) *At the Very Edge of the Forest: The Influence of Literature on Storytelling by Children*. London: Cassell.

Frater, G. (2000) Observed in practice. English in the National Literacy Strategy: some reflections. *Reading*, 34(3): 107–12.

Geekie, P., Cambourne, B. and Fitzsimmons, P. (1999) *Understanding Literacy Development*. Stoke-on-Trent: Trentham Books.

Gentry, R. (2000) A retrospective on invented spelling and a look forward. *The Reading Teacher*, 54(3): 318–32.

Gibbons, L. (1999) Literature for children, in B. Thompson and T. Nicholson (eds) *Learning to Read: Beyond Phonics and Whole Language*. Newark, DE: International Reading Association.

Glynn, T. (1980) Parent–child interaction in remedial reading at home, in M.M. Clark and T. Glynn (eds) *Reading and Writing for the Child with Difficulties*. Birmingham: University of Birmingham, Educational Review.

Glynn, T., Crooks, T., Bethune, N., Ballard, K. and Smith, J. (1989) *Reading Recovery in Context*. Auckland: New Zealand Department of Education.

Goddard, N. (1974) *Literacy: Language Experience Approach*. London: Macmillan Educational.

Gollasch, F.V. (ed.) (1982a) *Language and Literacy: The Selected Writings of Kenneth S. Goodman. Vol. I: Process, Theory, Research*. London: Routledge.

Gollasch, F.V. (ed.) (1982b) *Language and Literacy: The Selected Writings of Kenneth S. Goodman. Vol. II: Reading, Language and the Classroom Teacher*. London: Routledge.

Goodacre, E.J. (undated) *Hearing Children Read*. Reading: Centre for the Teaching of Reading, University of Reading.

Goodman, K. (1969) Analysis of reading miscues: applied psycholinguistics. *Reading Research Quarterly*, 5: 652–8.

Goodman, K. (1986) *What's Whole in Whole Language?* Portsmouth, NH: Heinemann.

Goodman, K. (1992) I didn't found whole language. *The Reading Teacher*, 46: 188–99.

Goodman, K. (1993) *Phonic Phacts*. Richmond Hill, Ontario: Scholastic Canada.

Goodman, K. (1994) Reading, writing and written texts: a transactional sociopsycholinguistic view, in R. Ruddell, M. Ruddell and H. Singer (eds) *Theoretical Models and Processes of Reading*. Newark, DE: International Reading Association.

Goodman, K., Shannon, P., Freeman, Y. and Murphy, S. (1988) *Report Card on Basal Readers*. New York: Richard C. Owen.

Goodman, K., Bird, L.B. and Goodman, Y. (eds) (1991) *The Whole Language Catalog*. Sauta Rosa, CA: American School Publishers.

Goodman, Y. (1989) Evaluation of students, in K. Goodman, Y. Goodman and W. Hood (eds) *The Whole Language Evaluation Handbook*. Portsmouth, NH: Heinemann.

Goodman, Y. (ed.) (1990) *How Children Construct Literacy: Piagetian Perspectives*. Newark, DE: International Reading Association.

Goodman, Y. (1991) The history of whole language, in K. Goodman, L.B. Bird and Y. Goodman (eds) *The Whole Language Catalog*. Santa Rosa, CA: American School Publishers.

Goodman, Y. and Altwerger, B. (1981) *Print Awareness in Pre-School Children: A Working Paper*. Tucson, AZ: Arizona Centre for Research and Development, University of Arizona.

Goodman, Y., Watson, D. and Burke, C. (1987) *Reading Miscue Inventory: Alternative Procedures*. New York: Richard C. Owen.

Goodwin, P. and Redfern, A. (2000a) *Non-fiction in the Literacy Hour*. Reading: Reading and Language Information Centre, University of Reading.

Goodwin, P. and Redfern, A. (2000b) *Reading Aloud to Children*. Reading: Reading and Language Information Centre, University of Reading.

Goswami, U.C. (1994) Phonological skills, analogies, and reading development. *Reading*, 28(2): 32–7.

Goswami, U.C. and Bryant, P. (1990) *Phonological Skills and Learning to Read*. Hove: Lawrence Erlbaum Associates.

Graham, J. (1991) *Pictures on the Page*. Sheffield: NATE.

Graves, D. (1983) *Writing: Teachers and Children at Work*. Portsmouth, NH: Heinemann.

Graves, D. (1994) *A Fresh Look at Writing*. Portsmouth, NH: Heinemann.

Gregory, E. (1996) *Making Sense of a New World: Learning to Read in a Second Language*. London: Paul Chapman.

Guppy, P. and Hughes, M. (1999) *The Development of Independent Reading: Reading Support Explained*. Buckingham: Open University Press.

Hall, N. (1987) *The Emergence of Literacy*. Sevenoaks: Hodder & Stoughton.

Hall, N. (ed.) (1989) *Writing with Reason: The Emergence of Authorship in Young Children*. Sevenoaks: Hodder & Stoughton.

Hall, N. (1998) *Punctuation in the Primary School*. Reading: Reading and Language Information Centre, University of Reading.

Hall, N. (1999) *Interactive Writing in the Primary School*. Reading: Reading and Language Information Centre, University of Reading.

Hall, N. (2001) Developing understanding of punctuation with young readers and writers, in J. Evans (ed.) *The Writing Classroom: Aspects of Writing and the Primary Child 3–11*. London: David Fulton.

Hall, N. and Abbott (eds) (1991) *Play in the Primary Curriculum*. London: Hodder & Stoughton.

Hall, N. and Robinson, A. (eds) (1996) *Learning about Punctuation*. Clevedon: Multilingual Matters.

Harris, A.J. (1979) The effective teacher of reading, revisited. *The Reading Teacher*, 33: 135–40.

Harrison, C. (1992) The reading process and learning to read, in C. Harrison and M. Coles (eds) *The Reading for Real Handbook*. London: Routledge.

Harrison, C. and Coles, M. (eds) (1992) *The Reading for Real Handbook*. London: Routledge.

Harste, J.C., Woodwaid, V.A. and Burke, C.L. (1984) *Language Stories & Literacy Lessons*. Portsmouth, NH: Heinemann Educational.

Heath, S.B. (1983) *Ways with Words: Language, Life and Work in Communities and Classrooms*. Cambridge: Cambridge University Press.

Hewison, J. and Tizard, S. (1980) Parental involvement and reading attainment. *British Journal of Educational Psychology*, 50: 209–15.

Hill, S. (1999) *Guiding Literacy Learners*. York, ME: Stenhouse.

Hilton, M. (2001) Are the Key Stage Two reading tests becoming easier each year? *Reading*, 35(1): 4–11.

Hinds, D. (2000) Boys can read too – once they've learned to sit still. *The Independent*, 14 September, pp. 2–3.

HMI (1991) *The Teaching and Learning of Reading in Primary Schools*. London: Department for Education and Science.

HMI (1992) *The Teaching and Learning of Reading in Primary Schools 1991*. London: Department for Education and Science.

Hoffman, J., Assaf, L. and Paris, S. (2001) High-stakes testing in reading: today in Texas, tomorrow? *The Reading Teacher*, 54(5): 482–92.

Holdaway, D. (1979) *The Foundations of Literacy*. London: Ashton Scholastic.

Hoodless, P. (ed.) (1998) *History and English in the Primary School: Exploiting the Links*. London: Routledge.

Hornsby, D. (2000) *A Closer Look at Guided Reading*. Melbourne: Eleanor Curtain.

Huey, E. (1972) *The Psychology and Pedagogy of Reading*. Cambridge, MA: MIT Press (first published 1908).

Hunt, L.C. (1970) The effect of self-selection, interest and motivation upon independent, instructional and frustrational levels. *The Reading Teacher*, 24: 146–51, 158.

Johnson, P. (1995) *Children Making Books*. Reading: Reading and Language Information Centre, University of Reading.

Kalman, I. (1991) Who invented invented spelling?, in K. Goodman, L.B. Bird and Y. Goodman (eds) *The Whole Language Catalog*. Santa Rosa, CA: American School Publishers.

Kenner, C. (2000) *Home Pages Literacy Links for Bilingual Children*. Stoke-on-Trent: Trentham Books.

Kohn, A. (2000) *The Case Against Standardized Testing: Raising the Scores, Ruining the Schools*. Portsmouth, NH: Heinemann.

Lalley, M. (1991) *The Nursery Teacher in Action*. London: Paul Chapman.

Laminack, L. (1991) *Learning with Zachary*. Richmond Hill, Ontario: Scholastic Canada.

Lefevre, C. (1964) *Linguistics and the Teaching of Reading*. London: McGraw-Hill.

Littlefair, A.B. (1991) *Reading All Types of Writing: The Importance of Genre and Register for Reading Development*. Buckingham: Open University Press.

Littlefair, A.B. (1992) *Genres in the Classroom*. Widnes: UK Reading Association.

Lunzer, E. and Gardner, K. (1979) *The Effective Use of Reading*. London: Heinemann.

Mackay, D., Thompson, B. and Schaub, P. (1970) *Breakthrough to Literacy: Teacher's Manual*. London: Schools Council/Longman.

MacLeod, F. (1991) Down at the chippy, in N. Hall and L. Abbott (eds) *Play in the Primary Curriculum*. London: Hodder & Stoughton.

Manning, K. and Sharp, A. (1977) *Structuring Play in the Early Years at School*. London: Ward Lock Educational.

Martens, P. (1996) *I Already Know How to Read: A Child's View of Literacy*. Portsmouth, NH: Heinemann.

Matterson, E. (1969) *This Little Puffin . . . Finger Plays and Nursery Games*. London: Puffin.

McCarrier, A., Pinnell, G. and Fountas, I. (1999) *Interactive Writing*. Portsmouth, NH: Heinemann.

McCracken, R.A. (1971) Initiating sustained silent reading. *Journal of Reading*, 14: 521–4, 582–3.

McQuillan, J. (1998) *The Literacy Crisis: False Claims, Real Solutions*. Portsmouth, NH: Heinemann.

Meek, M. (1982) *Learning to Read*. London: Bodley Head.

Meek, M. (1988) *How Texts Teach What Readers Learn*. Stroud: Thimble Press.

Meek, M. (1990) What do we know about reading that helps us to teach?, in R. Carter (ed.) *Knowledge about Language and the Curriculum*. London: Hodder & Stoughton.

Millard, E., Taylor, C. and Watson, S. (2000) Books for babies means books for parents too: the benefits of situating the earliest stages of literacy in the framework of the wider community. *Reading*, 34(3): 130–3.

Miller, L. (1998) Play as a route to literacy. *Reading*, 32(3): 32–5.

Miller, L. (1999) *Moving Towards Literacy with Environmental Print*. Royston, Herts: UK Reading Association.

Mills, H., O'Keefe, T. and Stephens, D. (1992) *Looking Closely: Exploring the Role of Phonics in One Whole Language Classroom*. Urbana, IL: National Council of Teachers of English.

Minnis, P. (2000) Literacy in reception classes, in R. Drury, L. Miller and R. Campbell (eds) *Looking at Early Years Education and Care*. London: David Fulton.

Minns, H. (1997) *Read It to Me Now! Learning at Home and at School*. Buckingham: Open University Press.

Moon, C. (2000) *Individualised Reading*. Reading: Reading and Language Information Centre, University of Reading.

Mooney, M. (1990) *Reading To, With and By Children*. Katonah, NY: Richard C. Owen.

Moore, P. and Tweddle, S. (1992) *The Integrated Classroom: Language, Learning and I.T.* London: Hodder & Stoughton.

Morgan, R.T.T. (1976) 'Paired reading' tuition: a preliminary report on a technique for cases of reading deficit. *Child Care, Health and Development, 2:* 13–28.

Morrow, L.M. (1989) Designing the classroom to promote literacy development, in D.S. Strickland and L.M. Morrow (eds) *Emerging Literacy: Young Children Learn to Read and Write.* Newark, DE: International Reading Association.

Morrow, L.M. and Rand, M.K. (1991) Promoting literacy during play by designing early childhood classroom environments. *The Reading Teacher, 44:* 396–402.

Moustafa, M. (1997) *Beyond Traditional Phonics: Research Discoveries and Reading Instruction.* Portsmouth, NH: Heinemann.

Neate, B. (1992) *Finding Out About Finding Out: A Practical Guide to Children's Information Books.* Sevenoaks: Hodder & Stoughton.

Nicholson, T. (1992) Reading wars: a brief history and an update. *International Journal of Disability, Development and Education, 39:* 173–84.

Nulty, D. (2001) The magic of writing with IT, in J. Evans (ed.) *The Writing Classroom: Aspects of Writing and the Primary Child 3–11.* London: David Fulton.

NUT (1991) *Miss, the Rabbit Ate the 'Floating Apple'! The Case Against SATs.* London: National Union of Teachers.

Opie, I. and Opie, P. (1959) *The Lore and Language of School Children.* Oxford: Oxford University Press.

Opitz, M. (2000) *Rhyme and Reason.* Portsmouth, NH: Heinemann.

Pahl, K. (1999) *Transformations: Children's Meaning Making in a Nursery.* Stoke-on-Trent: Trentham Books.

Parkes, B. (2000) *Read It Again! Revisiting Shared Reading.* Portland, ME: Stenhouse.

Phinn, G. (2000) *Young Readers and their Books: Suggestions and Strategies for Using Texts in the Literacy Hour.* London: David Fulton.

Price, J. (1989) The Ladybird Letters, in N. Hall (ed.) *Writing with Reason: The Emergence of Authorship in Young Children.* Sevenoaks: Hodder & Stoughton.

QCA (1999a) *The National Curriculum Handbook for Primary Teachers in England Key Stages 1 and 2.* London: Qualifications and Curriculum Authority with Department for Education and Employment.

QCA (1999b) *Target Setting and Assessment in the National Literacy Strategy: Guidance on Setting Learning Targets and Assessing Children's Progress.* London: Qualifications and Curriculum Authority.

QCA (1999c) *Target Setting and Assessment in the National Literacy Strategy: Children's Work Exemplifying the Learning Targets and Suggested Criteria and Texts for Independent Reading.* London: Qualifications and Curriculum Authority.

QCA (1999d) *English Tasks Pack Key Stage 1.* London: Qualifications and Curriculum Authority with Department for Education and Employment.

QCA (2000) *Curriculum Guidance for the Foundation Stage.* London: Qualifications and Curriculum Authority with Department for Education and Employment.

Read, C. (1971) Pre-school children's knowledge of English phonology. *Harvard Educational Review*, 41(4): 1–34.

Redfern, A. (1996) *Practical Ways to Teach Phonics*. Reading: Reading and Language Information Centre, University of Reading.

Reid, J.F. (1974) *Breakthrough in Action: An Independent Evaluation of 'Breakthrough to Literacy'*. London: Schools Council/Longman.

Rhodes, L. (1981) 1 can read! Predictable books as resources for reading and writing instruction. *The Reading Teacher*, 34: 511–18.

Riley, J. (1996a) The ability to label the letters of the alphabet at school entry: a discussion on its value. *Journal of Research in Reading*, 19(2): 87–101.

Riley, J. (1996b) *The Teaching of Reading: The Development of Literacy in the Early Years*. London: Paul Chapman.

Riley, J. and Reedy, D. (2000) *Developing Writing for Different Purposes: Teaching about Genre in the Early Years*. London: Paul Chapman.

Rosen, C. and Rosen, H. (1973) *The Language of Primary School Children*. Harmondsworth: Penguin.

Rosenblatt, L. (1976) *Literature through Explanation*. New York: Appleton-Century-Crofts (first published in 1938 by Noble and Noble, New York).

Roser, N. and Martinez, M. (eds) (1995) *Book Talk and Beyond: Children and Teachers Respond to Literature*. Newark, DE: International Reading Association.

SCAA (1997) *Baseline Assessment Scales*. London: School Curriculum and Assessment Authority.

SCDC (1989) *Becoming a Writer: The National Writing Project*. Walton-on-Thames: Nelson.

SCDC (1990) *Writing and Micros*. Walton-on-Thames: Nelson.

Schickedanz, J.A. (1990) *Adam's Righting Revolutions*. Portsmouth, NH: Heinemann.

Short, K. (1995) Foreword, in B. Campbell Hill, N. Johnson and K. Schlick Noe (eds) (1995) *Literature Circles and Response*. Norwood, MA: Christopher-Gordon.

Short, K. (1999) The search for 'balance' in literacy instruction. *English in Education*, 33(3): 43–53.

Slaughter, J.P. (1992) *Beyond Storybooks: Young Children and Shared Book Experience*. Newark, DE: International Reading Association.

Smith, C. and Whiteley, H. (2000) Developing literacy through the literacy hour: a survey of teachers' experiences. *Reading*, 34(1): 34–8.

Smith, F. (1978) *Reading*. Cambridge: Cambridge University Press.

Smith, F. (1982) *Writing and the Writer*. London: Heinemann.

Smith, F. (1992) Quotable. *Reading Today*, 10(2): 34.

Smith, J. and Elley, W. (1994) *Learning to Read in New Zealand*. Katonah, NY: Richard C. Owen.

Southgate, V. (1968) Formulae for beginning reading tuition. *Educational Research*, 11: 23–30.

Southgate, V., Arnold, H. and Johnson, S. (1981) *Extending Beginning Reading*. London: Heinemann.

Stauffer, R.G. (1970) *The Language-Experience Approach to the Teaching of Reading.* New York: Harper & Row.

Strickland, D.S. (1998) *Teaching Phonics Today: A Primer for Educators.* Newark, DE: International Reading Association.

Strickland, D.S. and Morrow, L.M. (eds) (1989a) *Emerging Literacy: Young Children Learn to Read and Write.* Newark, DE: International Reading Association.

Strickland, D.S. and Morrow, L.M. (1989b) Interactive experiences with storybook reading. *The Reading Teacher,* 42: 322–3.

Strickland, D.S. and Morrow, L.M. (eds) (2000) *Beginning Reading and Writing.* Newark, DE: International Reading Association.

Taylor, D. (1983) *Family Literacy: Young Children Learning to Read and Write.* Portsmouth, NH: Heinemann.

Taylor, M. (1990) Books in the classroom and 'knowledge about language', in R. Carter (ed.) *Knowledge about Language and the Curriculum.* London: Hodder & Stoughton.

Teale, W. (1984) Reading to young children: its significance for literacy development, in H. Goelman, A. Oberg and F. Smith (eds) *Awakening to Literacy.* London: Heinemann.

Teale, W. and Sulzby, E. (1989) Emergent literacy: new perspectives, in D.S. Strickland and L.M. Morrow (eds) *Emerging Literacy: Young Children Learn to Read and Write.* Newark, DE: International Reading Association.

Temple, C., Nathan, R., Temple, F. and Burris, N.A. (1988) *The Beginnings of Writing.* London: Allyn & Bacon.

Thompson, B. (1999) The process of learning to identify words, in B. Thompson and T. Nicholson (eds) *Learning to Read: Beyond Phonics and Whole Language.* Newark, DE: International Reading Association.

Topping, K.I. and Lindsay, G.A. (1992) The structure and development of the paired reading technique. *Journal of Research in Reading,* 15: 120–36.

Trelease, J. (1995) *The New Read-Aloud Handbook.* London: Penguin.

Turbill, J. and Cambourne, B. (eds) (1997) *The Changing Face of Whole Language.* Carlton South, Victoria: Australian Literacy Educators' Association.

Veatch, J. (1991) Whole language as I see it, in K. Goodman, L.B. Bird and Y. Goodman (eds) *The Whole Language Catalog.* Santa Rosa, CA: American School Publishers.

Vygotsky, L.S. (1962) *Thought and Language.* Cambridge, MA: MIT Press.

Vygotsky, L.S. (1978) *Mind in Society.* Cambridge, MA: Harvard University Press.

Wade, B. (ed.) (1990) *Reading for Real.* Buckingham: Open University Press.

Wade, B. and Moore, M. (2000) *Baby Power.* Handforth, Cheshire: Egmont World Ltd.

Waterland, L. (1988) *Read with Me: An Apprenticeship Approach to Reading.* Stroud: Thimble Press.

Waterland, L. (ed.) (1989) *Apprenticeship in Action: Teachers Write about Read with Me.* Stroud: Thimble Press.

Weinberger, J. (1996) *Literacy Goes to School.* London: Paul Chapman.

Weinberger, J., Hannon, P. and Nutbrown, C. (1990) *Ways of Working with Parents to Promote Literacy Development*. Sheffield: University of Sheffield Division of Education.

Wells, G. (1986) *The Meaning Makers: Children Learning Language and Using Language to Learn*. London: Hodder & Stoughton.

Wepner, S. and Ray, L. (2000) Sign of the times: technology and early literacy learning, in D.S. Strickland and L.M. Morrow (eds) *Beginning Reading and Writing*. Newark, DE: International Reading Association.

Wheldall, K. and Entwistle, J. (1988) Back in the USSR: the effects of teacher modelling of silent reading on pupils' reading behaviour in the primary school classroom. *Educational Psychology*, 8: 51–66.

White, D. (1984) *Books Before Five*. Portsmouth, NH: Heinemann (first published 1954).

Whitehead, M. (1987) Narrative, stories and the world of literature, in G. Blenkin and A. Kelly (eds) *Early Childhood Education: A Developmental Curriculum*. London: Paul Chapman.

Whitehead, M. (1999) *Supporting Language and Literacy Development in the Early Years*. Buckingham: Open University Press.

Woods, P. (1995) *Creative Teachers in Primary Schools*. Buckingham: Open University Press.

Wray, D. and Lewis, M. (1997) *Writing Frames*. Reading: Reading and Language Information Centre, University of Reading.

Wray, D. and Lewis, M. (2001) Developing non-fiction writing: beyond frames, in J. Evans (ed.) *The Writing Classroom: Aspects of Writing and the Primary Child 3–11*. London: David Fulton.

Wray, D. and Medwell, J. (1991) *Literacy and Language in the Primary Years*. London: Routledge.

Wyse, D. (1998) *Primary Writing*. Buckingham: Open University Press.

Children's books

Base, G. (1986) *Animalia*. New York: Harry Abrams.

Bourma, P. (1987) *Bertie at the Dentist's*. London: Bodley Head.

Carle, E. (1969) *The Very Hungry Caterpillar*. New York: Philomel Books.

Carle, E. (1982) *The Bad Tempered Ladybird*. London: Penguin.

Carle, E. (1988) *Do You Want to be My Friend?* Boston, MA: Houghton Mifflin.

Dodd, L. (1983) *Hairy Maclary from Donaldson's Dairy*. Harmondsworth: Puffin Books.

Dodd, L. (1993) *Slinky Malinki, Open the Door*. Harmondsworth: Puffin Books.

Hill, E. (1966) *Spot's First Words*. London: Heinemann.

Hill, E. (1983) *Where's Spot?* London: Penguin.

Hughes, S. (1981) *Alfie Gets in First*. London: Bodley Head.

Hutchins, P. (1968) *Rosie's Walk*. London: Bodley Head.

Hutchins, P. (1972) *Good-Night Owl*. London: Bodley Head.

Lacome, J. (1993) *Walking Through the Jungle*. London: Walker Books.

Oxenbury, H. (1993) *It's My Birthday*. London: Walker Books.

Quest Books (1979) *Famous Cities: London*. London: Chambers.

Seuss, Dr (1957) *The Cat in the Hat*. New York: Beginner Books/Random House.

Seuss, Dr (1960) *Green Eggs and Ham*. New York: Beginner Books/Random House.

Sunshine Books (1980) *Dizzy Dog*. London: Frederick Warne.

Waddell, M. (1988) *Can't You Sleep Little Bear?* London: Walker Books.